THE NAME & THE NAMED

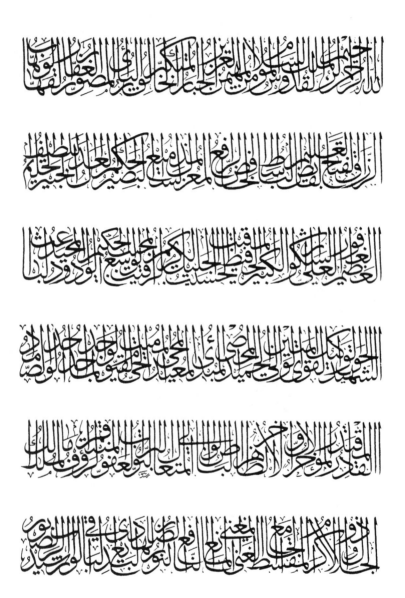

The Name &
the Named

The Divine Attributes of God

Compiled by Shaykh Tosun
Bayrak al-Jerrahi al-Halveti

Introduction by
William C. Chittick

Including Al-Ghazali's
*Al-Maqṣad al-Asnā̄ fī Sharḥ
Maʿāni Asmāʾ Allāh al-Ḥusnā*
THE NOBLEST OF AIMS
IN THE EXPLANATION OF
GOD'S FAIREST NAMES

FONS VITAE

Fons Vitae Edition published 2000

Co-published with THE BOOK COMPANY

Printed in Canada

Library of Congress Catalog Card Number: 00-106819

ISBN-1-887752-29-3

PUBLISHER'S NOTE

The word "Hadrat" found in the text should be understood as
the "title of an exalted personage." The Arabic phrase 鷺 is the
prayer used after mentioning the Name of the Prophet Muhammad,
meaning "May Allah commend and salute him." *Allah* is not translated as *God* in this English text due to the sacramental nature of His
Name. *Allah* is the personal Name of the one and only god, which
no other can assume.

Fons Vitae
49 Mockingbird Valley Drive
Louisville, KY 40207-1366
email: grayh101@aol.com
website: www.fonsvitae.com

Clothe yourself with the excellent qualities of
God Most High . . . God has nine and ninety
virtues: whosoever puts on one of them will
surely enter the Garden [Heaven].

Prophetic Saying

The creature's [man's] portion [lot, share in]
respecting this Name ought to be *al-ta' alluh*
[becoming Godlike, deification, divinization,
"putting on" God].

Al-Ghazālī

Your preoccupation with this world: eating, drinking, seeking more and more to eat, to have, to enjoy: your slavery at the hands of your flesh and your ego have made you inattentive to everything else. Only when the bird of the soul flies from the cage of the flesh will this dream evaporate, and you will find yourself alone with your deeds. Then you will see that single companion whom you hug and press to your chest. Is it something warm and friendly, or is it full of snakes and scorpions and poisonous thorns? Then you will know what you presumed to be good was Hell, and what you thought was suffering was Paradise

'Abd al-Jami' is the servant in whose being visible character and morals and hidden truths of the heart are combined into one. Both his exterior and interior are beautiful. The manifestations of all the beautiful Names of Allah are gathered in him. He is able to bring together all that which is dissimilar, different, and opposite inside and outside of himself.

Al Jami'—The Gatherer

CONTENTS

7

8

9

The original disposition (*fiṭra*) of Adam is the original disposition of all the cosmos. . . ; it is the Self-disclosure of Allah. . . . So within him is the capacity (*isti'dād*) of every existent thing in the cosmos. Hence he worships by every religion, he glorifies God with every tongue, and he acts as a receptacle for every Self-disclosure—on condition that he fulfills his humanity and knows himself. For he does not know his Lord except through knowledge of himself. If anything of himself veils him from seeing the whole, he has committed a crime against himself, and he is not a perfect man. . . . By perfection is meant knowledge of self, and knowledge of self is identical with knowledge of the Lord. Adam's original disposition was his knowledge of God, so he knew the original disposition of all things. That is why God says, "He taught Adam all the Names"

Ibn al-'Arabi

INTRODUCTION*

by
William C. Chittick

The Koran encourages few practices as often as it encourages *dhikr Allāh*, the "remembrance of God." The word *dhikr* means not only "remembrance" but also "mention," and the Koran clarifies that remembrance of God demands mentioning His name or names (whether verbally or mentally) in several passages where it speaks of *dhikr ism Allāh*, "the mention of God's name." Observant Muslims remember and mention God's name through performing the daily prayer, reciting the Koran, and many other ritual practices.[1] Those who take seriously the Prophet's command to "act beautifully" (*ihsān*) attempt to serve and worship God "as if they see Him," and they find that the best way to keep His image present to their mental gaze is to remember Him constantly.

Muslim theologians and Sufis have written numerous commentaries on the names of God. In the process they frequently describe the effects that each name may have on the souls of those who remember it. Among these theologians,

---

* This introduction is a slightly revised version of the article "Microcosm, Macrocosm, and Perfect Man," originally published in *Islamic Culture* in 1990.

1. On the Koranic basis for *dhikr* and the role that it plays in Sufism, see Chittick, *Sufism: A Short Introduction* (Oxford: Oneworld, 2000), chapter five.

Muḥyī al-Dīn ibn al-'Arabī (d. 1240) has long been known by the Sufis as the "greatest master" because of his unparalleled expositions of the theoretical basis for Islamic teachings. His works are full of explanations of why full humanity—which he calls the station of "perfect man" (*al-insān al-kāmil*) can only be achieved by men and women who focus themselves upon the fullness of reality, which is nothing but the reality of God Himself. That reality is revealed to us only through God's names, and focusing upon it can only take place through remembrance. A brief review of Ibn al-'Arabī's teachings on human perfection can help clarify why the divine names play such a central role in Islamic teachings and practices.

According to Islamic cosmology in general and Ibn al-'Arabī's teachings in particular, God created man as the last of the creatures, since He employed all the other creatures to bring him into existence. As the final link in the "great chain of being" man brings together and combines (*jam'*) in himself all previous links. Not only does he have animal, vegetal, and mineral components, he also replicates the whole invisible and visible cosmic hierarchy, beginning with the First Intellect and including the Universal Soul, Prime Matter, the Universal Body, the Throne of God, God's Footstool, the starless sphere, the sphere of the constellations, the seven planets, and the four elements. In some mysterious way, man contains everything in the cosmos.

Ibn al-'Arabī discusses the cosmological links between man and the various strata and creatures of the macrocosm in many contexts. In a brief overview we can do no better than to discuss the most fundamental determinant of man's existence, the fact that he was made in the divine image. According to the Prophet, "God created man in His own image," or, slightly more literally, "Allah created Adam upon His own form." It is important to note the use here of the divine name "Allah," which is called the "all-comprehensive name," since it brings together every other name of God. When one mentions Allah, one mentions implicitly all of God's names, such as All-merciful, All-forgiving, Just, Creator, Generous, Powerful, Exalter, Abaser, and so on down the list of the ninety-nine, or 1001, or infinite divine names. No name other than Allah includes in itself all the names, since each of the other names has its own specific and limiting characteristics which sets it apart from the others. Only Allah is truly a universal name.

Since man was created "upon the form of Allah," he was also created "upon the form of" the other names. That is why the Koran says that God taught Adam *"all* the names" (2:30). Hence man displays an indefinite variety of divine aspects or "faces" (*wajh*) If all human attributes and activities for the whole of human history could be brought together in one place, we would begin to have an idea of what manifesting "all the names" implies. It is precisely this human all-comprehensiveness which allows for every sort of human possibility, every imaginable attribute, every conceivable act, whether good or bad, high or low, just or unjust, compassionate or cruel. If, in contrast, Adam had been created upon the form of the Gentle, the world would be free of anger and cruelty; if he had been created upon the form of the Vengeful, no one would ever forgive his enemy; if he had been created upon the form of the All-mighty and the Glorious, he would never obey God or anyone else. But since he was created upon the form of all the names, any conceivable attribute can appear from him. For, what are the divine names but the archetypes of every possibility of existence?

Again, since man comprehends *all* the names, each human individual reflects every divine attribute to some degree. But during the course of a human life the divine names manifest themselves in all sorts of combinations and interrelationships which may or may not produce a harmonious and balanced individual. In the last analysis it is the mode in which the names appear in man which determines his destiny in this world and the hereafter. From the human point of view this mode is completely unpredictable, and thus our situation stands in stark contrast to all other creatures, since they are created within known and fixed stations (*maqām ma'lūm*). But man has no fixed station, and he can become anything at all. His station does not become fixed until the moment of death.

Only one creature other than man was created upon the form of the name Allah—the cosmos in its entirety. "Cosmos" or "universe" (*al-'ālam*) is defined as "Everything other than Allah." God and the cosmos include everything in existence, while the one is the mirror image of the other. So, every name of God is reflected in the universe. As Ibn al-'Arabī puts it, the cosmos itself is the sum total of all the "properties" (*aḥkām*) and "traces" (*āthār*) of the Divine Names. The fundamental difference between God and the total universe is that God exists by His very essence and has no need of the cosmos, while the universe has no existence in its essence and has every need for God. In the last analysis, says Ibn al-'Arabī, even to speak of the "existence" of the cosmos is a metaphor (*majāz*), not a reality. The cosmos only exists after a fashion, much as a reflection may be said to exist in a mirror. But God cannot not exist.

Man and cosmos are similar in that each was created upon the form of God. However, the cosmos manifests the Divine Names in a differentiated mode (*tafṣīl*). As a result, each and every name displays its own properties and traces both separately and together with every other name and combination of names. Hence in its spatial and temporal totality, the cosmos represents an infinitely vast panorama of existential possibilities. In contrast, man displays the properties and traces of all the names in a relatively nondifferentiated mode (*ijmāl*). All the properties of the Divine Names are drawn together and concentrated within him.

14

God created the cosmos upon His own form primarily in respect of the multiplicity of His names, but He created man primarily in respect of the unity of the names, the fact that each and every name refers to a single Reality. Ibn al-'Arabī often expresses these ideas by employing the terms "small world" and "great world"—that is, microcosm and macrocosm. More commonly, he uses the expression "small man" or "micro-anthropos" for man and "great man" or "macro-anthropos" for the universe.[2]

Since man is a part of the cosmos, the cosmos is not a complete divine image without him. Hence, at the beginning of the *Fuṣūṣ al-ḥikam*, Ibn al-'Arabī writes that man is the spirit of the cosmos and that the cosmos without man is like a proportioned and well-balanced body, ready and waiting for God to breathe His Spirit into it, but lifeless as long as man has not appeared. It is for this reason that Ibn al-'Arabī calls perfect man the "pillar" of the cosmos; without him the cosmos would collapse and die, which is precisely what will happen at the end of time when the last perfect man departs from this world for the hereafter. Cosmologically speaking, the corruption and decay of the natural environment is one of the outward signs of the fact that there are fewer and fewer perfect men on the face of the earth.

Though the cosmos is not complete without man, man is complete without the cosmos, since he himself is a total divine form and a total world; that is why perfect man loses nothing through death. Quite the contrary, when he dies he is released from the limitations of the spatio-temporal world and actualizes the full ontological expansion demanded by the Divine Form. He himself blossoms into a limitless world, independent of this world and dependent only upon God.

---

2. On occasion Ibn al-'Arabī employs the term "great man" for perfect man, e.g., *Al-Futūḥāt al-makkiyya*, Beirut, n.d., vol. II, p. 120.23; vol. IV, p. 45.28.

THE GOAL OF CREATION

That the universe without man is incomplete should be enough to alert us to the fact that the cosmos has no purpose in and by itself; its only purpose is to bring man into existence. For perfect man is the "Sought-after Goal" (al-'ayn al-maqṣuda), God's reason for creating the universe. Ibn al-'Arabī writes,

> The whole cosmos is the differentiation of Adam, while Adam is the all-comprehensive book. In relation to the cosmos, he is like the spirit in relation to the body. So man is the spirit of the cosmos, and the cosmos is the body. Through bringing together all of this the cosmos is the "great man" as long as man is within it. But if you look at the cosmos alone, without man, you will find it like a proportioned body without a spirit. The perfection of the cosmos through man is like the perfection of the body through the spirit. Man is "breathed into" the body of the cosmos, so he is the goal of the cosmos.[3]

Man is also the goal of the cosmos since no other creature can truly know God. In the famous hadith of the Hidden Treasure, God says, "I was a Hidden Treasure and I wanted to be known; so I created the creation that I might be known." Every creature knows God after its own fashion, but only perfect man knows Him under the guise of Allah, the all-comprehensive name. Ibn al-'Arabī constantly quotes the Koranic verses that tell us, "Everything in the heavens and the earth glorifies God" (57:1, 59:1, etc.). This

---

3. *Futūḥāt*, II, 67.28.

glorification, he says, is grounded in a knowledge of God possessed by each and every created thing. The creatures glorify God inasmuch as they know Him. Flowers glorify Him as the Lord of the sun, the earth, and the rain, and bees glorify Him as the Lord of flowers. Men glorify Him as the Lord of their goals and desires, whatever these may be. It is God who is Provider, Sustainer, Life-Giver, Merciful, and so on, and all people glorify Him by such names by making use of His bounties, whether or not they verbalize their glorification. Only perfect man glorifies God by the name Allah, a glorification which comprehends the glorifications of all things.

Perfect man is the only creature complete in itself. Not even the cosmos is complete unless man exists within it. All other creatures within the cosmos are partial images of God and possess an incomplete knowledge of Him.

> Everything in the cosmos is ignorant of the whole and knows a part, except only perfect man, for God taught him all the Names and gave him the all-comprehensive words.[4] So his form was perfected, since he combined the form of God and the form of the cosmos. . . . God sees His own form in the mirror of man. . . , since all the divine names are ascribed to him.[5]

To summarize: Man, or more precisely perfect man, is the microcosm, since he was created upon the form of every

---

4. Here Ibn al-'Arabī alludes to Koran 2:30, "He taught Adam all the names," and to a well-known saying of the Prophet, "I was taught the all-comprehensive words," which, according to Ibn al-'Arabī, refers to an even higher stage of perfection than that possessed by Adam.

5. *Futūḥāt*, III, 398.15.

divine name and thereby contains within himself the realities which brought the whole cosmos into existence. The universe as a whole is the macrocosm, so long as perfect man exists within it, since without him it is but a body without a spirit.

As for the reality of perfect man, the "Muhammadan Reality," that is the Form of God in God Himself, or the Divine Face turned toward the creation of both macrocosm and microcosm. In other words, microcosm and macrocosm are two Forms of God *manifest* (*zāhir*) within the created order; but the reality of perfect man is the Form of God as *nonmanifest* (*bāṭin*), or in other words, that which is designated by the name "Allah." Ibn al-ʿArabī writes,

> Perfect man is sought after for his own sake, since he is the manifest of the Form of Allah. But God Himself is both the Manifest and the Nonmanifest.[6]

THE PATH TO PERFECTION

Because perfect man contains all the realities of both God and the cosmos, he recognizes God in all things. He sees with a vision whereby all veils are lifted. For him the words of the Koran are concretely realized: "Wherever you look, there is the face of God" (2.115). For perfect man, everything is a divine Self-disclosure (*tajallī*). Ibn al-ʿArabī writes,

> The original disposition (*fiṭra*) of Adam is the original disposition of all the cosmos. . . ; it is the Self-disclosure of Allah. . . . So within

---

6. Ibid., III, 109.13.

18

him is the capacity (*isti'dād*) of every existent thing in the cosmos. Hence he worships
by every religion, he glorifies God with
every tongue, and he acts as a receptacle for
every Self-disclosure—on condition that he
fulfills his humanity and knows himself. For
he does not know his Lord except through
knowledge of himself. If anything of himself
veils him from seeing the whole, he has
committed a crime against himself, and he is
not a perfect man. . . . By perfection is meant
knowledge of self, and knowledge of self is
identical with knowledge of the Lord.
Adam's original disposition was his knowledge of God, so he knew the original disposition of all things. That is why God says,
"He taught Adam all the Names" (2:30).[7]

Achieving perfection depends upon knowing oneself,
and to know oneself is to know Allah. In Ibn al-'Arabī's
vocabulary, those who do not achieve perfection are known
as "animal man" (*al-insān al-hayawān*). Though Adam was
created perfect, imperfection and animality have gradually
come to be the dominating characteristics of his children.
But we should not take man's present animal state as nor-
mative. Hence it is incorrect to define man as a "rational
animal," since, as Ibn al-'Arabī puts it, "Man is defined
specifically by the Divine Form."[8] He writes,

A person who does not reach perfection in
this world is a rational animal, a part of the
Divine Form, nothing else. He does not reach

7. Ibid., II, 69.25.
8. Ibid., III, 154.19.

19

the degree of man. On the contrary, he is related to man as a corpse is related to a human being, since a corpse is a man in shape, but not in reality; the corpse lacks all powers, just like him who does not reach perfection.[9]

Ibn al-'Arabī refers to the process whereby human beings come to possess the divine names in fact and not just virtually as "assuming the traits of the Names of Allah" (*al-takhalluq bi asmā' Allāh*), or "assuming God's character traits" (*al-takhalluq bi akhlak Allāh*). He identifies this assumption of divine traits with the spiritual path.[10] It is clear that a man must assume the divine traits because he does not possess them in his present situation, and it would be a terrible error to imagine that man is perfect simply by virtue of being human. How then does one become perfect?

To summarize Ibn al-'Arabī's answer: one must follow the "Universal Balance" (*al-mīzān al-kullī*), that is, the divine guidance which God has revealed through the prophets. Only in this way can man bring his beliefs, his thoughts, and his activities into conformity with the Divine Form upon which he was created. Ibn al-'Arabī often refers to the Universal Balance as the Balance of the Law (*al-mīzān al-shar'ī*), i.e., the Law or "Shari'a" revealed by God and exemplified in its highest form through the Koran and the example of Muhammad. Only the external, formal, particular pronouncements of God can protect man from his own egocentric ignorance and the whims and desires of others. Only a norm revealed by God Himself can allow man to assume God's character traits and names. The most danger-

---

9. Ibid., II, 441.4.

10. Cf. ibid., II, 42.3, 267.11. A term used synonymously is "Gaining similarity to God" (*al-tashabbuh bi Allāh*), II, 93.30, 126.9, 385.13.

ous course a person can follow is to fall back upon his own interpretation of the nature of things or upon an interpretation that is not firmly rooted in the Universal Balance. Many passages from Ibn al-'Arabī's works could be quoted to illustrate these themes. One example will have to suffice:

> Beware of throwing the Balance of the Law from your hand! . . . If you understand from the Law something different from what the people understand, such that your understanding prevents you from performing the apparent and exoteric statute of the Law, do not rely upon your own understanding! For it is the ego's deception taking a divine form but coming from a direction of which you are unaware.

> We have met sincere people . . . who were confused in this station. They preferred their own unveiling (*kashf*) and their own understanding to the established statute of the Law, thereby nullifying the statute. They depended upon this in their own case, and then they let other people observe the statute exoterically. But in our view this unveiling is nothing. . . . Anyone who relies upon it has suffered a dreadful confusion and has left the framework of the path of the People of God, thereby joining those who are the "greatest losers," those about whom the Koran says, "Their striving has gone astray in the present life, while they think they are working good deeds" (18:104).[11]

---

11. Ibid., II, 234.6.

The Universal Balance provides the only means whereby one can hope to assume the character traits of God, yet, paradoxically, following it does not mean that one actively strives "to assume God's character traits". In other words, one does not try to imitate God's generosity, His justice, His forgiveness, and so on. A little reflection upon the diversity and multiplicity of God's names should be enough to show that this sort of task is totally beyond the reaches of our forgetful human nature and that the very attempt to imitate God would involve a tremendous arrogance. The goal of striving on the path is not to acquire God's attributes for ourselves, but to negate our own attributes. Man does not gradually grow in stature until he becomes a kind of demigod rivaling God Himself. On the contrary, man is gradually reduced in stature until there is nothing left of him. But since nothing belongs to man in the first place, once he eliminates his own attributes and effaces his own self, there remains only that which truly is: the face of God turned toward creating him, the Divine Form, the Reality of Muhammad.

This explains why Ibn al-ʿArabī often describes the station of perfect man in negative terms, since positive terms can only refer to the Self-disclosure of God Himself. On the metaphysical level, Ibn al-ʿArabī explains that perfect man returns to his own immutable archetype, which is nonexistent in relation to the cosmos. Ibn al-ʿArabī tells us repeatedly that all existence belongs exclusively to God. Our *existence* as separate creatures is illusory, since existence is not our essential attribute. However, our *reality* as separate creatures derives from the Eternal Divine Knowledge, so our reality is eternal and immutable. When perfect man negates his own existence as a separate creature, he returns to his nonexistence, which is his true nature; but by the same token he dwells in eternity, at ease in the Being and bliss of God.[12]

Humanly speaking, the station of perfection is described by the term "servanthood" (*'ubūdiyya*). As Ibn al-'Arabī often remarks, it is impossible to gain nearness (*qurb*) to God without being His servant.[13] Perfect man is the utter and absolute servant of God. He does nothing on his own, since his separate existence has been negated. Whatever he does is done by God through him. In many passages Ibn al-'Arabī speaks of servanthood as the highest human station, achieved primarily by Muhammad, the most perfect of the perfect men, who is known to all Muslims as "God's servant and His messenger" (*'abduhu wa rasūluh*). First Muhammad is God's servant, then only is he worthy to be His messenger. It goes without saying that in order to reach this extremely exalted station of servanthood, one must first follow the commands of one's Master to the last detail. In other words, servanthood cannot possibly be actualized outside the framework of the Universal Balance—the revealed Law.

One more point needs to be brought out. By now it should be clear that according to Ibn al-'Arabī, being a perfect man is not only the *highest* possible human aspiration, it is also, properly speaking, the *only* human aspiration. If man does not actualize the Divine Form upon which he was created, he remains less than human, no matter what sort of great deeds he may have accomplished in this world. The

---

12. Ibn al-'Arabī calls this station "the ease of eternity" (*rāḥat al-abad*). He writes, the greatest of the men of God "are protected from attributing acts to themselves when the acts become manifest from them. They say, 'The acts belong to His names which become manifest within His loci of manifestation. So how should we claim them? We are a no-thing (*lā shay'*) in the state of being loci of manifestation for God and in every other state.' This station is called 'the ease of eternity'" (*Futūḥāt*, II, 96.33; cf. III, 48.21).

13. E.g., ibid., IV, 231.2.

station of perfection is the mark of being human, and it has only been achieved by a relatively small number of those whom we normally refer to as "human beings." By reaching perfection man becomes the absolute servant of God, totally effaced as an independent individual but fully affirmed as a Divine Form. Perfect man lives in every situation exactly as that situation demands according to the Wisdom of God, not according to any human norms. Perfect man is fully and completely merciful, compassionate, forgiving, loving, generous, just, and so on, exactly as demanded by the divine Reality Itself.

One could go on listing the attributes of perfect man indefinitely. I merely want to point out that the station of perfection as described by Ibn al-'Arabī is beyond our wildest fantasies of what it means to be human. If this is so, would it not be better for all of us to give up the idea of being perfect? Certainly not, says Ibn al-'Arabī, since in any case we have to live up to the Truth which is incarnate within ourselves; in any case we owe to God to follow the Universal Balance, which He revealed to guide our activity; and in any case He has guaranteed happiness in the hereafter to those who follow the Law to the extent of their capacities, whether or not they reach perfection. But as human beings, we must always strive to attain to our true archetype, the Muhammadan Reality itself. I close with one further quotation from the "Greatest Master":

> You should think about the degree of animal man in relation to perfect man, and then you should try to understand which kind of man you are yourself. For you have the capacity to receive perfection, if you understand. That is why you have been admonished and notified by the whole

world. If you did not have the capacity to receive perfection, it would be incorrect to admonish you, and letting you know about perfection would be vain and useless. So blame only yourself[14] if you do not reach that to which you have been called![15]

---

14. Allusion to the words of Satan to his followers when they enter the chastisement of hell: "So do not blame me, but blame yourselves" (Koran 14:22).

15. *Futūḥāt*, III, 266.21.

PREFACE

When we look at this world we see beauty, grandeur, sublimity, strength, the power of joy or the power of destruction manifested in it. We are attracted or repulsed by these manifestations. We feel drawn into some, absorbed or even annihilated sometimes. We feel threatened by some or inspired by awe. There is an inevitable link between what we see and feel, and ourselves.

That link is provided by the attributes of Allah. Each object manifests some power of Allah. His joy or His anger, His love or His magnificence emanates through these objects. That is why we are attracted or repelled. There is no end to these manifestations so long as the process of creation exists.

Allah's various powers are described by His Names. That is why we see that the entire creation manifests Allah's Names.

The first human being, Adam, peace be on him, was taught all the names of everything (Baqarah 31). These are the names of all objects that had come into existence by the time of his creation and all that will come into existence till Doomsday. "Teaching the Names" means making man conscious of the essence of these things. This consciousness implies full knowledge. Full knowledge is impossible without the essence becoming part and parcel of the being. Teaching the names of things therefore implies the implanting of the essences within the being of Adam and hence the

27

implanting of the Names of Allah in Adam's self. The attributes of Allah that were, are, and are going to be manifested in this creation until Doomsday, were planted within the being of Adam. That is why Adam (عليه السلام) could represent Allah as his *khalifah*, his deputy, and become worthy of receiving the salutation of the angels. That is why Allah granted him and through him to humanity the mastery of this entire creation:

> *It is He Who made you (His) agents, inheritors of the earth* (Surah An'am 165).

Allah, therefore, tells us to remember Him and draw near Him by reciting His Name or His Attributes. His Name is His proper name "Allah" and His Attributes are innumerable. The Qur'an teaches us some of His Attributes. By describing the meaning and significance of those attributes which have been referred to in the Qur'an, Tosun Bayrak has satisfied a long-felt need. Though many books and philosophical treatises have been written on the Names or Attributes of Allah, there is hardly a book which sums up so succinctly the explanations that every Muslim, non-Muslim believer, and even non-believer would like to know. Who knows, this book may kindle the light of faith in many hearts. May Allah make this book a means of guiding them in the right path, Amen.

Syed Ali Ashraf (r.a.)
Former Director General
The Islamic Academy
Cambridge, 1984

THE MOST BEAUTIFUL NAMES

DEDICATION

In the name of Allah, All-Merciful and Compassionate

Praise be to Allah, the Everlasting, and benediction to our Master Muhammad, his family, his descendants and his companions, one and all.

This humble servant, full of faults, dust under the feet of the lovers of Allah, in humble compliance with the requests of my spiritual children, the light of my eye, put this composition together, after consulting the works of many saints, lovers, and beloveds of Allah, who are the hand of power and the tongue of power of Allah, sanctified be their souls. For Allah says in a divine tradition about them, ". . . *I become his hands . . . .*"

Thus ordered by my companions on the Path to Truth, I translated from the works of these masters and when it has seemed suitable a commentary has been incorporated. Let there be no doubt that this abject person and the pen in his hand is similar to "the archer and the arrow in his hand."

Should any of my spiritual brethren and the sincere seeker deign to peruse this book, I beg their forgiveness for my forgetfulness and errors, and I pray to them to remember this humble servant of Allah in their prayers of supplication. My plea to be successful is from Allah. I lean on Him and I count on Him.

31

FOREWORD

Allah says that

He taught Adam all the names (Surah Baqarah 31)
and

Allah's are the most Beautiful Names, so call on Him thereby (Surah A'raf 180).

The Messenger of Allah says: "Allah has ninety-nine Names, one less than a hundred; whoever counts them, enters Paradise" (Sahih Bukhari, Sahih Muslim).

The Divine Truths, commandments, attributes, His Beautiful Names, given to humanity number ninety-nine. Whoever realizes these in himself enters Paradise. But one truth over and above the ninety-nine belongs to God, the Lord of Power alone, and is His greatest Name. This one Name is the master of all names. The universe, the whole of existence, is contained within these one hundred Names.

Hadrat Ibn 'Arabi says that the whole universe revolves around four heavenly realms: the Highest Realm, the Evolving Realm, the Regenerating Realm, and the Realm of Interrelated Worlds. Of the ninety-nine Names God taught man, twenty belong to the realities in the Highest Realm of the greater universe, twenty-five belong to the Evolving Realm, the Regenerating Realm has four, and the Realm of the Interrelated worlds contains ten. All these realities, truths, and qualities exist also in the human being. The principal realities particular

33

to the greater universe are another thirty-nine Names. All these are also included in the human being. Thus the whole universe contains a total of ninety-eight attributes, while humanity holds one additional special attribute that connects us personally to our Lord, and is a secret between us. It is this which makes the human being worthy to be God's deputy on earth.

The Lord said to the angels: 'Behold I will create a deputy on earth . . .' (Surah Baqarah 30).

And He said to humanity,

I have created everything for you, and you for Myself (Hadith Qudsi).

Allah says:

I have not created jinn and man but to know Me (Surah Dhariyat 56).

Some interpreters give the meaning of the word *li-ya'budun* as "to worship Me" or "to serve Me", but the greatest of commentators, Ibn 'Abbas, gives it the meaning of *li-ya'rifun*, "to know Me." And the Messenger of Allah says, "He who knows himself knows His Lord."

And Allah in order to

. . . teach humanity that which it does not know (Surah Alaq 95)

has placed

. . . on the earth signs for people of assured faith and also in themselves; will you not then see? (Surah Dhariyat 20–21).

If we do not know that we exist, we cannot know the meaning of existence. We know that the Lord exists, because we and the whole universe exist, because we were created by Him. He is the One who also created knowledge, the knowledge within His names that he taught to Adam. That knowledge, inherited by all human beings, is from Him, for Him, and the way to Him; the way to the All-Knowing One.

The life of a human being is also from Him and for Him, and our return is to Him. To see, to hear, to speak; power, will, generosity, compassion, love, ability to forgive all: these are not just words, but divine qualities given to humanity out of God's own attributes. In identifying with these names, we can know ourselves and know our Lord, for these attributes are common to both.

But all these divine attributes are hidden deep inside of us. It is difficult, indeed it is almost impossible, to raise them into our consciousness and to live according to them.

Yet we must realize that the one and only way to peace, salvation, happiness, and Paradise in this world and in the Hereafter, the only means of achieving perfection as a human being, is to connect with our Lord. And the sole hope of being with Him is to assume His Beautiful Names, His divine character and morals. We must try.

To be able to begin on this path of felicity, to come close to our Lord, we have to cleanse our hearts from the love of and preoccupation with this world. Consider a simple student, realizing the beauty and perfection of the knowledge of his teacher and wishing to receive it. If he is hungry for food, the need of his flesh will prevent him from learning.

The place of humanity in the creation is between animals and angels. We contain aspects of each. The needs and desires of the flesh reflect the animal side of man. The instinct of survival dominates the life of animals. The meaning of life for them is to stay alive and they depend on their five senses to survive. Beyond seeing, hearing, smelling, touching, and tasting, they have no understanding. To realize something only with one's senses, one has to be in proximity. Anything further than the eye can see is beyond comprehension. The only emotions animals feel are either lust or anger. That is also the nature of the animal side in man.

The angels are free from all negative feelings, as well as all lust and desires of the flesh, and their actions are not motivated by such drives. Neither are they restricted by distance from perceiving and knowing a thing. Their understanding and knowledge are not limited by materiality: the realization of material existences alone is merely the lowest form of knowledge. The principal meaning of existence and the only course of action for the angels is their desire to know, to find, and to be with their Lord. This is also the situation of the angelic side of man.

The first step on this path to Truth is therefore to step away from the animal in us toward the angelic side. The means of locomotion are the ninety-nine Names of God.

It does not suffice to hear them, to read them, to recite them from memory, to know their dictionary meanings, even to believe sincerely that these are truly eternal attributes of God. An animal can hear them, a parrot can be taught to repeat them, and anyone who speaks Arabic can know the meaning of them. A child who has barely learned to speak will believe in them.

Those who have heard the ninety-nine Names of God, read them, memorized them, learned their meaning, and believed in them have certainly not done so in vain. They are better than the ones who do not know. Yet they are people who know only what they have heard from others. They know the Name but not the Named. They are like someone who is hungry and who tries to satisfy his hunger by saying "bread, bread, bread;" all the benefit such a person may hope for is that his repetition may increase his wish and effort to find bread and eat it.

There must be an inner preparation to come close to our Lord. First we have to try to get rid of the animal self which is dominant in everyone. To assume the angelic character

36

which is innate but hidden in the human being, we have to choose from divine attributes as we can, and try to live our daily lives according to them. Then, if Allah wills, this effort will help our imitation become real.

Secondly, in applying to our life the traces of the Lord's attributes in ourselves, we have to magnify the value of these qualities. For instance, if we find in ourselves an ability to be compassionate, a feeling of pain because someone else is in pain, we should realize that that feeling is a minute portion of only one percent of God's compassion, which He gave to all of His creation from the beginning till the end of time. When our heart is filled with the awe of the enormity of God's compassion, this will encourage us to be compassionate to the limit of our capacity.

Effort like this will enable us to reach the final level of detecting the connection between the Lord's attributes and their traces in us. Now we must establish our relation to the universe around us, to see the similarities between the whole of the material existence and ourselves, to see that the human being is the microcosm of the macrocosm where God's attributes are reflected.

Now, God's attributes, reflected in His creation and concentrated in man, are not God! Yet neither are they other than God. The common qualities between God and man do not make man like God. One thing may resemble another because they may both have similar qualities. Black and white are opposites, yet they have many similar aspects: they are identities, properties of objects; they are both colors, they are both visible, to name a few.

God exists and we exist; God hears, sees, knows, wills, lives, has power; so does man. God's existence is eternal, ours temporal. He is self-sufficient; our existence depends on Him. His existence is not within a space; ours is limited in space and time. His divine attributes reflect His infinity: He is all-seeing, all-hearing, all-knowing, infinitely. This status cannot be compared to the minute traces of these qualities in us.

God says of Himself:

And there is nothing like Him (Surah Ikhlas 4).

Yet He taught our father Adam His beautiful Names and placed in him traces of His divine attributes, to make Adam able to know Him.

But even the ones who love Him most and who have devoted all their lives to Him, like the saint Hadrat Junayd Baghdadi, say, "Only Allah knows Allah." So said the one whom God loves most, our Prophet Muhammad (ﷺ), who was given one Name which reduced the 70,000 veils between the Creator and the creation to only a single veil remaining between them by the verse

Glorify the Name of thy Lord, the Most High (Surah A'la 1).

The beloved of Allah and all the Muslims repeat the Name *A'la*, the Most High, over and over again, saying, *subhana rabbiy al-A'la,* Glory to my Lord Most High, in prostration during their prayers. We are taught that we can rise to the highest place and come close to our Lord only by humbling ourselves to our utmost before Him. Yet even the Prophet (ﷺ), who was brought to his Lord through ascension during his worldly life, said, "I swear by God that no one but Allah can know Allah, either in this world or in the Hereafter."

If someone has assumed the traces of divine attributes, and beautified his character with the Most Beautiful Names, and sees God's hand in His creation and similarities between himself and the rest of creation, it is justifiable if he says, "I know God." It is as if he is shown a beautiful work of art, and asked if he knew the artist, whom he has not met. He could say, "No, I do not know him," and that would be true. Or he could say, "Yes, I feel that I know him. I can see that he is a genius, sensitive, creative, observant, powerful, loves that which is beautiful, and is able to express his feelings in a wonderful way. How can I say I do not know him? Besides, I feel an affinity with him. . . . " This statement is as true as the first. The difference between the two is that whoever says he knows the One who created all this profits more from what he sees, and is closer to the Creator, than whoever says, truly, that he does not know Him.

GUIDANCE FOR THE STUDY OF THE MOST BEAUTIFUL NAMES OF GOD

$\mathbf{W}$e have introduced the meaning of each Name, which is like a drop from an ocean. The drop is not the ocean, yet it is from the ocean.

Next, we have suggested how man can relate to that Divine Name and see the traces of it in himself.

Then follows the description of the one who can succeed in assuming traces of each Divine Attribute, and make it a part of his life, becoming truly a servant of God.

And finally, we have reluctantly included traditionally accepted uses of the Divine Names as the means to cure many human ills. We must warn the ones who are tempted to use God's name in vain. Although we have no doubt that these Names are salutations of great power, a sword in the wrong hand will wound the hand which holds it. The following story is the best explanation of our warning.

A man met the saint Hd. Junayd al Baghdadi on one of his travels, and asked the saint if he could be his companion on that trip. The saint accepted. They came upon a river which they had to cross, but there was neither a bridge nor a boat. The saint said to his companion, "We will cross this river, walking with the permission of God. You hold my hand and I will recite a prayer, and you say 'as the sheikh

says'; we will then walk over the water." The companion
was amazed, but thought it was worth a try, so he held the
hand of the sheikh. The sheikh said, "Ya Allah," and the
man said, "As the sheikh says;" they indeed started walking
on the water. Towards the middle of the river, the man
thought that while he had initially believed that the sheikh
was going to recite secret prayers which he did not know, he
just kept repeating "Ya Allah," and he felt ridiculous repeating "As the sheikh says!" So he decided to say "Ya Allah"
himself, and immediately sank into the waters. The sheikh,
pulling him out, exclaimed "You stupid man, do you think
you have the heart and the mouth to say the Beautiful Name
of God?"

Allah

ALLAH

الله

Allah is *al-ism al-a'zam*, the Greatest Name, which contains all the divine and beautiful attributes and is the sign of the Essence and the cause of all existence.

Allah, the cause of all existence, does not resemble in any way any of His creation. *Allah* is Allah's name only. Nothing else can in any way assume this name nor share it. As it is said in the Qur'an

> *Do you know anyone worthy of the same name as He?* (Surah Maryam 65).

The name *Allah* contains five meanings, qualities that indicate the non-resemblance of Allah to anything else. They are:

Qidam: He is before the before. He did not become: He always was.

Baqa': He is after the after, eternal: He always will be.

Wahdaniyyah: He is unique, without partner, without resemblance, the cause of all. All is in need of Him, all has become by the order "Be!" and has died by His order.

Mukhalafatun lil-hawadith: He is the Creator, bearing no resemblance to the created.

Qiyam bi-nafsihi: He is self-existent, without any needs.

Allah is perfection. The extent of this perfection is infinite. The Greatest Name, *Allah*, contains eight essentials indicating the perfection of Allah:

Hayah: Allah is ever-living, eternal in the past and eternal in the future, uninterrupted. He is independent of everything except His own eternal knowledge of being alive. This life

45

independent of anything like flesh and bones or anything material is pure and unlike any other living being.

'Ilm: Allah is all-knowing of all things, visible and invisible, at all times. He knows "the black ant on a black stone in the darkest of nights;" the vibrations that make an atom; what is in the depths of your heart ; and the thoughts of which even you are not aware. He knows the secrets of secrets. He knows every existing thing before it is even created, and He knows it after it is gone.

Sam 'Basar: Allah is all-hearing and all-seeing. He sees that which is visible and invisible, hears that which is audible and inaudible. Neither does distance prevent Him from hearing, nor does darkness prevent Him from seeing. He does not hear with ears, nor see with eyes. He hears and sees with His eternal Essence and pre-existence all sounds, words, forms, colors, air, wind, motion, silence, thoughts, and memories. . . .

Iradah: All will is His. Allah decides a thing to be this way and not another, and no one is able to change it. All things that exist do so because He willed them to exist. Everything will be when He decides it to be, and is the way He wishes it to be, and will be gone when He wishes to erase it at the end of its appointed time.

Qudrah: All power is His. There is nothing that Allah cannot do. His power is only conditional upon one thing: His will. The whole of eighteen thousand universes and what is beyond are in His hand of power. His power does not depend on any other means. He is the One who does everything and cannot be asked when, how, or why!

Takwin: All existence and actions depend upon Him. He is the only creator. The whole, the parts, the essence and attributes of everything are created by Him in the most beautiful, perfect and just manner. Men, jinn, the worlds and the heavens; devils, beasts, plants, rocks, and jewels; all that can be perceived, felt, and imagined all are created from nothing. Only He existed before anything existed. Then He created the creation, not because He needed it, but to manifest His love, His will, His wisdom, His power, and His compassion.

Kalam: The word, all that is said and heard, is His. Allah's commands, ordinances, and judgments that apply to all His creation are in His words, and these are contained in the last divine book, the Holy Qur'an, which includes all the other holy books. The Qur'an is His final word, whose meaning is infinite and forever. Allah's word is soundless, does not depend on the movement of the tongue and the lips, nor on sound waves, or molecules hitting each other. It does not need ears to be heard, nor does it have letters needing eyes to read.

The servant of Allah can relate to the divine name, *Allah,* which encompasses all names, is devoid of all faulty attributes, and contains all attributes of perfection by pursuing the wish he may find in himself to become a perfect human being. In the attempt, he will try to eliminate what is faulty in himself, and try to increase what is good in himself.

'Abdullah is a servant who has received the highest level and honor it is possible to attain in this creation, because the Creator has manifested in him with the secrets of all His attributes. Therefore Allah Most High has called His beloved Prophet by this name. In Surah Jinn (19) Allah identifies His beloved, saying:

. . . *the servant of Allah stood up praying to Him.*

In reality, this name belongs only to Hadrat Muhammad (ﷺ) and to the *qutb*s, the individuals of highest spiritual stature in any given time. These are the true inheritors of His divine wisdom. Since the Name *Allah* is the Greatest Name, the name of the Essence of God, it is bound by the qualities of the Unity and Oneness of Allah. Therefore, even

47

if a servant has lost his proper identity in unison with Allah, his being called 'Abdullah is only metaphorical.

AR-RAHMAN

He is the one who wills mercy and good for all creation, at all times, without any distinction between the good and the bad, the faithful and the rebel, the beloved and the hated. He pours upon all creation infinite bounties. The proof is in the Qur'an:

My Mercy encompasses everything (Surah A'raf 156).

The ones who know have interpreted the meaning of Rahman as the divine will toward the total good, al-iradat al-khayr, and say that Rahman, like Allah, is a proper name of the Creator, and cannot be attributed to others. Allah says:

Say: Call upon Allah or call upon The Compassionate (ar-Rahman): by whatever name you call upon Him, to Him belong the most beautiful names (Surah Isra' 110).

The meaning of mercy begins with a fineness of feeling, a pain and concern felt when one knows that someone is in distress. The pressure of this pain moves us to help the one in distress. But the feeling of pity is not sufficient. Real compassion is in force when one is able to alleviate the pain and distress which the pitied one is suffering. Allah is beyond all these conditions, yet He opted for compassion rather than punishment before He ever created creation. He has created all creation with His mercy. Everything which

48

has come to be since the beginning is blessed with mercy. He has created all creation, including His supreme creation, the human being, without defect and pure. He has blessed His creation with infinite bounty. In His mercy, He has shown the dangers of loss and perdition. He has given humanity and only humanity the freedom of choice between good and bad.

Find in yourself the light of *Rahman* by using your freedom of choice for the good of yourself and of others. Feel the pain of the misguided one as well as the unfortunate one, not with condemnation, but with pity and assistance, and find hope in Allah's promise that His compassion far surpasses His wrath .

Abu Hurayrah reports that the Messenger of Allah (ﷺ) said, "Allah Most High has one hundred portions of mercy. He has sent only one portion upon the universe and divided it among all His creation. The feeling of mercy and compassion that His creatures feel among themselves is out of that share. The other ninety-nine portions He has saved for the Day of Judgment when He will bestow them upon the faithful."

Another hadith reflecting the will and wish of Allah to offer His compassion and beneficence to the creation is: "If someone does not need and ask of Allah [for His compassion and beneficence], Allah will direct His anger toward him."

'Abd ar-Rahman is the one in whom Allah expresses His mercy upon the universe. Every son and daughter of Hadrat Adam takes his or her share of mercy from the Merciful in accordance with their potential. None are excluded from this expression of the Merciful, as the Prophet (ﷺ), Allah's mercy upon the universe, says in a tradition: "Allah has created the human being in the form of His mercy."

AR-RAHIM

He is the source of infinite mercy and beneficence, who rewards with eternal gifts the ones who use His bounties and beneficence for the good. This is mentioned in the Qur'an:

He is compassionate and beneficent [only] to the faithful (Surah Ahzab 43).

Ar-Rahim indicates beneficence toward those who have a choice, and who use it according to Allah's will and for His pleasure. When Allah says, "I have created everything for you . . ." that is the expression of His *rahmaniyyah*. When we find this bounty hidden in everything, including ourselves, and use it as He wills us, caring for it as we are asked to do for His sake, we are rewarded with eternal salvation. Allah says, ". . . and I created you for Myself." This great honor is the expression of His *rahimiyyah*.

Hadrat Mujahid said, "*Rahman* belongs to the people of this world; *Rahim* belongs to those of the Hereafter." The ones who know pray: *ya Rahman ad-dunya wa Rahim al-akhirah"* O *Rahman* of the world and *Rahim* of the Hereafter." *Rahman* is mercy upon the *nafs*, the worldly being. *Rahim* is mercy upon the heart. *Rahman* gives sustenance in this world. *Rahim* gives eternal salvation in the Hereafter.

The manifestation of *rahimiyyah* in the faithful occurs as thankfulness to Allah, who gives us everything, and also as the ability to be compassionate, caring, and giving, which He also gives us. Absence of pride in being instrumental in doing good deeds, and realization that He is the Creator of the ones in need as well as the satisfaction of their needs: all this reflects *rahmaniyyah*.

If you should encounter difficulties, unthankfulness, and resentment, you should bear it for Allah's sake, because you will receive your reward here and a tenfold reward in the Hereafter. Do not show off your good deeds, especially to their recipients. Be thankful to them: if their conditions did not exist, your compassion and generosity could not be exercised.

As for the recipients of compassion and care, they should be thankful to their benefactors and remember them well at all times, because "The one who cannot be thankful to people cannot be thankful to Allah." But such people should not make gods out of their benefactors, becoming their servants instead of Allah's servants. They should know that good comes only from Allah; but that the tool He chooses is a beautiful tool, worthy of respect.

The ones who find the taste of Allah's attributes of *Rahman* and *Rahim* in their beings, and come close to their Creator through them, cannot have doubt and sadness in their hearts. They know that whatever happens, Allah, *ar-Rahman, ar-Rahim*, will have mercy upon them, save them, and reward them.

On the other hand, the ones who think that Allah's compassion, mercy, and beneficence appearing in them are their own qualities will become arrogant, and are bound to become doubters. That doubt, in extreme cases, may push people to take their own lives.

'Abd ar-Rahim is the pious person whose fear and love of Allah are constant. Such a life is a constant effort toward perfection in accordance with the prescriptions of Islam. This is the person with whom Allah is pleased, who is honored with the manifestation of Allah's compassion and beneficence, which he expresses toward other believers in Allah.

Those who, with a sincere feeling of compassion in their hearts, recite *ya Rahmanu ya Rahim* 100 times after each

51

obligatory prayer, may be saved from forgetfulness, heed-lessness, and hard-heartedness.

Whoever recites 100 times *ya Rahim* after each morning prayer may receive mercy and compassion from all creatures.

AL-MALIK

He is the Owner of the universe, of the whole creation the absolute Ruler. Allah is the only Ruler of the entire universe, visible and invisible, and of all creation, from before the beginning and after the end. There is none like Him because He is the Creator of His kingdom, which He created from nothing. Only He knows the size of His kingdom, the number of its population, and the strength of its armies. Only His will, His rule, and His justice exist. What happens is what He wills; what He does not will will never happen. He does not need His kingdom, His kingdom needs Him. He rules by Himself; He does not need any help to rule. He has created the universe as a workplace for His creation, and He has created the Day of Judgment as a great court of justice. In this world, we plant our deeds. On the Day of Judgment, we reap their rewards. Everyone will receive the result of his or her doings. There is none other than He in whom to take refuge.

Servants of Allah who come to know their Master, finding the meaning of that Divine Name in themselves, will become sober from the drunkenness of believing their fortunes, their high positions, and their fame to be their own. Those who have served worldly kings as gods will wish instead for the Master of their masters. All will know that they are not left on their own in this divine kingdom, but that there is an absolute Ruler who sees "a black ant crawling on a black rock on the darkest of nights," as well as the most secret thoughts and feelings passing through minds and hearts. Everything that we are, and everything that we do, is watched and recorded; all will be accounted for on the Day of Judgment.

A person who knows *al-Malik*, even if he is a king, will know that at best he is a shepherd charged for a short time to care for a flock that is not his. To the extent of his conscientiousness, hard work, and devotion, he may expect to be rewarded by his master. If he is a bad shepherd, killing and roasting the lambs, drinking all their milk, letting the wolves ravage the flock, he certainly will be punished. When his duty as a shepherd ends, he will have to give an accounting. It is better to put one's accounts in order before the day that they must be submitted.

'Abd al-Malik is the one for whom his Lord is enough. He does not need anything from anyone except from his Lord. People who reach such a state are given power and control over their own life and actions. Their Lord appoints them as His deputies, rulers in their own realms, for the kingdom of man is his own being. Our subjects are our tongue, our eyes, our hands, and our other members. Our armies are our ambitions, our desires, our lust, our anger. If we can control them, and if they obey us, Allah will let us control the lives of others as well. Thus, *'Abd al-Malik* is a servant who has been given the power and control over his own life and actions as well as the lives of others to the extent of the orders and will of Allah. The manifestation of the name *ya Malik*, the absolute King of the universe, upon a servant of Allah is the hardest to bear and the most powerful of the attributes manifested in human beings.

If someone truly comes to a state where his Lord is sufficient for him and keeps remembering this Name, he will appear to everyone as awesome and be respected by all.

According to tradition, Khidr (عليه السلام) taught the following prayer to be recited 100 times over a sick person: *"Allahumma antal-Malik ul-Haqq ulladhi la ilaha illa anta. Ya Allahu, ya Salamu, ya Shafi"* and thrice *"ya Shifa al-qulub."* ("Our Allah, you are the True King, other than whom there is no other god. O Allah, O Source of Peace, O Healer; O medicine of hearts!") If Allah so wills, a cure will follow.

AL-QUDDUS

He is the most pure one, devoid of all blemish, shortcoming, weakness, heedlessness, and error.

Al-Quddus is the equivalent of the attribute *mukhalafatun lil-hawadith*. He is the Creator "bearing no resemblance to the created." This is one of the five qualities that indicate the non-resemblance of Allah to anything.

Al-Quddus is the unique purity that is Allah's, whereby His essence, His attributes, His names, His words, His actions, His justice, are devoid of all blemish. He bears no resemblance, in any of His attributes or actions, to even the most perfect of His creatures. Even the most perfect creatures have something lacking in their essence, attributes, actions, judgments, or words. For one thing, they are temporal, while Allah the most perfect, the most pure, is eternal, free of time and place. Before existence there was no time and no place, but Allah existed.

The believers who understand and feel this divine purity will wish to praise Allah for His perfection (*taqdis*) and will remember to avoid attributing any qualities that are defective or any temporal imperfect state to Allah (*tasbih*).

To find the feeling of *al-Quddus* in ourselves, we should protect our understanding and knowledge of things from being limited to observations and impressions received through the senses, for they will not take us past the animal realm. In addition, the knowledge fit for human beings should not be a product of our imagination. One should work on cleansing one's faith by eliminating doubts. Faith is a whole: the existence of a single doubt blemishes it. One should try to cleanse one's devotions and prayers by sincerity. Sincerity in prayer is to pray to Allah for Allah's sake, for no other purpose, seeking no other benefit. Otherwise the prayer itself becomes *shirk*, the unforgivable sin of associating equals with Allah. One should try to cleanse one's heart by abandoning bad habits: bad habits are like garbage and thorns, and our hearts are Allah's houses.

'Abd al-Quddus is the one whose heart is cleansed and purified, and contains nothing but Allah. A heart filled with Allah is safe from everything else. The manifestation of the name *Ya Quddus*, the Most Pure, can only appear in the pure heart described by Allah in the Holy Tradition: "I do not fit into the heavens and the earth, but I fit within the heart of my faithful servant."

If someone with a pure heart recites *ya Quddus* 100 times a day, his heart will become free of all the thoughts and concerns by which we cause ourselves trouble, worry, and pain.

AS-SALAM

In the Qur'an Allah says that the Beneficent Lord sends a *salam,* or peace, blessing, protection, salvation, and salutation to the faithful in Paradise (Surah Ya Sin 57). In this verse Allah *al-Rahim* rewards the faithful with the security and joy of the wished-for Paradise. He is the one who saves believing servants from all dangers, bringing them peace, blessing, and security in the Hereafter. *As-Salam* is this state of being free of all fault, error, danger and trouble. In this it resembles the divine name *al-Quddus*, but it pertains to the future. It also means the one who is persisting, uninterrupted, unfaltering, unweakening, continuing to eternity. Allah is always the source of safety from all that is bad for His creation. None of the Lord's actions are aimed at harming His creation, although at times of pain and trouble which we cause ourselves, we may think that our suffering is His will. When an arm has gangrene and must be amputated, one rarely considers how such a loss will save one's life. In every pain a blessing is hidden.

Those who find the peace and security of *as-Salam* in their hearts believe in and depend on Allah in all their affairs, and know that by the grace of that name they will be saved from all dangers and difficulties. When they are saved from a danger by someone, they see the real Savior, although they are also thankful to the intermediary. A Turkish proverb says, "Don't lean on a tree that will only dry up and decay. Don't depend on people, they will only age and die." The one who depends on Allah *as-Salam*, the Savior, will never panic. Allah's strength will show itself in such a person as the fearlessness of the believer. This is the manifestation of *as-Salam*.

Patience is also a manifestation of *as-Salam*. Allah says, "If I give a pain to my servant either through his body or possessions or his family or children and he encounters this with the strength of patience and belief in Me, I would be embarrassed to weigh his deeds and to look into the books of his actions on the Day of Judgment."

'Abd as-Salam is the one who has cleansed his heart from hatred, envy, treachery, and vengeance. He is able to

56

protect all his members from performing wrong and unlawful acts, and has saved his being from the slavery of his ego. Once he has reached such a state, Allah protects him from all trouble, need, and shame.

If such a person, who is the master of his ego and under the protection of his Lord, recites *ya Salam* over a sick person 160 times, by the will of Allah that person may find health.

AL-MU'MIN

He is the illuminator of the light of faith in hearts.

He is the Comforter, the Protector of the ones who take refuge in Him. Faith is the security that protects one from all dangers; therefore it is the greatest gift of Allah. The absence of fear in the heart of the believer is commensurate with the degree of his faith.

We all have enemies who continuously try to harm us, to disturb our peace, to lead us astray. The worst of these enemies are our own egos and the accursed Devil. The tyrants, the maligners, the enviers, come after them. When one says "I take refuge in Allah," one takes refuge in the attribute of *al-Mu'min*. He never refuses anyone who takes refuge in Him. But to have faith in *al-Mu'min*, one first has to have faith! In Islam there are three degrees of faith.

1. Confirmation of our faith by our words so that others hear that we believe in Allah, in His Prophet (ﷺ), and in the truth of all that he said and did.

2. Confirmation by our acts: doing what is lawful and abstaining from what is unlawful.

3. Confirmation by our hearts: the firm belief, without any conditions or doubts, in the truth of the Prophet's message.

What is essential is faith in the heart. If that leaves, may Allah protect us, one enters the ranks of the nonbelievers. Whoever confirms his faith with his words while his heart is not with Allah is a liar. Whoever goes as far as acting as if he had faith is a hypocrite. But if a person is faithful at heart, and for some reason cannot declare it or cannot act upon his faith, he remains faithful.

Watch your faith and your actions as a believer: that is the reflection of *al-Mu'min*. Be the dependable one in whom others find security. Be a person who does not deny help to those who take refuge with you, and you will have a taste of *al-Mu'min*, the Most Secure.

'Abd al-Mu'min is one who has been given refuge by Allah from all disasters, pain, and punishment. The property, honor, and life of others is safe with and saved by the servant in whom the name *al-Mu'min* is manifested.

If a person in whom the name of *al-Mu'min* is manifest calls on *ya Mu'min* 36 times and takes refuge in Him when he encounters hostility or danger, by the will of Allah he will be safe.

AL-MUHAYMIN

He is the Protector and the Guardian. He is the one who sees to the evolution and growth of His creation, leading them where they are destined to go. Nothing escapes His attention for a moment. He is the one who watches the good deeds and rewards them fully. He counts the sins exactly, not adding to their punishment even an amount the size of a mustard seed.

We may find the reflection of *al-Muhaymin* in ourselves through consciousness and awareness by intently watching

Allah Al-Mu'min, Al-Muhaymin, Al-'Aziz,
Al-Jabbar, Al-Mutakabbir

our actions, words, thoughts, and feelings, and by trying to control them.

'Abd al-Muhaymin is the one who sees the existence and the rules of Allah in everything. In expression of the name *ya Muhaymin* he watches over himself and others, guarding them against wrong and helping them to secure the things to which they have a right.

Al-Muhaymin, as one of God's Names containing divine secrets, is mentioned not only in the Holy Qur'an but in all the ancient divine books. If someone who is aware and attentive in both his daily life and his inner life writes this Name on a piece of silk, holds it over the smoke of burning musk, amber, and sugar, recites *ya Muhaymin* over it 5000 times a day for seven days, and then puts it under his pillow, by the will of Allah he will dream of the events which will affect both his material and spiritual life in the future.

AL-'AZIZ

He is the Victorious One whom no force can overwhelm.

There is no strength in this universe that can stand before this will. *Al-'Aziz* appears often in the Holy Qur'an in relation to verses of punishment. Although Allah's power is victorious over all, like the true victor, He delays punishment. He does not hurry to destroy the one who persists in revolt and sin.

A person who leads a life obeying Allah's orders to become strong and invincible, but refrains from exercising his strength, and is not vengeful, reflects the beautiful name of *al-'Aziz*. We may find the traces of *al-'Aziz* in ourselves if we are able to suppress the demands of our ego and flesh and to satisfy our lawful needs through clean, honest, lawful means. If we stay within the limits of wisdom and clearsightedness in all our thoughts and actions, we may see our portion of Allah's attribute of *al-'Aziz.*

'Abd al-'Aziz is the one whom Allah has rendered safe from all attacks, while granting victory over all opposing powers.

If a person who is needed by people in need recites *ya 'Aziz* for 40 days after morning prayers, he will not need help from anyone, and will be able to help others.

AL-JABBAR

He is the repairer of the broken, the completer of the lacking, the one who can enforce His will without any opposition.

Hadrat 'Ali used to pray, *Ya Jabbira kulli kasirin wa ya musahilla kulli 'asirin*—"O *Jabbar,* who puts together all that is broken and brings ease to every difficulty."

At the same time *al-Jabbar* is the one who is able to enforce His will at all times and places without any opposition. This forcefulness makes submission a necessity. His forcefulness is within the destiny of all His creation. The sun cannot say, "I will not rise again." The wind cannot say, "I will not blow again." Yet the human being is given a choice. We are also given the wisdom to know what is right and what is wrong. We are given freedom yet the purpose of our creation is to know Allah, to find Allah, and to become the servant of Allah. But this is not enforced on us. Allah has left it to our wish.

We find *al-Jabbar* by knowing that the only place to go to repair our broken hopes, to find peace in the confusion in which we find ourselves, is to Allah. On those unhappy occasions of disobedience and revolt, if we run to take refuge in Allah's mercy before the coming of His punishment (from which no force can save us and from which there is nowhere to hide), we will find in this moment the recollection of Allah in His capacity as the Forceful One.

'Abd al-Jabbar is the one who reflects Allah's force, who dominates everything and enforces Allah's will in the material and spiritual creations.

Whoever sincerely believes in the invincible power of Allah and counts on it may recite *ya Jabbar* 21 times in the mornings and evenings. By the will of Allah this brings safety from the threat of tyrants.

AL-MUTAKABBIR

He is the Greatest, who shows His greatness in everything, on all occasions. The manifestation of greatness belongs only to Allah. No creature, whose being or not-being depends on the will and the single order of Allah, has the right to assume this Name.

Out of all creation, the first to become arrogant and claim greatness was the accursed Devil. Since then there are those who have followed the Devil, who think that the power, intelligence, knowledge, position, fame, and fortune that Allah has lent to them momentarily are theirs, so that they become proud.

If man thought of his beginning and his end, which are very close to each other, he would remember that his beginning was a drop of sperm transplanted into his mother from his father's urinary tract. His end will be as a limp, cold, yellow corpse that cannot be endured even by the ones who loved him and that will be placed into a hole in the ground. Where are the Pharaohs, the Nimrods, the Napoleons and Hitlers?

Al-Mutakabbir is an honor fit only for Allah. The created one cannot assume this attribute. Allah *al-Mutakabbir* is the adversary of the proud man. He will humiliate him, making him the lowest of the low. Just as the rain that comes from the skies does not gather on the tops of high mountains, Allah's blessings and compassion gather in lowly places.

The ones who wish to feel the divine attribute of *al-Mutakabbir* will find it only when they work hard to try to achieve the highest level of their potential, while never boasting of or even revealing their greatness.

'Abd al-Mutakabbir is he who is shown his smallness and the greatness of Allah. His egotism and pride are effaced and replaced by the greatness of Allah reflected in him. He is safe from being belittled and bows to none other than the Truth.

A servant of Allah in whom the name of *al-Mutakabbir* is manifest leaves the passions and pleasures of this world and is able to ignore the influence of everything which might prevent his heart from being attached to his Lord.

If such a person recites *ya Mutakabbir* 10 times before making love to his wife, they may have a righteous child.

AL-KHALIQ

He is the one who invents and creates from nothing, establishing at the same time the states, conditions, and sustenance of all that He has created. He establishes how, when, and where creation will take place. He creates in accordance with this order. Everything from the beginning to the end of created existences has been established in goodness and wisdom. In accordance with this perfect order, everything follows the path it will follow. There are no accidents in the universe.

Allah *al-Khaliq* did not need the creation, nor does He receive any benefit from it. Perhaps the reason for creation is that He may thus acknowledge His eternal greatness and power, and see His own beauty and perfection. For He says, "I was a hidden treasure. I loved to be known, so I created creation."

Allah existed. None existed with Him, yet there was nothing lacking or missing before He created the creation. When He created the universe, nothing was added, nor was anything diminished.

A human being, as the supreme creation, should know that "Allah has created all for humanity and humanity for Himself." All creation, and the order that it follows, is entirely beneficence and wisdom. One must find these benefits and this wisdom, use them, and feel the blessing of being a part of this creation which is a reflection of the Creator.

'Abd al-Khaliq is the one whom Allah has rendered able to do all things in accordance with His will. The one in whom *al-Khaliq* is manifest sees the universe reflected in him, for he knows everything that surrounds him. Thus he knows himself: he even knows the unseen, spiritual beings. Such knowledge is the recreating of the created in our minds. That is the true extent of human creativity.

If such a person recites the Name *al-Khaliq* nightly, while keeping its meaning in his heart, Allah will create an angel especially for him who will pray for him till the end of time.

AL-BARI'

He is the one who orders His creation with perfect harmony—not only is each thing harmonious within itself, but everything is in accordance with everything else. This infinite-seeming universe works like a clock. See how everything in you is connected, working together, and how, when one part fails, all else is affected too.

The functions of one and all depend upon each other. Try to see to it that this harmony that is in your nature is manifested in your life. Allah *al-Bari'* gave you intelligence to help you to know your Creator. He also gave you freedom of will and choice so that you may choose the right over the wrong. But if you use your will to opt for the wrong, and your mind to deny the existence of the Creator, then you will be attempting to destroy the universal harmony; you will end up destroying yourself.

'Abd al-Bari' is the one who is saved from incongruity, error, injustice, and confusion. Such a person is made to act in perfect uniformity with the divine laws working in nature, and can help and inspire others to do the same. The attribute of *al-Bari'*, the one who creates harmony, is actually part of Allah's attribute *ar-Rahman*, the Beneficent. As it is mentioned in Surah Mulk (3),

> *Thou seest no incongruity in the creation of the Beneficent. Then look again, canst thou see any disorder?*

Consequently *'Abd al-Bari'* is necessarily beneficent in his harmoniousness.

AL-MUSAWWIR

The perfect artist who gives everything the most unique and beautiful form is *al-Musawwir*. He is the one who, without using any model, shapes everything in the most perfect shape. No two things are the same. Look at your fingerprints. Each and every creation is a choice creation, an expression of Allah's infinite beneficence and wisdom.

These three beautiful Names of Allah the Creator, the Maker of Perfect Harmony, and the Shaper of Unique Beauty are the divine attributes manifested in the nearest and liveliest way in human beings. People make, build, shape many beautiful and useful things, manifesting these attributes in ourselves but we misjudge.

The artist says that he "creates" beauty. The engineer "invents" a flying machine. They think that it is they themselves who do this. They even forget the other people who might claim that they "created" the paint and the brush, and the sciences of geometry, physics, and mathematics, without whose "creation" their "creation" could not have been possible. They forget about the sources that produced the materials for that "creation."

Who created the mind, the eyes, and the hands that put all this together? That which people make depends on many conditions, materials, and helpers. Allah's creative act does not depend on any model, material, time, tool, helper, or anything else. When He creates, He says *Kun*, "Be!" and a whole universe becomes. Allah's treasure is between two letters, "K" and "N" or between "B" and "E." What man must do, instead of claiming to be a "creator," is to try to see the divine power of creativity. He should try to lead others who seek to find Allah *al-Khaliq*, *al-Bari'*, *al-Musawwir*, and help them to find Him through His creative manifestations.

'*Abd al-Musawwir* is the maker of things in accordance with the beauty manifest in all that Allah has created, because no beauty is possible in opposition to the beauty created by Allah or outside of it.

If a woman who cannot have a child and believes that Allah is the only Creator fasts for seven days, reciting at each fast-break *ya Khaliq, ya Bari', ya Musawwir* 21 times over a glass of water, and if she then breaks fast by drinking this water, it is to be hoped that she may have a child.

AL-GHAFFAR

Allah exposes that which is good and beautiful and hides that which is ugly. Sin is ugly. Repentance is the realization of an ugliness which is offensive to others as well as to one-self, together with an attempt to change the ugly thing, or at least to hide it.

Allah is the one who accepts repentance and forgives. If we are guilty of the disruption of harmony within ourselves and around ourselves, which is perhaps the greatest sin, and we realize, will, and beg Allah's help not to do it again, if we beg with tears of shame and ask Allah *al-Ghaffar* for forgiveness, Allah will forgive us . . . and perhaps even transform our sin into a good deed.

A sinner is like a poor fellow who has fallen into a sewer. What is the first thing he must do? He cannot face others in that state, nor can he stand himself. Unless he is insane, not realizing his offensive state, he will rush to wash and cleanse himself. The soap and water with which to wash our interiors is repentance. Woe to those who neither see nor smell the dirty stench filling their inner being!

Repentance is between each person and Allah; no one else need hear it. It need not even be pronounced. Allah knows what passes through our hearts. However, repentance must also be accompanied by a firm intention not to perform the sinful act again. The sign of the acceptance of our repentance, and the accordance of forgiveness by Allah *al-Ghaffar*, is that He will not permit us to repeat that sinful act again.

'Abd al-Ghaffar is the one who is given the quality of forgiving a fault, of covering and hiding a fault from others, of having the compassion of not seeing a fault as a fault. Such a person acts this way in cases and toward people whom Allah the Forgiver has forgiven. The Messenger of Allah says, "Whoever forgives and hides the wrongdoing of another, Allah will forgive him and hide his sins on the Day of Judgment."

If a person has compassion in his heart for the human foibles he sees around him, and recites *ya Ghaffar* 100 times after the communal prayers on Fridays, Allah may forgive his faults of the previous week.

When anger flares up in one's heart, if one remembers and recites *ya Ghaffar,* it may subside.

AL-QAHHAR

He is the Ever-Dominating One, who has surrounded all His creation from without and within with His irresistible power. Nothing can escape Him. The worlds and the heavens bow their heads before Him. How many universes, peoples, and nations has He destroyed in punishment!

Allah counters His attribute of *al-Qahhar* with His attribute *al-Latif.* They are within each other. He has also

Allah Al-Ghaffar, Al-Qahhar, Al-Wahhab

created causes and means that separate His punishing destructive force from His delicate loving finesse (*al-Latif*). He has created the means of faith, sincerity, justice, compassion, generosity, wisdom, and other beautiful characteristics upon which the light of *al-Latif* shines. He has created the causes of rebellion, denial, arrogance, ignorance, tyranny, and hypocrisy, upon which the darkness of His terror is reflected.

Try to find the traces of these ascending and descending causes, and these two mirrors one full of light, the other, of darkness in and around you. We take refuge from Allah *al-Qahhar* in Allah *al-Latif*.

'Abd al-Qahhar is the one who is given the power to obliterate tyranny. The greatest tyranny that people suffer is from our evil commanding ego, and *'Abd al-Qahhar* is able to enslave that tyrant. None can influence nor overcome him. Such a person becomes all-powerful to execute that which is right.

If a person with a sincere wish in his heart to free himself from the domination of his ego and from overwhelming worldly ambition remembers and recites *ya Qahhar* as often as he can, he may become able to control his ego.

AL-WAHHAB

He is the donor of all, without conditions, without limits, without asking any benefit or return, giving everything to everyone, everywhere, always. He gives money to the poor, health to the sick, children to those who are barren, freedom to the trapped, knowledge to the ignorant.

From the smallest necessity to the greatest fortune, He is the creator of everything of those who are in need, their needs, and the satisfaction of their needs. If *al-Wahhab* were not such a giver, no one would receive anything, ever.

When *al-Wahhab* gives to you, no one can prevent that good from coming to you. And when He gives to someone else, no force in the world can divert that good to you.

Allah has created a creation of donors who give without expecting return. But because they are not the creators of the things given through their hands, they are but signs of Allah's attribute of *al-Wahhab*. A person, like a tree, can give only so much to so few, for a limited time only. The ones who receive from these love them and are thankful to them. How much thanks, then, is due to the One who gives infinitely to all His creation?

A person gives, but is in need of a response, at least of recognition or thankfulness from the recipient. Above all, we need to receive the thing first, in order to give it. A tree that gives fruit, a goat that gives milk, need care, water, food.

Allah needs nothing, so His is the true gift.

'Abd al-Wahhab is the one through whom Allah gives whatever He wishes. Such a person becomes the donor of infinite gifts, without expecting any return, for no particular object, to those who are in need and who are worthy.

Sometimes a person may be imprisoned, or in desperate need of something, or stricken with poverty, and in spite of all efforts to advance materially or spiritually in life, has not realized any of his hopes. If he performs two cycles of prayer after midnight for three or seven consecutive nights, raising his open hands to his Lord and reciting *ya Wahhab* 100 times before begging for his need, Allah may accord his wish.

AR-RAZZAQ

He is the Sustainer. Sustenance is needed to maintain the creation, and there is both a physical and a spiritual sustenance. Physical sustenance gives energy to the body and keeps it alive for a fixed period of time, while spiritual sustenance gives us eternal life. In the case of human beings, one should count as physical sustenance not only food, drink, air, and clothing but also our mother and father, husband or wife and children as well. Even our possessions and knowledge are part of our sustenance.

All that falls under what we call the laws of nature is also included in material sustenance. There is nothing empty or useless in the universe. Every single creation is a treasure, as is indicated in the verse

Our Lord, You have not created this universe in vain (Surah Al 'Imran 190).

All material sustenance is pure in origin. Only if it is soiled by human hands does it become undesirable, hateful, and unlawful. Therefore we must first seek and find the elements of sustenance in everything. Whoever cannot receive his sustenance because he does not make any effort is one of the unsustained, which is a curse. And again, if a person soils with his dirty hands the pure sustenance given to him, he is one of those who partake of what is unlawful.

The spiritual sustenances are contained in the holy books, but some holy books, although originally pure, have also been soiled by human hands. Not so the Holy Qur'an, the last and final sacred book, which has not been tampered with: not even a dot has been changed. But just as we have to make efforts to gain our material sustenance, we will receive our spiritual sustenance from the Holy Qur'an to a degree equal to the extent of our efforts.

'Abd ar-Razzaq is the one whom Allah has rendered rich and who knows that those riches come from Allah and from no one else. *'Abd ar-Razzaq* is sustained not only by material riches but also by a knowledge leading to truth, by a tongue that teaches the path to salvation, and by a heart filled with love and compassion. Such a one becomes a source through whom others gain their sustenance with ease and in abundance.

If a person who truly believes that our sustenance comes from Allah finds that his household is in need, he may, after morning prayers, recite *ya Razzaq* 10 times at the four corners of his house, starting from the corner in the direction of qiblah. Allah may increase the sustenance of his family.

People who have this name written out and hanging in their workplace may be more successful. To recite *ya Razzaq* 100 times after Friday communal prayers may help people who are stressed and depressed.

AL-FATTAH

He is the Opener and the Solver, the Easer of all that is locked, tied, and hardened. There are some matters that are closed to us. There are states and problems that are tied in a knot. There are hardened things that we cannot see through or pass through. Some of these are material things: professions, jobs, gains, possessions, places, friends that are unavailable to us. There are also hearts tied in a knot with sadness, minds tied up in doubts or with questions they are unable to answer.

Allah *al-Fattah* opens them all. There is nothing unavailable to the beloved servant of Allah, for whom *al-Fattah* opens all gates. No force can keep those doors locked. But if Allah does not open the doors of His blessings, no force can make those doors open. He has the key to the treasure of sacred secrets that is the human heart, Allah's very own house.

Stand at the gate of Allah's mercy, and knock on the door of *al-Fattah*. He certainly will open it sooner or later. Pray and seek things from Allah unceasingly, always. You are poor, He is Rich. You are in need, He is the Satisfier of needs. You are in the dark, He is the Light. If Allah wills you will see *al-Wahhab* when He opens the door.

You yourself, open your doors of mercy and generosity! Help those who are weaker than you are, so that you may be saved from the tyranny of those who are stronger than you are. Help the ones who have fallen so that you too will be helped when you fall. Above all, do not hurt anyone, because that is the key which locks the doors of mercy and blessings.

'Abd al-Fattah is the one who has raised himself, through his efforts, to the level of perfection, where with his wisdom and experience he can solve both his own wordly and spiritual problems and those of others. Then Allah gives him the key to the secrets of all knowledge. He opens knots believed to be fast, secrets which are hidden, hearts which are tight, bounties which are reserved.

For people who sincerely wish to cleanse their hearts from imagination, mischief, egoism, anger, and other dirt, it is recommended, after morning prayers, to press one's right hand over one's heart and recite *ya Fattah* 70 times.

AL-'ALIM

He is the one who knows all. He knows what has happened, what is happening, and what will happen from the beginning to the end. All existence is present at all times in the knowledge of *al-'Alim*. Nothing can be left out, no one can hide himself. All existence exists by His creation, within the limitations of the conditions He has created; it knows as much as Allah has permitted it to know. Yet there is no limit to Allah's knowledge.

Human knowledge is derived from things that exist, while existence is derived from Allah's infinite knowledge. In comparison to what we know of this creation, what we do not know is infinite. This world of ours is like our very own house. For these millions of years we have inhabited it, yet we still do not know what is hidden in the closets, in the attic, and in the basement. Sometimes we are like someone who is dying of hunger who has a treasure buried a foot under him. Our knowledge stays on the surface of a very few things. When we attempt to look under the surface, we see our impotence. And what about the future? We do not know what is going to happen to us in the next moment. What is this human life in comparison to the infinite past and the infinite future? It is a blink of the eye. How much can we see? Happy is he who can see that he cannot see.

Indeed Allah bestows upon us all sorts of blessings, perfections commensurate to us. He taught us His Names, and what is right and what is wrong. But our life is limited. Our power is limited. Our knowledge is limited. We are limited. Try to feel the unlimited perfection, the unlimited knowledge of Allah, Knower of all, and seek His pleasure. Eternal salvation is contained within all that.

'Abd al-'Alim is the one who is given wisdom without learning anything from anyone, without studying or thinking, through the purity and light out of which we were created. The knowledge which *'Abd al-'Alim* receives is called *'irfan*: to know Allah the All-Knowing. But people can know only the attributes and actions of Allah. Only Allah knows the Essence of Allah. *'Abd al-'Alim* knows the real Reality and the true Truth.

If one recites *ya 'Alim* 100 times after one's prayers, one may be made able to see certain things which escaped one's notice until then. If one makes a habit of reciting this Name 150 times daily, one's mind and understanding may improve .

AL-QABID, AL-BASIT

He is the one who constricts, and He is the one who releases. All existence is in the palm of Allah's Hand of Power. He may close His hand and prevent wealth, happiness, family, children, and comfort from coming to us. The rich turn poor, the healthy become sick, the happy become sad. The comfortable heart becomes constricted, the clear mind becomes depressed. These are manifestations of Allah's attribute *al-Qabid*.

Then He opens His hand and releases abundance, joy, relief, and ease. These are manifestations of His attribute *al-Basit*.

Allah knows all. He is the All-Merciful, He is the Judge, He is the One who guides the life of His creation. His is the will. The life on this planet is a test for us, but Allah does not test His servants above their ability. He tries us with trials that He knows we can pass.

At the times of constriction, your self and your flesh will suffer, but your essence should balance that state with patience (*sabr*), which is the companion of faith.

Allah loves those who are patient (Surah Al 'Imran 146).

Profit from the times of constriction (*qabd*), which may be means of strengthening your faith, bringing you closer to your Creator, making you His beloved.

Do not be spoiled by the periods of comfort and ease (*bast*), when all is going well, forgetting Allah in your excitement and pleasure, by becoming arrogant, thinking that you are the cause of your success and your security. Those are the times to remember the other companion of faith, thankfulness (*shukr*).

Adab, right behavior, is the means by which we can encounter and solve the problems which may arise in the states of constriction (*qabd*) and ease (*bast*). It can prevent us from falling into a state of disorientation, confusion, and doubt at times of depression, *qabd*, and overexuberance at times of ease, *bast*.

Keep a balanced state with the knowledge that "all good and bad comes from Allah," and that a fine wisdom, unknown to us, is in Allah's judgment. Whatever happens, tie your heart to Allah's prescriptions and Allah's pleasure, and continue doing your duties as Allah's good servant.

Such faithful ones, well balanced and serious, will certainly gain Allah's help, approval, and love.

'Abd al-Qabid is the one who closes his own being to prevent unworthy influences from entering, and who helps others to do the same. At the same time, he knows that it is not right to hold too tight to one's own and others' egos, as Allah is the Best Judge and knows best. If one held the control of one's ego too tight, it would be like trying to control one's destiny. *'Abd al-Qabid* holds

77

with the hand of Allah and as tight as Allah, *al-Qabid*, wills.

Ya Qabid is the litany of the angel of death Azrael. Whoever is tyrannized is advised to recite *ya Qabid* 903 times. Either the tyrant or the tyranny will eventually be eliminated, or that person will be protected from it.

'Abd al-Basit gives freely of his efforts, and from what he possesses in accordance with Allah's will, brings joy to the hearts of Allah's servants. He is generous in the exterior world and generous in his inner being. In him, the secret of *al-Batin*, the Inner Existence, is also manifested. He brings that which is innermost in himself and in others to the surface but in this and in other actions, he does nothing which is contrary to the *shari'ah*, Allah's prescriptions.

Ya Basit is the litany of the archangel Israfil. Whoever makes a habit of reciting this Name often receives peace of heart, is rid of stresses and problems, finds increased income, is loved and respected, and is enabled to give happiness to others.

AL-KHAFID, AR-RAFI'

He is the Abaser and the Exalter.

Allah Most High is the one who raises His creatures to honor and fame, and who can cast them down to be the lowest of the low. Often this action of the Creator is manifested in the states of those who do not recognize Allah, refuse to obey His rules, and exalt themselves in arrogance, becoming tyrants who dismiss the rights of others. The one abased by Allah can only be raised by Him. Allah is merciful. Such

78

treatment may shake the heedless out of their sleep. Then, although painful, the state of abasement at the hand of *al-Khafid* becomes a great gift for the one who wakes up and sees the hand that raises and the hand that lowers.

Know that although it is Allah who exalts and abases, the reason is always you. In His mercy, He delays His harsh lessons so that you may realize yourself and change your ways. Do not feel secure, for your state, your actions both material and spiritual, unmistakably will always result in the terrible abasement or the rewarding exaltation.

Allah exalts those who have the conduct of angels, who have sweet tongues, who prefer to give rather than receive, who hide the faults of others instead of criticizing, who build instead of destroying, who are strong yet gentle. He exalts them, enlightening their hearts with faith, knowledge and truth, and makes His creatures love and respect them. As long as they persist in their enlightened way, Allah further heightens their state.

But those who refuse to acknowledge the purpose of their creation, letting their egos ride them and lead them astray into lies and cheating, setting traps for each other, fighting each other shamelessly—these are the unfaithful ones who are like animals dressed up in the fine clothes of kings. They make a lot of noise and raise a lot of dust; in that they attract attention, but they are no more than dogs fighting for a bone.

Allah the Abaser strips them of their fine clothes and shows their real shape. It is hoped they will learn; it is hoped they will serve as lessons to others.

'Abd al-Khafid protects himself and others from abasement. The protection of Allah's servant from influences that cause degradation is an opportunity to see the Truth. Such a person exalts the truth, abases the lie, supports the right and fights the wrong. Allah says in a divine tradition, "Your piety in this life is for your own peace

and comfort; your worship, prayer, and calling on Me is for the honor you receive in acknowledging Me. Have you done anything for My sake alone: have you supported the ones who were right, have you fought against the ones who did wrong?"

The numerical value according to mnemonic formula (*abjad*) of *ya Khafid* is 889. Whoever recites this Name 889 times at the appropriate time will appear invincible to all enemies.

If a group threatened by an enemy fasts for three days and gathers on the fourth day to recite 70,000 *ya Khafid* divided into shares according to their number, Allah will protect them and abase their enemy.

'Abd ar-Rafi' sees the magnificence of the Creator in the created, including himself. With this vision he rises into high levels of consciousness, coming closer to Allah. Such a person is exalted, yet humble, and he exalts others who are worthy in turn. The Prophet (ﷺ) says, "Allah exalts the humble and abases the arrogant." Whoever tries to rise only does so through wishing and begging to reach Allah's Beneficence. Thus a person in whom the name *ar-Rafi'*, the Exalter, is manifest, also receives the expression of Allah's attribute of *ar-Rahim*, the Compassionate; beneficence comes through him to all around him.

If someone who wishes to become exalted among people only in order to help them and lead them to the right way recites *ya Rafi'* 100 times, daily and nightly, the necessary high position and power may arrive.

AL-MU'IZZ, AL-MUDHILL اَلْمُعِزُّ اَلْمُذِلُّ

He is the one who honors and the one who humiliates.

In raising and lowering there is the implication of honor and humiliation. Whoever is honored has received a state of pride and dignity (*'izzah*). But the state of pride and dignity obtained from Allah the Honorer is very different from the pride that people imagine they deserve (*kibr*). The pride and dignity of those who are honored by Allah is not pride in themselves, but respect paid to the honor given them, and to the One who gives honor.

Indeed, the honored ones are still human beings. They need to eat and drink and they do that lawfully and in good measure. For Allah, as part of the honor He bestows upon them, gives them the wisdom and joy of obtaining the necessities and enjoyments of this world with His good pleasure. Such servants of Allah will not stray from Allah's permission and pleasure even if it means death for them, because within the gift of the Honorer to the honored is a safeguard against the disgrace of the divine gift.

However the honor that we attribute to ourselves or that is attributed to us by other creatures of Allah is a curse that distorts our reality, making us imagine that we occupy a state other than our own. Knowledge of oneself leads one to one's Lord. But imagining oneself to be other than one is leads to the Devil. His feature is arrogance: arrogance was the cause of his expulsion from Allah's presence. That expulsion was the first act of Allah in His manifestation as the Humiliator.

Then there are those who have neither the dignity and honor awarded by Allah nor the false pride that people make up themselves but who are undignified, shameless, and

81

disgraceful. Their hearts are on fire with the ambition of this world. No good comes from them to anything or anyone because they are selfish and stingy. There is no limit to the degree to which they will humiliate themselves to beg for the goods of this world. They are guilty of *shirk*, attributing equals to Allah, because they take the temporal hands that throw bones to them as their gods.

A person who asks and hopes from Allah alone knows that all honor is His and can come only from Him. Those who think they are the fashioners of their own destinies and can get what they want by themselves, who seek the praise of creatures and are arrogant, these are the followers of the Devil. They will receive the punishment of the Devil, and will be expelled from the presence and care of Allah. Those who lower themselves and worship creatures, hoping to receive good from them, will be further humiliated by Allah, and tyrannized by the very creatures whom they take for their temporal gods.

'Abd al-Mu'izz is the faithful person whose lot from Allah suffices, and who does not ask for more from the others. He is given the strength to defend himself against his evil-commanding ego. Honored with the friendship of Allah, he rises to the highest summit of honor and fortune, and appears in that state to the whole creation.

If someone who feels rich without having riches, who is strong without guns and muscles, and is able to keep his ego at bay in his attempt to help others, should encounter strong enemies and suffer tyranny, he may recite *ya Mu'izz* after the night prayers on Sundays and Thursdays. He will then be fearless and appear invincible to his enemies.

'Abd al-Mudhill is dissatisfied with what he has and is envious of others. He is the slave of his ego and has lost all sense of measure, and is made an example of degradation to others. Often Allah manifests His attribute of Abaser in His enemies.

If a person is tyrannized by someone who depends on his position of power, his wealth, and his stooges to oppress him, the oppressed one may recite *ya Mudhill* 40 times on Friday nights, and after taking ritual ablution recite it 75 times more, then go to prostration and pray, saying, "O Lord, save me from the tyranny of so and so. . . ." Allah may make him appear strong to his enemy and protect him from the tyrant's power.

AS-SAMI'

He is the one who hears all that which comes from the lips, passes through the minds, is felt by the hearts; the rustling of leaves in the wind, the footsteps of the ants, and the atoms' moving through the void. There is no screen that prevents the sound from reaching Him, nor is one sound heard less than another though an almost infinite number of voices is speaking.

As-Sami', the All-Hearing, is an attribute of perfection because its opposite, deafness, is an imperfection. There are two levels of perfection, absolute and relative. Absolute perfection does not depend on means, conditions, or limitations. Relative perfection depends on means and conditions and is limited. In the universe, from beginning to end, from one end to the other, without interruption, an almost endless number of sounds and voices arise. Some are as loud as the greatest explosion; some are minimal, almost imperceptible. All are heard by the All-Hearing one by one at the same time, one as clear as the other. This hearing is not in vain, for all is registered: the meaning understood, the need satisfied, the answer given, the call responded to, the wrong corrected.

Of this infinite ability to hear, if an atom is given to humanity, it is in order that it guide us toward this absolute perfection. It is in order that we know His perfect attributes, which He has given in traces, in signs in and around us. It is so that we may know Him and find Him and love Him and be with Him.

But when the ones who have even the best ears and the most sensitive machinery listen, if they ever begin to compare their hearing to Allah the Hearer of All, they will be liars. Worse still, they will be guilty of *shirk*, attributing equals to Allah. There is none like Him in any of His attributes and manifestations. The traces and signs of His attributes in human beings and upon the universe are at best a reflection, a symbol, a word, a means, a path to understand and reach truth.

'Abd as-Sami' and *'Abd al-Basir* are the ones who hear and see the Truth with the eyes and ears of Allah, as Allah says in a divine Hadith: "My servant comes close to me with his continuous devotion until I love him and when I love him I become his ears with which he hears and his eyes with which he sees and his tongue with which he speaks and his hand with which he holds."

If a preacher or a public speaker who believes that Allah hears what he says makes a habit of reciting *ya Sami'* as often as possible, his words have greater effect on the listeners.

Allah Mudhill, As-Sami, Al-Basir, Al-Hakam

AL-BASIR

He is the one who is All-Seeing.

He sees all that has passed, all there is, and all that will be until the end of time from before the time when He moved the sea of nothingness in *'alam al-lahut* until after Doomsday and the Last Judgment. He has also given to His creatures the ability to behold His creation. Some of His creatures see shapes and colors and movements better than people do. Human perception is limited in registering only preexisting objects at a certain distance, and can differentiate those objects only when the eye or the object moves and changes. The eyes are incapable of seeing what is under the surface.

The least we can do is to believe that these eyes are given to us to observe the universe around us as signs and attributes of our Creator, and take a lesson from what we see.

Someone asked Jesus (ﷺ), "Could anyone among us be like you?" He answered, "Whoever speaks only what God makes him say; whoever, when silent, is only silent in remembrance of God; and whoever, when he looks at things knows that what he sees is not God but from God, and learns and takes a lesson from what he sees, is like me."

Allah has also given us an eye of the heart for seeing deeper things than our ordinary eyes can see; an inner eye to see the inner man. That eye is called the *basirah*. Although we cannot see Allah, only He can see Himself, with the *basirah* we can see ourselves. In doing so we will know that though we cannot see Him, He is looking at us, seeing not only what is on the outside of us, but what is in our minds and in our hearts. He who sees himself and knows himself knows that Allah sees him.

When you are in front of someone whom you respect and fear, you behave properly with good conduct. You stand respectfully. You watch what you do and what you say. Yet that person can only see your outside; your respect and fear of him depend only on your temporal worldly interest and concern. The One who has created you and those who came before you; the One who truly controls your life, sustains you, loves you, protects you, has mercy on you, is with you night and day; the One on whom your life depends for eternity in the Hereafter, He is closer to you than your jugular vein. He has also told you clearly through His prophets and in His holy books what He wishes you to do, how He wishes you to behave, to the minutest detail. Yet right in front of His eyes, you do not hesitate to perform the most shameful and careless acts, without respect or fear.

Is it because you do not see Him that you believe that Allah *al-Basir* cannot see you?

If an intended action is not selfish but for God's sake, then if one recites *ya Allahu ya Basir* 100 times before Friday communal prayers, Allah will treat one with His compassion and grant success in the intended act.

AL-HAKAM

He is the one who orders.

He is the bringer of justice and truth. He judges, and executes His justice. There is no justice but His. None can oppose His decree and none can prevent or delay the execution of His orders. He is the cause of the judged, the judge, the justice, and the judgment. All that happens in the universe is the effect of that one and only cause.

What is destiny? It is an immutable cause, of a definite quality and quantity, which cannot be changed in either its attributes or its measure, directed toward a distinct aim upon which it will create a preconceived effect at a specific time.

How can a human being, who is shortsighted, see the beginning and end of a chain of events? Even if we are heedful, we can only realize these things after they have happened. Everything is predestined, and causes are directed to their effects. All is hidden in *al-Lawh al-Mahfuz*, the Secret Tablet. The Lord looks upon it 300 times a day and orders the angels to execute that which is to happen.

But Allah, in His mercy, has also written His divine law in His holy books. A human being understands it to the extent of his purity, sincerity, faith, knowledge, wisdom, and finally to the extent of his lot. Again according to his lot, a person obeys or rebels and is rewarded or punished accordingly.

How often grandchildren pay for the sins of grandfathers, and fathers pay in advance for the sins of future generations! Do not judge Allah's justice. Often poison for one is medicine for another.

In Allah's attribute of the great Judge, *al-Hakam*, there are good tidings to the faithful, and a warning to nonbelievers. Those whose destiny is felicity in this world and the Hereafter can only receive it if they obey Allah and worship Him. One has to encounter the cause to be able to receive the effect. That is why the Messenger of Allah (ﷺ) says, "Only if you act can you receive that which was destined for you."

Among the faithful there are four attitudes in respect to destiny:

1   There are those who are practical and try to judge what will happen to them next by taking lessons from what has happened to them already. That practicality also

includes their concern for what will happen to them in the Hereafter.

2   There are those who show regret and repent for troubles which have befallen them as well as for troubles which have befallen other people through them. They accuse themselves and fear Allah's judgment. They are thankful to Allah for the good things that happen to them, and also thankful for the good things that have happened to others through them. They believe that everything wrong is from themselves and everything good and right is from Allah.

3   There are those who are not concerned either about the past or the future for they know that everything is in Allah's Hand. They are the children of the Now in which they live and try to live right.

4   And there are those who are concerned neither with the past and the future, nor with the present. Their hearts are totally occupied with their Lord: they are with Him. Whoever is blessed with this state is the best in the eyes of God and creatures.

O believer, first know that your destiny is on the way and there is no stopping it! It will happen. And as there is no need to worry about what will happen, neither is there reason to regret whatever has happened, for regret will change nothing. Accept, and you will be rewarded with satisfaction and peace. Instead of questioning Allah's judgment, be a true judge of yourself. Neither tyranize yourself nor excuse and pamper yourself. Then judge others as you judge yourself. If you have any power to execute your judgment, make sure that your judgment is not other than Allah's decree, and that your power is none other than that which is in His hand.

'Abd al-Hakam is he who executes Allah's judgment upon His servants as He wills. Allah says

The decision belongs to Allah alone (Surah An'am 57).

And He says

But no, by thy Lord [O Muhammad,] they can have no (real) faith until they make thee judge in all disputes between them and find in their souls no resistance against thy decisions but accept them with the fullest conviction (Surah Nisa' 65).

If someone takes ablution in a state of purity and peace of mind, and then, in the middle of the night, recites *ya Hakam* until he falls asleep, his heart will be filled with divine secrets. His words will be effective and accepted by his opponents.

AL-'ADL

His is the absolute justice. Justice is the opposite of tyranny. Tyranny causes pain, destruction, and disturbance. Justice secures peace, balance, order, and harmony. Allah the Just is the enemy of tyrants: He hates those who support tyrants and their friends, sympathizers, and acquaintances. In Islam, tyranny in any form or shape is unlawful. To be just is an honor and a distinction befitting a Muslim.

These opposites—justice and tyranny—have wide implications more important than their simple moral and social consequences. They are equivalent to harmony versus disharmony, order versus chaos, right versus wrong. If in expression of his generosity someone gave money to the rich, swords to scholars, and books to soldiers, he would, at one level, be considered a tyrant for swords befit soldiers, books, scholars, and the poor need the money. Yet if Allah did the same, His act would be justice, for He sees all, the before and the after, the inner and the outer. He is All-Knowing, the Beneficent, the Merciful, the Absolute Justice. He creates some beautiful and others ugly, some strong and others weak; then He renders the beautiful ugly, and the strong, weak; the rich, poor; the wise, stupid; the healthy, sick. All is just. All is right.

It seems unjust to some of us that there are people who are lame, blind, deaf, starving, insane; and that the young die.

Allah is the creator of the beautiful and of the ugly, the good as well as the bad. In this are mysteries difficult to understand. Yet we understand at least that one often needs to know the opposite of a thing in order to understand it. Whoever has not experienced sadness cannot know happiness. If there were no ugliness we would be blind to beauty. Both good and bad are necessary. Allah shows one with the other, the right against the wrong, and shows us the consequences of each. He shows the rewards versus the punishments; then He leaves us free to use our own judgment. Each according to his lot may find salvation in misery and sickness, or damnation in riches. Allah knows what is best for His creation. Only Allah knows our destinies. The realization of destinies is His justice.

Out of respect for the beautiful name of Allah, *al-'Adl*, we must learn to exercise *shukr*, *tawakkul*, and *rida'*—thankfulness, trust in God, and acceptance. We must be thankful for the good, and accept, without personal judgment or complaint, whatever falls to our lot that does not seem to be good. In so doing, perhaps the mystery of

Allah's justice will be revealed to us, and we will be happy with both the joy and the pain coming from the Beloved.

'Abd al-'Adl is the one who applies to himself first that which he intends to do to others. His actions are never under the influence of anger, revenge, or self interest: they are never to the detriment of others. He behaves and acts according to the rules of Allah. Yet such a person knows that divine justice is not equality as human beings imagine it to be. He gives their rights in right measure to those who have the right.

Someone may be fair in his treatment of others yet opposed by them. If such a person writes this divine Name on a mouthful of bread and eats it on a Friday night, his opponents will see the truth and obey him, if Allah so wills.

AL-LATIF

He is the most delicate, fine, gentle, beautiful one. He is the one who knows the finest details of beauty. He is the maker of a delicate beauty and the bestower of beauty upon His servants, for He is All-Beautiful. The finest of His beauties are hidden in the secrets of the beauties of the soul, the mind, wisdom, the divine light. He contains the minutest details of a divine puzzle where all things fit into each other. The fetus fits within the mother's womb, the pearl within the oyster, the fine silk within the silkworm, the honey in the bee, and in the heart of the human being, the knowledge of Allah Himself. But a heart that does not contain the beautiful light of knowing Allah, like a bee without honey, becomes a hornet with a poisonous stinger, stinging whoever comes close by.

Open the eyes of your heart and look hard to see the manifestation of *al-Latif*. Sometimes it is a fine delicate mist of quietude within the turbulence of worldly activity. Sometimes it is a gentle blessing within His harsh punishment. Happy are those who can see, because for them there is no doubt, anxiety, or hopelessness.

'Abd al-Latif is the one whose finer inner eye is opened to see the inner beauty in all. Thus he receives beauty himself and relates to all creation beautifully, rendering it beautiful. He points out to the believers the infinite blessings Allah pours upon His creation, and leads them to thankfulness. He is gentle, beautiful in words and action. His efforts are like the rain in spring: wherever they fall, things flower. Like the sunshine, he enlightens every corner of people's lives.

To recite *ya Latif* 129 times may help if one is depressed and stressed. If one made it a habit to recite *Allahu Latifun bi 'ibadihi yarzuku man yasha'a wa huwal-Qawiyy ul-'Aziz* "Allah is Gentle with His servants, He sustains whomsoever He wills, and He is the Strong, the Mighty" nine times every day, it would lead to an easier and happier day, if Allah so willed.

AL-KHABIR

He is the one who is aware of the hidden inner occurrences in everything. He is the one whose cognizance reaches the deepest, darkest, hidden corners of His kingdom, where neither human intelligence nor His angels can penetrate. Everywhere in the universe, an infinite number of things are happening, some universal, some minute, over and under, inside and outside each other. He is aware of all these from their very beginning until their end, in infinite detail. Occurrences that are not yet actualized, but are in a state of formation, or are being planned, or are hidden, like secrets within secrets, are manifest to Him. None can escape His attention.

Know that there is nothing that you do in secret or think of doing that is not known by *al-Khabir*. Know also that your most secret needs and wishes for which you have not asked in prayer are known to Him and are often accorded to you without your asking.

'Abd al-Khabir is blessed with total understanding. Such a one has been made aware of the conditions and consequences of events, as well as their nature. The prerequisite of this gift is to know oneself; to be one's own doctor. First we must diagnose the sicknesses of arrogance, hypocrisy, envy, selfishness, anger, excessive love of the world, and other negativities which we all have. Then we must make a great effort to cure them.

If one is afflicted with certain bad traits of character and is sincerely ashamed and wants to get rid of them, it helps to recite *ya Khabir* as often as one can. If a faithful person is worried about the outcome of an action, he will be shown the result of his action in his dreams if he recites the verse *a-la ya'lamu man khalaq, wa huwal-Latif ul-Khabir*

> *Does the one who created not know? And He is the Gentle, the Aware* (Surah Mulk 14)

many times till he falls asleep at night.

94

AL-HALIM

He is forbearing in the punishment of the guilty.

He waits, giving time to the sinner to realize his guilt and ask forgiveness in order that He may forgive rather than punish. He has absolute power and is just. Yet He is gentle and compassionate: He prefers to pardon the guilty rather than take vengeance.

So many among us deny Him, revolt against Him, disobey Him, tyrannize His good servants, mistreat His creation, and tyrannize themselves. And they keep doing this, not even getting a bellyache from eating what is stolen from orphans. Do not think that they will go unpunished. Allah *al-'Alim* knows. Allah *al-'Adl* judges. But the gentle *al-Halim* waits, preferring to see them regret, change, repent, compensate for the harm they have done, so that He may forgive them and transform them into good servants rather than destroy them.

In this compassionate attribute of Allah there is a breath of relief for all of us. Is there a day or an hour that passes in which we have not sinned? If Allah were prompt in His punishment, not giving us time to realize what we have done and its consequences, to beg His forgiveness and hope for His mercy, there wouldn't be a person alive on the face of the earth. Allah says

> *If Allah were to punish people according to what they deserve He would not leave on the back of the (earth) a single living creature: but He gives them respite for a stated Term* (Surah Fatir 45).

Allah loves those pure and clean hearts that, like clear mirrors, reflect His beautiful attributes. Allah loves the

95

gentle *halim* man who is not ready to condemn, to avenge, but rather waits and hopes that his adversary will change and become *halim* himself.

'Abd al-Halim is blessed with perfect character. His manifestation is gentleness and forgiveness. Although having the power to punish and to take revenge, he will forgive and treat kindly the ones who tyrannize him. He will be forbearing in the face of the treachery of the deceitful and the stupidity of the vile. Yet he is always victorious over the mean with his gentleness.

If someone who is choleric recites *ya Halim* 88 times when he is about to flare up, his anger may subside.

If one of the partners in a marriage falls out of love, to write this Name on an apple and eat it may help to restore affection.

If this Name is written on a paper and dissolved in water and the water is sprinkled on a field or garden, the earth bears better crops, if Allah so wishes.

AL-'AZIM

He is the Greatest on the earth below and in the heavens above, in realms where our sight cannot reach and of which our minds cannot conceive. His is the absolute and perfect greatness. All the greatness we know is relative, and all of it is a witness to His being the Greatest. No greatness can be compared to His. The greatest thing we are able to know still has needs. How could the absolute Greatest have needs? Allah al-'Azim has none. He is the satisfier of all needs.

We call some among us great: human greatness depends upon one's work, one's achievement. We call some among our great ones "greatest:" they are the ones whose work is greatest. But the greatest work of the greatest of these is nothing in comparison to the billions of much greater works of Allah *al-'Azim*. The greatest man is one of Allah's works. The greatest work that he has done is one of Allah's works. A blade of grass with its pulsating cells transforming the earth, the water, the air, the light of the sun into life, color, and sustenance for Allah's creatures within it is a factory containing mysteries that no botanist could venture to imagine. Yet it is one of Allah's humblest works! For seeing the greatness of the Greatest, that blade of grass is a witness vast enough to surpass our comprehension. You who cannot even understand the mystery in the creation of that blade of grass must compare it to countless other things visible and invisible, reachable with all your telescopes and microscopes, unknowable in your wildest imagination, to see His greatness.

In your minuteness and awe, you must prostrate and glorify Him, and pray to be included among those servants who meet His pleasure and are accepted by Him.

'Abd al-'Azim is he to whom Allah appears in His perfect greatness. And from the power generating from the right, he sees to the condemnation of those who oppose the right and to reward those who support the right. He appears above others in magnificence and strength as his inner greatness is reflected in his outer appearance. Our master the Prophet (ﷺ) said, "He who learns, teaches what he knows, and acts upon his knowledge is called *'Abd al-'Azim* in the Heaven."

According to a tradition of the Prophet (ﷺ), if you recite *subhanallahi wa bi-hamdihi subhanallah il-'azimi astaghfirullah* 100 times between daybreak and sunrise, it will help you to avoid chasing after success in this world, because the successes of this world will chase after you.

If you fear harm from a powerful enemy and recite *ya 'Azimu dha thana' il-fakhri wal-'izzi wal-majdi wal-kibriya'i fa-la yadhillu 'izzuhu ("O Greatest One who possesses of the praise of honor and might, glory and eminence; and His might is not humbled")* 12 times and blow upon yourself each time, you may become impervious to the harm your enemy wants to inflict upon you.

AL-GHAFUR

He is the Most Forgiving One. An aspect of forgiveness is to hide our faults and treat them as if they had never existed. Allah displays that generosity through all dimensions of this Name. There are three meanings to the forgiveness of Allah, three separate and related divine attributes: *al-Ghaffar*, *al-Ghafir*, and *al-Ghafur*.

Al-Ghafir is His quality of hiding His servants' shameful acts in order that they be able to live with each other, have faith in each other, and be able to depend on, love, and respect each other. Otherwise, if Allah *al-Ghafir* in His mercy did not hide our faults, our adverse opinions, ugly thoughts and hateful feelings, everyone would run away from everyone else. There could be neither a society nor a single family.

Next Allah *al-Ghafur* hides our faults in the realms of the spirits and the angels just as He does in the human realm. The angels see things we cannot see in this world. Allah hides our faults from them so that we will not be ashamed in the Hereafter. Through this Name we may find the same respect and closeness from the spirits and the angels from whom our sins are hidden by Allah *al-Ghafur* that His forgiveness has permitted us among other people.

Allah's name *al-Ghaffar* is the most encompassing in forgiveness. A man whose faults are hidden from others is saved from being ashamed in front of them, but he may still be ashamed of himself within himself. Everyone has a degree of conscience which suffers from his actions. Allah *al-Ghaffar* in His mercy hides a person's faults even from himself and makes him forget in order to alleviate his suffering.

Remember *al-Ghafir*, the veiler of our faults from the eyes of other people; *al-Ghafur*, who keeps the knowledge of our faults even from the angels; and *al-Ghaffar*, who relieves us from the suffering of continual remembrance of our faults. To such a compassionate one should we not be thankful? Should we not confess our sins, repenting with tears in our eyes, asking His forgiveness?

'Abd al-Ghafur is the forgiver of wrongs and the hider of faults.

If someone feels guilty and is therefore heavy of heart, reciting *ya Ghafur* 100 times after Friday communal prayers may relieve the pain. And if Allah so wills, He will forgive that sin.

ASH-SHAKUR

He is the one who repays a good deed with a much greater reward.

Thankfulness is to return good with good. To be thankful is a human being's duty toward Allah. He is the one who created us and poured upon us all His bounties. He has left us free to see His gifts and to be thankful, or to be blinded by arrogance, denying even His existence.

Blessed are they who choose the path of thankfulness, spending what Allah bestows upon them in Allah's way. Then Allah *ash-Shakur* returns their thankfulness with rewards infinitely superior to their good deeds, and this in turn paves the way to further good deeds.

The thankful know that all they are and all they have is from Allah. They use every part of their bodies, their minds, their tongues, their hands, only for the purposes for which they were created. They use all that they have, their talents, their strength, their money, for Allah's pleasure on Allah's creation. Allah helps the thankful and increases their wisdom, their abilities, and their fortunes.

People who deny the bounties of Allah and hide them in secret rooms all for themselves are misers. They pretend that they have nothing therefore, although they have a lot, it is just as if they don't have anything: they want more and more. Never finding enough, they suffer destitution in the midst of abundance. Allah leaves them alone with their egos, their insatiable greed. All the bounties that they have received decay, stored in some secret place, unused. They pass from one loss to another, from one disaster to a worse one. If they do not take heed of these lessons, their unthankfulness will lead them to eternal damnation. We take refuge in Allah from such an eventuality.

'Abd ash-Shakur sees all as good and as nothing but good, and knows that all good comes from Allah. Such a person is in a state of continuous thankfulness. Yet he also realizes that Allah's bounties are distributed through the hands of His good servants, and is thankful to them as well. The Messenger of Allah (ﷺ) said, "He who is not thankful to people will not be able to be thankful to Allah."

Ya 'Ali, Ya Kabir

AL-'ALI

He is the Highest One.

Allah is higher than the whole of the created universe. This does not mean that His highness is closer to the high mountains, to the stars above, to the higher intellects, or to the ones who occupy high positions. Neither is He further from the deepest depths and the lowest of the low. He is close to every atom of His creation in all places, and closer to human beings than their jugular vein.

As His essence and attributes do not bear any resemblance to the essence and attributes of His creatures, so His nearness and farness and His being high cannot be measured by the limits of human intellect.

He is higher than the unimaginable heights. None resemble Him. He is higher than all perfect attributes in power, knowledge, judgment and will together. *Al-'Ali* is He who is highest by Himself, in Himself, in the qualification that applies only to Him.

Some, with good will but lesser mental and spiritual comprehension, think of Allah as a Being residing in high heavens on His throne, and imagine Him as if king of a vast kingdom, ruling the universe through His agents, officers, priests, and potentates.

Allah Most High has no place, for He is the place of all places.

He has no time, as He is the time of all times.

He needs no agent to act in His name.

He is the highest in the sense that He is above and encompasses all that has been, all there is, and all there will be.

'Abd al-'Ali understands that the highest among people are those who believe themselves the lowest. He knows that

to be Allah's servant is the highest station to which a human being can aspire. The gift of humbleness makes him virtuous and generous, and he supports and helps all those around him. Thus he is valued and considered by all as the highest among them.

This Name benefits whoever carries it, written, upon his person, and recites it as often as possible. If he is poor, he will be richer; if he is troubled, he will be better; if he is lowly, he will be higher; if he is lonely in exile, he will soon come home among those who love him.

AL-KABIR

He is the Greatest, whose greatness stretches from before the beginning until after the end. The greatness of all conceivable greatnesses from the beginning to the end is only His creation and is proof of His own greatness.

We use the term "infinite" in relation to the heavens and to time. We only attribute infinity to created things because a proper conception of them will not fit into our understanding. If we had a vehicle as fast as our thoughts and our imagination, and if we were carried in it in a straight line, in one direction, into the depths of the heavens, across immeasurable distances passing millions of suns in every second, and if we had a life of billions of centuries, we would travel through only a very little of the created universe and created time.

All this which cannot fit into our comprehension was created with a single word and with His will. If He so wills, He could do it again and again, and more and more, without losing any of His strength. There is no difference for Him between the creation of an atom and the creation of the infinite-seeming universe. This is His grandeur as much as we can understand it. He is greater than that.

The realization of His grandeur should raise in us the fear and love of Him, and the wish to be nothing but His servants. Fear of Him is not the fear of a tyrannical strength that could crush us, whether rightfully, in vengeance, or arbitrarily. He is the Merciful, the Compassionate, the Wise, the Just, the Generous, the Loving. The fear of Allah is a fear that is an outcome of loving Him, wishing to be loved by Him and fearing to lose His love, to face His disappointment in you. The greatest loss for a human being is to receive Allah's disappointment and anger, and the greatest gain for a human being is to be the beloved of Allah.

How much effort do we spend for the approval and love that we hope to receive from those whom we consider great! What a loss of effort to seek the servant's love instead of the Master's!

'Abd al-Kabir grows and is perfected by the hand of Allah alone, without any effort on his own or support from others.

If people have lost their jobs or been demoted unjustly, or have debts which they cannot pay, if they fast for seven days, and each night at fast-break recite *ya Kabiru anta lladhi la tahdil-'uqulu li wasfi 'azamatihi* ("O Greatest, you are the one whose magnificence intellects are unable to describe") 1000 times, they will have their positions back and be able to pay their debts, if Allah wills.

To recite *ya Kabir* 232 times over some food and feed it to a couple who are having marital troubles may help to solve their problems.

AL-HAFIZ

He is the one who remembers all that was and all that is, keeping in His divine protection all that will be.

He is aware of, remembers, and keeps in His memory all that you do, or say, or think at all times. He preserves all: nothing is lost. In His preservation, there is also protection.

He protects His creation from all harm and disharmony. That is how all the heavenly bodies speeding in great haste revolve and travel within their destined orbits, instead of clashing with each other. As a manifestation of His name *al-Hafiz*, He has placed in each of His creations an instinct for survival. He protects us by teaching that that which is bad for us is unlawful. Lawful food, aged and spoiled, becomes unlawful. Lawful bread, burnt and carbonized, becomes unlawful. They have turned into poison.

So the poisons of alcohol, adultery, gambling and gossip are unlawful, and arrogance, hypocrisy, envy, and ignorance are poisons to one's spiritual being. As a blessing of *al-Hafiz*, the Protector, Allah has sent His prophets, His books, His teachers, to teach wisdom, intelligence, the divine law to protect man from material and spiritual harm. But those who are heedless of Allah, His prophets, and His books, who disbelieve and revolt, they are thankless. With their own small will they turn away from the protection and preservation of Allah. So Allah does not treat them with His attribute of *al-Hafiz*, but with His attribute of *ar-Raqib*, the Watcher who responds according to each action.

Use well Allah's means of preservation and protection which He has bestowed upon you. Protect yourself from evil, from revolt, from sin; help and protect others; remember and preserve Allah's words in His Holy Qur'an, His sacred law, and the words of His prophets, and help others to do the same.

'Abd al-Hafiz is protected in all his states, actions, and words, outwardly and inwardly, by Allah the Protector. The protection of Allah over him is so strong that the ones who are close to him, who are around him, who know or touch him are also protected. It is said that the friends and acquaintances of Hadrat Abu Sulayman Darani (رضي الله عنه) who stayed in his company for thirty years never suffered adversity, nor did a bad thought ever come to their minds, nor a negative feeling come to their hearts during that time.

It is believed that if one wears around one's neck the written Name *ya Hafiz* and remembers to recite it at least 10 times a day, one will be safe from any kind of hostility, even from wild animals and jinn.

AL-MUQIT

He is the nourisher of all creation.

Allah creates the nourishment for each of His creatures before He creates it. No one can take away the nourishment destined for any element of the creation.

The sustenance due to us will not run out until death overtakes us. Look at the plants, look at the birds. Think of twins in the womb of their mother, how each takes its destined nourishment without trying to wrest any away from the other and without fighting. Yet the same twins who tranquilly and peacefully received their sustenance through their mother's lifeblood, coming into this world and growing up, may kill each other for their mother's inheritance. Has Allah told them, "When you come into the world, go and fetch your own sustenance, I am done with you?" Has He forgotten to give them their sustenance?

Allah is *'Alim*. He is *Khabir*. He does not forget. He does not fall into error. He is *Qayyum*, *Muhaymin*, the Lord of the Universes. He does not lose sight of His creation, nor does He fail in His protection and care for it for even a split second. He gives nourishment without being asked to the ones who cannot ask and work for their own nourishment. For the ones who can, Allah has created means of sustenance. He needs no means. Yet because Allah wills it, His servants may choose between lawful and unlawful means.

Opting for the unlawful will not increase your sustenance. Whatever your nourishment is and wherever you receive it, it can only be your lot. The means do not create the sustenance. They do not even give the sustenance. The means are like pipes coming from Allah the Nourisher to each and every creation. The nourishment in them flows as death presses from the end of the pipes. Death will not come upon you until your nourishment is finished. It will certainly come upon you after your last mouthful and and your last breath.

Therefore a faithful servant of Allah, who believes that Allah *al-Muqit* is the creator and giver of his nourishment until the day of his death, counts on Allah's promise alone. He opts for the lawful means. He does not endanger his life here and in the Hereafter with evil ambition, treachery, and lying to try to get the sustenance due to others.

'Abd al-Muqit is given awareness of the needs of others as well as the means to satisfy those needs at the right time, in the right amount, without delay, and with nothing lacking.

Someone about to take a hard and dangerous voyage may recite *ya Muqit* seven times over a bottle of water, then write this Name on the bottle seven times. As long as he drinks from the bottle during his trip, he will find the strength to bear the difficulties and dangers which he may encounter.

AL-HASIB

He is the one who takes account of all and everything that His creation does or undergoes.

Certain affairs and concepts are best expressed in numbers. To reach a conclusion, certain calculations are necessary. In fact, the conclusion of most affairs in this created universe necessitates such calculation. But Allah knows the result of all these calculations without any need for performing such operations, because His knowledge does not depend on any causes or means, nor upon any analysis or thought.

On the Day of Judgment people will have to present their accounting to Allah: that is why that day is also called the Day of Reckoning. We will have to give the accounting of all that we have received and how we have spent it. Billions and billions of others like us will appear on the same day. Allah is such an accountant that He knows even the number of breaths taken from the first person He created to the last person whom He will take unto Himself. On that day, we will have to give our own accounting of all the capital Allah has lent us.

The greatest capital He has lent us is our life. Whatever we will gain, we will gain with that. Our capital is being spent day by day, hour by hour. With each breath, the time of the final accounting is closer, when we must return the capital of this temporary life to its owner. Then we will be rewarded for the gains and be responsible for the losses. Some of us will have gone bankrupt: the nonbelievers who have squandered Allah's capital.

Know that every minute that passes without benefit, every hour you are not working for Allah's sake, caring for

His creation, or remembering Him, thanking Him, praising Him, watching what you are doing is a loss. You have no hope of ever regaining that loss: you cannot buy back yesterday, even if you spend the rest of your life. Know the value of your life! Don't squander it in laziness, heedlessness, and dreams. Make your calculations now before you have to present your accounting to Allah *al-Hasib.*

'Abd al-Hasib watches over the good use of life, means, sustenance, and everything else that Allah has given to His creation in limited amounts. He sees to the good management of Allah's bounties upon His creatures.

If there is reason to fear an enemy, a mean neighbor, an envious person, or to keep one's house from being broken into, it is believed that if one recites *Hasbi Allah ul-Hasib* 70 times, day and night, for seven days, starting on a Thursday night, one will be safe.

If one writes this Name on a bottle and feeds a colicky baby from it, his crying may stop.

AL-JALIL

He is the Lord of Majesty and Might. His might and His greatness, His eternity, bear no resemblance to any energy, matter, or time. His essence, His attributes, His very existence are mighty and great; they are immeasurable in time, nor do they fit into any space, yet He is here, everywhere, at all times.

His knowledge is great: all is known to Him as He created all. His power is great: it encompasses all universes and each atom. His mercy is great: He forgives all. His generosity is limitless, His treasures inexhaustible. Whom should we respect, praise, love, and obey but the Mighty, the Great?

Who is the mighty and the great? The one who is powerful, who is wise, who is generous, who is compassionate. Even someone who possessed one of these characteristics would be considered great.

Allah is the owner and source of all attributes of greatness, known and unknown. He is the one who distributes specks of greatness to whatever and whomever He wishes in His creation. He is the owner of all good and perfection, the goal of all hopes.

Existence, life, death, gain and loss all are His will. The mind, the heart, the soul, the whole being of one who knows this is filled with His love and fear. Through loving Him, we also love the ones whom He loves, the ones who love Him, the ones who teach His words, and the words that they teach. All love is due to Him.

'Abd al-Jalil is the person of perfect character. His feelings, thoughts, and actions are in emulation of the Prophet(ﷺ) and in accordance with the Holy Qur'an, and therefore Allah has rewarded him with might. He casts fear into everyone's heart, as Allah has given him a share of His majesty.

AL-KARIM

He is the Generous One. His greatest generosity is His mercy, through which He forgives when He could punish. He fulfills His promises. He has promised rewards for good deeds. In His generosity, His rewards surpass all expectations. He also promises punishment for the sinner. That is called *al-wa'id*, the threat, in accordance with which all who sin should expect punishment. Yet He in His divine judgment finds extenuating circumstances, and in His generosity, forgives.

He is generous to those who take refuge in Him. You need not seek intermediaries to stand in His presence. He knows your difficulties and your needs before you know them yourself. In His generosity He gives help, satisfying your needs even before you ask.

The generous among human beings are those who have received more of Allah's generosity than others: their gift is generosity itself. Those are the people who are not content when they are not able to give or to help others.

The generous among human beings do not always receive recognition or thanks. On the contrary, they are bothered with increasing demands: petitioners from far and near crowd around them. The generous person should be thankful, and know that this is a sign that Allah has accepted the services of His servant, and has increased his honor.

One should not tire, one should not be proud. Those are the dangers. For people in need, hopelessness and doubt of the generosity of Allah are also dangers. And it is dangerous for the sinner, no matter how enormous his sin, to doubt Allah's mercy and His generosity.

'Abd al-Karim is a witness to the infinite generosity of Allah and acts in accordance with it. Such a person is able to fully appreciate Allah's generosity, knowing that none of that which is given to us is ours. Whoever receives the divine generosity is unworthy and certainly does not deserve it, yet as Allah hides our faults and weaknesses, so does *'Abd al-Karim* overlook our faults and hide them from others. As Allah forgives our unthankfulness, so does he. Allah says in Surah Infitar (6–7):

O man, what beguiles thee from thy Lord, the Generous, who created thee, then made thee complete, then made thee in the best of states?

It is said that when Hadrat'Umar (رضى) heard these verses, he answered Allah's question by saying: "It is Your generosity itself, O my Lord!" Hadrat Muhyiddin ibn al-'Arabi says that this comment of Hadrat 'Umar has as its purpose to attract others' attention to their state, which resembles that of spoiled children.

Compared to the immeasurable bounties of Allah the Generous, the sins and revolt of the servant become minute and inconsequential. The servant in whom He manifests His graciousness knows no bounds in his giving, and finds no fault in the ungratefulness of those who take his gifts.

Al-Karim, the Most Generous One, is often written in the Holy Qur'an together with *al-Jalil*, the Mighty One. This is because Allah's might and power may be associated with unescapable punishment, and lead the believer into hopelessness. A*l-Karim*, the Generous One, then becomes a refuge from His crushing might. Whoever recites *astaghfirullah ya Karim* often will feel safe from Allah's punishment and hope for His forgiveness.

It is believed that if one recites this name at night until one falls asleep, one will be appreciated, helped, and served by people, and one's well being will be enhanced.

Those who recite *ya Karim* 270 times daily may be freed from their debts by some means or another.

AR-RAQIB

He is the one who watches everything, always.

This scrutiny of every detail in the existence of all creation is in part protective. Allah watches His faithful servants proceeding on their allotted paths in harmony with each other and everything else, and protects them from the intentions and the actions of those who revolt, who are about to clash with what is rightful.

The ones under the watchful eye of *ar-Raqib*, who are heedful, aware, obedient, serving Allah for Allah's sake, should know that not a speck of their good deeds will be lost: all will be rewarded. The heedless ones who dream that they are their own masters and that they can do and have all that they want should know that not one of their moves against the divine order and harmony will pass unnoticed and unpunished.

In accordance with this attribute of Allah, humanity should realize that in addition to Allah *ar-Raqib*, the loving merciful watcher, there are two other watchers, deadly enemies who watch you all the time to find an appropriate time and a weak spot to attack you; to possess, to torture, to kill you. These two wakeful enemies are the accursed Devil and the insatiable egoist, the *nafs*.

You must will all the awareness within your power, and watch every minute the moves of these two enemies who have surrounded you from four sides and from the inside.

'Abd ar-Raqib is more aware of Allah watching him and everything else than he is aware of his very existence. Consequently he is unable to cross the borders of Allah's prescriptions. Nobody but a person blessed by the manifestation of this Name is totally conscious and totally in control of himself and others around him. In reality, *'Abd ar-Raqib* is an expression of Allah's watching over him and others.

This Divine Name is the litany of the faithful who have been given the gift of *ihsan*, the gift of the certainty that although they cannot see God, God at all times sees them—not only their form and their actions, but their most secret thoughts and feelings. If one such person recites this Name as often as possible in a hidden place for a month, the eye of his heart will see secrets which others cannot see. He even may understand the language of the beasts, vegetation, and lifeless things.

If someone misplaces or loses something, recitation of this Name may help him find it.

If someone fears a curse or spell cast upon him, recitation of this Name 312 times a day for a week will render the spell ineffective.

AL-MUJIB

He is the one who responds to all the prayers and needs of His servants.

Allah is closer to His creatures than they are to themselves. His proximity to all His creatures is the same. He is not any closer to a saint than He is to you or to a mustard seed. He knows all the needs of His creation before they arise, and provides their satisfaction even before it is needed.

The manifestation of *al-Mujib* in human beings is our attentiveness and responsiveness, above all to Allah, the One who created us and furnishes all our needs. We respond to Allah by glorifying Him and by begging for our needs from Him, by attending to our duties prescribed by Him, and by responding to the needs of His other creatures when Allah chooses to give to them through our hands.

'Abd al-Mujib is the one who obeys Allah's call when he hears Allah say in Surah Ahqaf (31):

O people, accept the inviter to Allah and believe in him.

As he accepts Allah's call, Allah accepts his call. That is when His attribute *al-Mujib*, the Responder, is expressed in His servant. When *'Abd al-Mujib* calls, all come: since he has responded to Allah, everyone responds to him. Allah confirms this in Surah Baqarah (186):

> *And when My servants ask thee concerning Me, surely I am near. I answer the prayer of the supplicant when he calls upon Me. So should they hear My call and believe in Me, that they may walk in the right way.*

Prayer is a generator of energy. If one learns how to use it, one will discover a treasure and a source of strength.

If a person recites *ya Mujib* 55 times after private prayers, especially at sunrise, his or her needs will be met.

The recitation of this Name helps to stop gossip and slander directed against oneself.

AL-WASI'

He is the limitless vastness, whose knowledge, mercy, power, generosity, and all other beautiful attributes are infinite. *Al-Wasi'* is also interpreted as the endlessness of the tolerance of Allah. The wrongs and sins of humanity are like a drop of dirt in the vastness of Allah's ocean of tolerance.

A sign of *al-Wasi'* is in the infinite variety of His creations. Look at people: although we are all made of the same material, no two faces, no two voices are alike. The all-reaching vastness of Allah is reflected among us in people of vast knowledge from whom many benefit; in people of great riches and greater generosity who help the needy far and wide; in people of compassion, gentleness, and great patience whose far-reaching justice inspires great confidence. All other unconditional and limitless good qualities in human beings are reflections of *al-Wasi'*.

Know that Allah's knowledge is vast, reaching all, everywhere. You cannot hide anything from Him. His power is overwhelming; nothing can escape it, so beware of sinning and revolting. His mercy is infinite, so turn to Him. He is tolerant in His commandments, and forgiving, so do not lose hope.

'Abd al-Wasi' has a wisdom that is all-inclusive. His being covers all the possible levels to which a human being may aspire to rise. He is vast and cannot be limited within any restrictions.

People who are under heavy loads of work and responsibility which they feel unable to carry may find strength and relief if they continue reciting this Name.

People who are afflicted with the sicknesses of envy and revenge may find a cure in repeating this Name.

Reciting *ya Wasi'* 137 times when depressed may relieve one's depression.

AL-HAKIM

He is the perfectly wise, in His knowledge and in His deeds.

There is no doubt or uncertainty in His knowledge, nor does it have a limit. Neither is there any doubt or uncertainty in His commandments. Whoever follows them will learn from the reflection of His perfect knowledge many crucial things otherwise unattainable, and evolve toward being a perfect human being. Whoever does not follow Allah's orders will receive neither good nor benefit: he will not grow, but will dry up, becoming fuel for Hellfire. That which teaches us wisdom is the fear of Allah. The one who is truly wise is the one who is the master of his ego: he prepares in this life for the Hereafter. The one who is a willing slave to the desires of his flesh, and still hopes for Allah's forgiveness, hopes in vain.

Look at the things Allah has forbidden you: Each of them is a calamity. Allah created these calamities, and the unlawful as well as the lawful. He forbade the former and permitted the latter. He is the one who gave you the force to obey and the weakness to disobey. He left you free to choose. This test is not to show Him whether you are faithful or faithless. Allah knew all about you before He created you. The test is for you and for others, so that you know yourself and others know you.

None of Allah's deeds is without benefit and wisdom. None of Allah's wisdom is for His own benefit. Allah needs nothing. The purpose of this wisdom is the order and continuity of the cosmos until the appointed time.

Look at your inner being, a microcosm, a model for the universe. See how every organ, every cell is perfectly created for a definite function, how everything without fail works harmoniously. The purpose of this wisdom of perfect cooperation is only to keep that being alive until the appointed time.

The totality of the knowledge of what keeps you alive— your body, your mind, your soul—is the human portion of *al-Hakim*. When you see that, you will see the mark of Allah's wisdom in you.

'Abd al-Hakim is shown the secrets of the reasons for creation. As he knows the purpose of each creature, his behavior and actions towards them all are in accordance with that knowledge. When he sees a deviation from a thing's purpose, he is able to correct it.

117

If someone finds himself incompetent in a task he is given, or in spite of all efforts is unsuccessful in things he does, if he keeps reciting this Name, things may turn out for the better.

AL-WADUD

He is the one who loves His good servants. He is the only one who is ultimately worthy of love.

Allah in His infinite and unconditional love of His good servants has given them all abilities but above all the ability to love Him. He has given them the possibility to receive and achieve Truth, which is beyond the understanding of ordinary intellect. *Fayd* is that special ability. Yet the gift in itself is not sufficient. To be able to profit from this enlightenment, *fayd*, there is yet another condition, which is faith, and faith put into action, which is devotion. Let the ones who seek enlightenment run to piety and worship.

Al-Wadud is that sole goal of the heart which seeks the love of Allah. But love is only possible if the lover is aware of the beloved, as well as of the beauty and perfection of the beloved.

For most people, awareness depends upon the senses, and the senses are many. Each one is attracted to different things. When the soul is aware of itself and one is aware of one's soul, then the senses follow the soul which is aware of the whole. Allah is the one Beloved of the soul, because all perfection is in Him. All the senses are ecstatic with the inexhaustible sweet taste of this perfection.

How does one reach that state of sensitivity and awareness when the flesh naturally loves its good life, its pleasures,

118

health, home, property, business, and so forth? No ordinary person needs education, intelligence, incentive, and guidance to love these things. But to love Allah, we do need at least intelligence and guidance in order to realize that everything we naturally love is Allah's possession and His gift, that all of it is only a sign of His care and love for us.

All that we love is temporary, as we ourselves are. Only our sacred soul, the greatest gift to us, and the Owner of that soul, our Creator, are eternal. The realization of this is a much greater gift than all we could possess in this world. For when Allah loves His servant, He gives that person understanding, consciousness, faith, and love of Him.

The *wadud* among human beings is the one who loves for others that which he loves for himself. Indeed, he prefers the needs of others to his own. Such a blessed one confided, "I pray that on the Day of Judgement I may be stretched over the whole of Hell so that the feet of sinners will not burn." Hadrat Ali (ﷺ) said, "If you wish to be loved by your Lord, draw close to those who abandon you. Give to those who are stingy toward you. Forgive those who harm you."

The Beloved of Allah said, "If a believer looks at the face of another believer with love, it is better for him than praying in my mosque for a whole year." He also said, "The faithful who love and care for each other are like one single body: when a part of that body is injured, the whole body aches."

Even when we suffer at the hands of those for whom we wish more than we wish for ourselves, we should say, as the Beloved of Allah (ﷺ) said when he was wounded in the battle of Uhud, "O my Lord, guide my tribe well, for they don't know what they are doing, they do not know the Truth."

'Abd al-Wadud is the one whose love for Allah and the ones who love Allah is perfected. When Allah loves his servant, he spreads the love for that servant far and wide so that all, except the heedless, love him too. Muhammad, the Beloved of Allah (ﷺ), said: "When Allah loves a servant,

He calls the archangel Gabriel (علا) and says, 'I love this servant of Mine, love him also.' Then Gabriel (علا) calls unto the heavens and says, 'O you who are in the heavens, Allah loves this servant, love him too!' So all that exist in the heavens love him. Then the love of that servant is proposed to the creatures of the earth, and they love him also."

Many saints have declared this blessed Name to be *al-ism al-a'zam*, the greatest Name. The seekers of Truth, those who wish to follow orders with love and pleasure and become good servants of Allah, should recite this Name often. Allah loves His servants. He says, in a divine tradition, "My servant draws not near to Me with anything more loved by Me than the religious duties I have enjoined upon him, and My servant continues to draw near to Me with supererogatory works so that I shall love him. When I love him I am his hearing with which he hears, his seeing with which he sees, his hand with which he strikes and his foot with which he walks."

If a husband and wife, or any two people who are in conflict and hostile to each other, eat from a dish upon which one has recited *ya Wadud* 1000 times, it is hoped that they will be reconciled .

If a person writes this Name upon a piece of white silk and carries it on himself, and remembers to recite it often, people will be more inclined to like him.

Ya Razzaq, Ya 'Alim, Ya Hakim, Ya Wadud, Ya Majid

AL-MAJID

He is the Most Majestic and Glorious.

Allah Most High is glorious and majestic in the whole of His creation and beyond. No hand reaches Him, no power can touch Him, yet He is closer to His servants than their own souls. He has love and compassion for them that are far greater than their own care for themselves. His bounties are infinite; there is no end to His mercy. His state is pure perfection and His acts are pure wisdom.

In the meaning of *al-Majid* there are two elements. One is His majesty, His power, which keeps Him above and beyond any attempt to reach Him, and for which He is respected and feared. The other is His glory and honor as shown in His beautiful actions and states, for which He is praised and loved.

It behooves good servants, in consideration of the glory and honor of our Lord, to be sincere, serious, and pure in our devotions to Him as well as in all our doings thereby seeking His pleasure. A servant should recoil from arrogance, hypocrisy, and lies. Those who realize the majesty and the honor of their Lord, who are faithful, and who join Him, seeking only His pleasure, receive strength and honor themselves.

'Abd al-Majid is the one whose character and morals are perfected. Such persons are honored among people and the rest of creation because of their beautiful behavior toward them. They are virtuous through the virtues of Allah.

If a believer of good character who has contracted psoriasis fasts during the 13th, 14th, and 15th of the lunar months, and at fast-break recites *ya Majid* 100 times, it has been known to help the sickness. This regimen also assists in cases of heart disease and depression.

AL-BA'ITH

He is the raiser from the dead.

Allah *al-Ba'ith* will give life back to all of creation on the Day of Judgment. He will raise people from their graves and bring out all the actions, thoughts, and feelings that occurred during their lifetimes on this earth. This attribute of Allah is so important that recognizing it is one of the seven affirmations of faith, its last condition for the faithful must declare their belief that they will be brought back to life after their death. This is true. It is real. It will certainly happen. Allah has made this Truth known in all the books He has revealed and through all the prophets He has sent. In the Holy Qur'an, almost all the chapters have some mention of it.

> *And the Hour is coming, there is no doubt about it; and Allah will raise up those who are in the graves* (Surah Hajj 7).
>
> *From it [the earth] We created you, and into it We shall return you, and from it raise you a second time* (Surah Ta Ha 55).
>
> *Allah is He Who created you, then He sustained you, then He will cause you to die, then bring you to life* (Surah Rum 40).

How are we to realize the meaning of *al-Ba'ith* while we think that we come into this life from nothing and nowhere, and go after death into nothing and nowhere? Death is not "nothing," neither is the revival after death like our birth. After death, there is the life of the tomb, which is either a pit of the fire of

Hell or a rose garden from the rose gardens of Paradise. The dead are either tortured beings in misery or blessed beings in bliss: they are not extinguished into nothingness.

The Messenger of Allah (ﷺ) stood on the edge of the pit where the enemies of Allah who had fought him at the battle of Badr were buried, and said in a loud voice, "I have now seen that [victory] which my Lord promised me. Are you also seeing that [punishment] which your Lord promised you?" When his followers asked him, "How could you talk with those who are dead and gone?" the Messenger of Allah (ﷺ) said, "They hear what I say to them better than you can, only they are not able to answer."

And Allah, addressing the martyrs of the battle of Uhud, revealed the following verses:

And think not of those who are killed in Allah's way as dead. Nay, they are alive being provided sustenance from their Lord. Rejoice in what Allah has given them out of His grace, and they rejoice for the sake of those who, [being left] behind them, have not yet joined them, that they have no fear, nor shall they grieve (Surah Al 'Imran 168–69).

The revival after death is not like birth. Neither are coming into this world and returning after death the only instances of receiving life. That is why Allah says,

Were We then worn out by the first creation? Yet they are in doubt about renewed creation (Surah Qaf 15).

Within this life are many deaths and revivals. How often the soul loses its control of the flesh and again regains it! It even happens medically: people die and are revived. Within your body, cells are continually dying and new ones are being born. Don't you see that in all these cases what dies and is revived is only the flesh? The soul is eternal.

To deny things that we have not experienced, that we do not know, is in human nature. Because in this life we have not experienced the Hereafter, nor returning to life after death, we do not believe in them. A child who has not come to the age of discernment and who has not yet burnt his hand will refuse to believe that fire is hot. If he believes his mother and does not touch the fire, he is a happy baby. To have faith in things we have not experienced here and cannot understand is to have faith in the unseen. This is the key to bliss.

Do not be of the unbelieving, like Ubayy ibn Khalaf, who crushed decayed old bones between his fingers and threw them in our Master's face, saying, "So you claim that He will revive these rotten bones?"

The Holy Prophet said, "Indeed, so will He recreate you, so that He will put you in His fire."

On that occasion, the following verses were revealed:

Says he, Who will give life to the bones when they are rotten? Say: He will give life to them, who brought them into existence at first, and He is knower of all creation (Surah Ya Sin 78–79).

Allah's promise to bring you back to life on the Day of Judgment is sure. You are going to die the way you lived; and you are going to be revived the way you died. Whatever you sow here, you will reap in the Hereafter. Choose the seeds of good deeds. Till the ground with your efforts. Water your seeds with your tears of love and compassion and warm your fields with the divine light reflected upon the mirror of your clean heart. Do not forget that Allah in His Holy Qur'an likened *'ilm*, knowledge, to *hayyat*, life, and *jahl*, ignorance, to *mawat*, death. Whoever revives himself from the death of ignorance into the life of knowledge, or whoever helps another to be reborn into knowledge from the dark tomb of ignorance, will then see the manifestation of *al-Ba'ith* and truly believe it.

'Abd al-Ba'ith is the one whose egotism, lust, fleshly desires, and love of the world have been killed, and whose heart has been purified and revived into eternal life. He has "died before dying" and is able to revive, through his knowledge and wisdom, dead hearts which have been killed by ignorance.

If a person is able to recognize that he is heedless and loose in living according to Allah's prescriptions, and knows that he does not fear Allah's punishment, but still suffers from this state and wishes to change, he should recite this Name often. Then he will fear, love and hope for Allah's compassion and change his ways.

If someone is wrongly accused, reciting *ya Ba'ith* 7070 times may save him.

ASH-SHAHID

He is the one who witnesses all that happens everywhere at all times.

Allah is close to all things, whether we think of them as near or far. He pays attention to all events, whether we see them as large or small. He knows everything through His attribute *al-'Alim*. He is aware of the secrets and inner aspects of everything through His attribute *al-Khabir*. He is a witness to everything that appears, whether there are other witnesses to it or not, through His attribute *ash-Shahid*. On the final Day of Judgment He will reveal Himself as the witness to every action of every human being.

Ibn Mas'ud (رضى) had gone with some of the other Companions for a stroll into the country near Medina when they saw a child shepherding a flock. They invited him to share their meal. The boy declined, saying that he was fasting. This excessive devotion amazed the Companions, as it was not the month of Ramadan. Partly as a pleasantry and partly as a test, they asked the boy to sell them a sheep, and promised him half of its meat as a gift. The boy said that the sheep were not his and he did not have the right to sell them. Then, with the intention of testing him, they said, "My son, who will know? You can always say that you lost a sheep." At that the boy screamed *ayn Allah*? "Where is Allah?" and ran away. As a reward, Ibn Mas'ud (رضى) bought the whole herd from its owner and donated it to the young shepherd, who thus profited immediately in the world for his awareness of *ash-Shahid*. Ibn Mas'ud, when he met the young man from time to time in Medina, would tease him by asking him, "Where is Allah?"

'Abd ash-Shahid witnesses the truth of everything as well as the absolute Truth, and sees that he, as well as everything else, is under the will of that absolute Truth.

A person guilty of revolting against Allah despite knowing well that he is doing something wrong may be able to control his actions if he undertakes to recite *ya Shahid* in a series of 21 repetitions at a time. The same recitation made while putting one's index finger upon the hand of a disobedient child may make the child more obedient.

AL-HAQQ

Allah is the Truth, whose being is ever unchanged.

Haqq is that whose essence is valid in itself, and whose essence is the cause and necessary condition for all other existence. As Allah does not gain His existence from other than Himself, He is eternal. Everything else is temporal. Since *Haqq* is existent by itself alone, not influenced by anything else, He is non-changing. His is the only true existence. Other things which appear truly to exist draw the truth of their existence from Him.

The intellect sees other existent matters as corresponding to that Truth. We call these "truths" as well. Yet the truths of all temporal existences change in their relationship to each other and finally, when they disappear, the belief in their being true becomes invalid.

There is nothing in creation whose existence is parallel to that of Allah, the Truly Existent, Who is forever before the before and after the after. This creation may be likened to the moon: at the beginning a fine bow, as thin as a string; then a crescent; a full moon; then reversing and disappearing again. That is the order of the universe. Everything except Allah the Truly Existent begins, changes, disappears, reappears.

The manifestation of the attribute *al-Haqq* appears for the believer in faith and in words. The truth is that which needs no proof, and whose denial is impossible. So the beliefs and words relating to the non-changing causal existence are called "true faiths" and "true words," because they too in a manner of speaking are constant. Allah keeps them constant and alive, and rewards the ones who speak them, listen to them, and believe in them.

'Abd al-Haqq has been saved from all falsehood, in action and in word. Such a person is aware of the truth at all times, everywhere, and thus of the unity and oneness of all. For such a one the Truth is constant and ever-present.

A believer who takes it as truth that on Judgment Day he will stand in front of his Lord and give an accounting of his acts may be poor in spite of his efforts. If he recites *la ilaha illa Llah ul-Malik ul-Haqq ul-Mubin* ("There is no god but

128

Allah, the King, the Clear Truth") 100 times each day, he will receive his sustenance from unexpected places.

AL-WAKIL

Allah is the ultimate and faithful trustee. He completes the work left to Him without leaving anything undone.

People think that they are able to do, but He is the one who does everything and He has no need for anyone to do things for Him. He can replace everything in the universe, but nothing can replace Him nor can stand on its own without being dependent upon Him. Neither His messengers nor His prophets are His trustees. He only manifests His messages and His trusteeship through them. They are His servants; He is the Lord and the Owner of all.

He does best everything that is left to Him, yet He is under no obligation. None can influence His will; no power can force Him to do a thing. He does for you what is good for you, and that which pleases Him.

Who is the one whom you may trust to do for you better than you can do for yourself? The trustee has to know better. He has to be more powerful. He has to be trustworthy. Someone who entrusts his affairs to another has to be sure of all that. He also has to have confidence in the compassion, love, and loyalty of the trustee toward him. Who among men is such a lawyer to represent you, and work for you? What payment are you prepared to give for the services of such a trustee? No human being is such a trustee. When people do things for each other, it is only a business transaction; they give and they take. Allah, the All-Knowing, the All-Powerful, the Most Compassionate, is the only one for His servants to trust.

In all we pretend to do in our business, for the maintenance of our health, for our family, for our children, we seek some benefit. We plan, we calculate, we take precautions, we consult with accountants, doctors, lawyers; yet daily all sorts of unforeseen hindrances, oppositions, and problems appear. The true servant does all this the best he can, not only for himself, but for others. Then he leaves the outcome for Allah in His bounty to assign. He prays to *al-Wakil,* whose hand controls his life, to do that which is good for him, as he himself admits that he does not know. This is the meaning of *tawakkul,* trust in Allah. Whoever has this absolute trust in the ultimate and faithful Trustee owns a greater treasure than the greatest treasures of this world, because even in the total loss of his efforts he does not fall into despair; he is at peace. If that peace is nonexistent, no worldly benefit, no material treasure can bring happiness.

The difficulties that prevent or destroy this peace of mind are excessive ambition, miserliness, competitiveness, fear, and imagination. No amount of money, no amount of security, is going to relieve the constricted hearts of those afflicted by these sicknesses.

Tawakkul, trust in Allah, does not mean ignoring the causes of things that happen. To sit and not care about the causes and their effects is laziness. Trust in Allah is an obligation in Islam, and laziness is a sin. Allah has revealed to His servants the causes and the solutions of things that will happen. In fact, He has made the realization of these causes and solutions a condition for the happening of those things. For a thing to be created, for a need to be satisfied, a reason, a cause, has to appear. This is Allah's law and order, called *hikmat al-tasbib,* causal reason. To ignore what is available to one is purposefully to throw oneself into the jaws of the dragon of ignorance, sickness, and poverty, which is unlawful and sinful according to Islam.

130

The Messenger of Allah says, "Tie your camel. Then entrust it to the hands of Allah." Thus, well aware of the causes of effects, one should strive for what one wishes, knowing that all one's effort is but an active prayer, a wish for Allah's help. Indeed, these active prayers of our efforts become a proof of our trust in Allah for the outcome, and nothing more. The Messenger of Allah says, "If you really trusted Allah, He would feed you in the way He feeds His birds." Those who act thus do not count on their efforts, but count on Allah the Beneficent who says, "Ask and I will give."

'Abd al-Wakil is the servant who has such total faith in Allah that he becomes the recipient of the attribute of *al-Wakil*. He evolves from a state in which he sees Allah's hand in the causes and reasons of things, to a state in which all causes and reasons disappear. He gives his life fully into the hand of the ultimate Trustee, and in turn becomes His trusted servant. Allah's trusteeship is thereby manifested in him.

If someone who has total faith in God is in danger of a natural disaster such as flood, fire, or earthquake, or of an enemy's assault, recites this Name continuously in series of 66, he will be saved.

It is reported that Hadrat Ak Shamseddin, the shaykh of Mehmed the Conqueror, the Turkish sultan who took Constantinople, kept reciting this Name during the conquest.

The Prophet (ﷺ) says, "If you recite *Hasbi Allahu la ilaha illahu 'alayhi tawakkaltu wa huwa rabb ul-'arsh il-'azim* ('Allah is sufficient for me, there is no god but He, in Him do I trust and He is Lord of the Tremendous Throne' Surah Tawbah 129) in the mornings and the evenings, Allah will be your Trustee, and will guide your affairs in this world and in the Hereafter, as it is best for you."

AL-QAWI

Allah is the strongest one, the Inexhaustible.

He possesses all strength. Allah is able to overcome all, and none may touch Him. On the action of His strength there are no conditions that are difficult or easy. He can create a billion universes with the same ease with which He creates a blade of grass. With His inexhaustible strength He sees to the continuation of the creation and the protection of the creatures, and guides their actions until the appointed time.

'Abd al-Qawi is the servant who is honored with the manifestation of the strength of *al-Qawi*. With Allah's power this servant defeats lust, worldly ambition, anger and negativity, and the other soldiers of the Devil. By the grace of the manifestation of that Name in him he becomes able to destroy, always and everywhere, all enemies; man, devil, or jinn. None can oppose him. He repels all opponents through the power of Allah, whose strength is victorious over all.

If a believer who has a tyrannical enemy against whom he has no chance to defend himself makes a dough from flour and water, then fashions from this dough 1000 little balls each the size of a chickpea, and throws them to the birds to eat one by one reciting the Name *ya Qawi* each time, Allah the possessor of all strength will protect him.

Ya Qawi is the litany of Azrael, the archangel of death.

The ones who recite this Name 116 times every day, if they are weak or tired doing their daily prayers, will find strength and enjoy them. If they suffer during a difficult and dangerous voyage, they will not feel the pain.

If a person is entering a dangerous place or situation, to recite *bismi Llah ir Rahman ir-Rahim wa la hawla wa la*

132

quwwata illa bi-Llah il-'Aliy il-'Azim ("In the Name of Allah All-Merciful and Compassionate, and there is no strength nor power save in Allah, the High, the Great") may eliminate the dangers or give one strength to face them.

AL-MATIN

Allah is perfect in His strength and in His firmness.

The attribute of *al-Qawi* pertains to the perfection of His power, while the attribute of *al-Matin* is the vehemence—the all-pervasive action—of this strength. None can be saved from this strength; no force can oppose it. Nothing causes difficulty for it, nothing can weaken it, nor does that strength need any aid.

Allah has compassion and He has punishment. When He extends His compassion to His beloved servants, none can prevent this beneficence from reaching its destination, nor can any conceivable power prevent His vengeance, anger, and punishment from hitting its target. The servant should hope for all good and beauty to come from Allah, and should fear only Allah's punishment. Thus all other fears disappear from the hearts of servants who are attached to their Lord.

'Abd al-Matin is the servant to whom the mystery of the attribute of the all-pervasive strength of Allah is given. That strength makes him hold to his religion with such strength and patience that nothing can tempt him away from it, no difficulty will tire him, and nothing can separate him from the Truth. In the defense of the Truth, no one can frighten him or silence him. His effect is upon everything, and none other than Allah can affect him.

If a believer realizes that he himself is a tyrant and is negative, and wishes to get rid of his bad character, making a habit of reciting this Name 500 times every day may assist him to become a better person.

If a mother is short of milk to suckle her baby, when she drinks from a cup upon which *ya Matin* is written, her milk may increase.

AL-WALI

Allah is the protecting friend of His good servants.

He helps His good servants; He eliminates their difficulties and gives them guidance, peace, and success in their affairs in this world and in the Hereafter. He takes them out of darkness into light and enlightens their hearts. Those hearts do not stay constricted and attached to the present, but stretch to times before the before and after the after. They come to know the Lord of these realms, acknowledge His unity and oneness, and are honored by the highest level that can be reached by human beings, His friendship through being a good servant to Him.

Allah's friends have eyes enlightened by and seeing with the divine light. They take lessons from all that they hear and see. Divine light shines through their faces: whoever sees them remembers Allah. There is neither fear nor sadness for them, for they do not know any other friend but Allah. They fear nothing except opposing Allah's pleasure. They are tied to no expectation of anything from anyone except Allah.

Try to gain Allah's friendship. Be friends with His friends and learn to be like His friends. Believe in what they believe, do what they do, reject what they reject, love the ones they love, and above all, love the One whom they love most.

'Abd al-Wali is the servant in whom the friendship of everyone who is faithful becomes manifest. He is a friend to all those who are pure and devout. The Prophet (ﷺ) says, "The one who is not troubled by the troubles of other believers, and does not suffer because other believers are suffering, is not truly faithful."

If a faithful person recites this Name 1000 times on Friday nights, all material and spiritual barriers will disappear. It is hoped that such a person will see the real reality and the meaning of things.

In a marriage where one spouse has a quarrelsome character, if the other keeps this Name in his or her mind during their encounters, their communications may stop turning into fights.

AL-HAMID

Allah is the Most Praiseworthy.

He is the one praised by all existence. Praising is honoring with respect and thankfulness the Great One who gives infinite gifts. All that exist praise Allah with their tongues, with their actions, or simply by their very existence. He is the only one who is finally worthy of devotion, of respect, of thankfulness, and of praise. How can one praise another than He in His presence, while all is from Him? He is the source of all gifts and all perfection.

He has given us life, a beautiful form, strength, intelligence, language, so many wonders directly. He has given us further gifts through the hands of other people or the mediation of His other creatures. These gifts praise Allah; the ones through whom these gifts came praise Allah. Should we not praise Allah? Man invented the computer, which works, speaks, writes, communicates, captures the forms and sounds of things. The machine itself, in doing these things, praises its inventor. It is in this way that all nature praises Allah with its existence and its function. The people who use and benefit from that computer praise its inventor: that is how the servant praises the Creator. Then the inventor praises himself! Allah the Inventor of all this praises Himself and is not in need of the praise of any other.

Allah in His mercy and generosity has ordered human beings to perform certain duties for our own good, and to escape from certain evils for our own peace and salvation. There are such duties to be executed at every hour of one's life. When we perform these duties at their appointed times, we receive both material benefit and spiritual joy and wisdom, especially if these tasks are consciously performed for Allah's sake. A reward of special enlightenment comes with such action. Humanity learned what it knows in that way, and has advanced in that way. With what Allah forbade people to do, He protects us from Hellfire.

The greatest of all sins is *kufr*, denial. Denial is the opposite of praise. Imagine the benefactor of a community who has helped everyone, from whom everyone has equally profited, and furthermore, on whom the life and harmony of that society depend. If someone insulted this benefactor, denied his good deeds, what would the community that loved and respected him do? They would all be angry, hostile, vengeful toward that person. Even though that person had not done any harm to the people directly, all the people would hate him and curse him and try to destroy him. Because he had insulted the benefactor, the people would consider the harm done to all of them.

136

That is how, if one denies Allah's existence, criticizes His canons, or minimizes His perfect qualities and beneficent doings, one is cursed not only by men, but by all creation. Since there is no place which is not His, such a one will not be able to escape. We take refuge from Him in Him. All praise is due to the Lord of the whole creation, who leads us from darkness to light, who clears hearts of the night of denial and fills them with the divine light of faith. As all Muslims say in reciting Surah Fatihah at every prayer, *Al-hamdu li-Llahi rabb il-'alamin:* Praise belongs to God, Lord of the worlds.

'Abd al-Hamid is the servant to whom Allah shows Himself with His most beautiful attributes. All those beauties become manifest in such a one. All people praise that person who praises only Allah.

If someone whose faith, worship, and character befit a Muslim recites this Name 99 times after morning prayers, Allah will enlighten that person's day. If someone recites this Name 66 times after morning and evening prayers, Allah will beautify his words and actions. If someone recites this Name 100 times after each of the five daily prayers, Allah will count that person among His devout servants who will be loved and served by all people and every living creature.

If someone has a foul mouth, his writing *ya Hamid* on a cup and drinking from it regularly may refine his speech.

AL-MUHSI

Allah is the possessor of all quantitative knowledge.

He sees and knows everything in its reality. In addition to knowing all existence as an inseparable whole and knowing every creation individually, He knows each thing analytically separated according to its kind, its class. He knows its parts, even its atoms. He counts and calculates to the exact number. He knows the number of all existences in the created universe, though it seems infinite to us, down to the number of breaths exhaled and inhaled by each of His creatures. He counts and weighs, one by one, all our good deeds and sins, registering all in a great ledger.

As with His attributes *al-'Alim*, the one who knows all, *al-Khabir*, the one who is aware of all inner occurrences, and *ash-Shahid*, the one who witnesses whatever exists, the recollection of *al-Muhsi,* the one who analyzes, counts, and records in quantities should encourage the friends of Allah who do right and admonish His enemies who do wrong. Even if a good deed or a sin is as small as a mustard seed, it is counted and not lost.

Good servants, aware of this attribute, should themselves analyze each thing they intend to do, calculating whether it is right or wrong. They should watch themselves at every breath and be aware. They should make their accounting often, five times a day, at the time of each prayer, and be thankful to Allah for the good which came through Him, assume the responsibility for their sins, and repent. Salvation is in making one's accounting now, well before the Day of Judgment, the terrible day of accounting before your Lord. And ask yourself each day, "What have I done for Allah's sake today?"

'Abd al-Muhsi is the one who is honored with the ability and will to count everything, to whom the quantity of all is made known. This person not only knows things in breadth and depth around himself, but also knows his own acts and words and being analytically, and lives accordingly.

For people who are having difficulty in understanding what they hear or remembering things, reciting this Name 148 times may help. Reciting this Name may also give people the courage for self-criticism.

AL-MUBDI'

Allah is the originator of all. He creates without model or material.

In the beginning, before time or space, Allah existed. There was none other than He, none who could profit Him or hurt Him. There were no models of things to be, nor material to make them from. Allah Most High, to manifest His existence, to make known His beauty and perfection, and to make felt His love and compassion, created the creation and produced the first models. In order that the creation proliferate and continue, He made each original creation a means of perpetuating its own kind in accordance with causes, conditions, and canons of a divine order, which He also created.

Those who think of these means as the originators of things that exist, and think of nature as God, must contemplate what it is that moved the void; who charged the proton and the electron; what force it is that is inexhaustible, that sustains the continuity of things.

Servants inspired by this attribute must seek to understand their origins. How, from nothing, did we and everything else come to be creatures that live, grow, see, hear, speak, think exquisitely, in perfect order? And such servants must confirm that none else but Allah, the originator of all creation, without the influence or help of anything, is responsible for all this. Anyone who thinks of attributing a partner to Allah becomes guilty of the only unpardonable sin.

'Abd al-Mubdi' is the servant who receives the secret of the Originator, to whom Allah reveals the origin and the source of everything, and who becomes a witness to the beginning of everything.

If a person is uncertain of a decision which he is about to take recites this Name 1000 times, he may be able to decide correctly.

If a pregnant woman fears miscarriage, putting her right hand upon her belly and reciting this Name 99 times daily may help her to keep her baby.

AL-MU'ID

Allah is the restorer of the things that He has created and destroyed.

The attribute of *al-Mubdi'*, the Originator, contains the meaning of the Inventor, while *al-Mu'id* is the Re-creator and the Restorer to previous form. Everything runs through its predestined period of life and passes away. Finally, as it was in the beginning, nothing exists except Allah. Yet all the doings of the creation, especially of humanity, are recorded within the eternally existent and eternally alive Allah.

Some have lived according to His laws, purely and decently. Others have claimed "freedom" and revolted, becoming murderous and tyrannical. The laws of men do not catch and punish one thousandth of them. Allah knows all; He is the Most Just; He does not love tyrants, and He takes vengeance against them. If all is resolved by death, there is no eternal justice. Then the sinner, the revolter, the tyrant, would escape punishment. Even human reason cannot accept this.

Without a doubt there will be a Day of Judgment, where the good and the evil will be separated from each other. The good will receive their reward, the bad their punishment. Allah promises this in His Qur'an, and Allah keeps His promises. On that day, Allah *al-Mu'id* will re-create all creatures, perfect to the details of their fingerprints, and return their souls to them.

The servant who is aware of this recognizes Him not only as his Creator, but as the one who will re-create him. He will be loyal to Him alone, and will not revolt against the Creator for the sake of the created.

'Abd al-Mu'id is the one within whom Allah has placed the knowledge of the secret that things are continuously being re-enacted. Often that servant helps in the re-creation of things and the recurrence of affairs. He helps to maintain the re-created and the recurrent.

If a person in a household disappears, or a valuable possession is lost, if one recites this Name 77 times upon the four walls of the house in the quiet of the night after everyone has gone to sleep, either the news of the person who disappeared or the person himself (or the object lost) may return to that household.

AL-MUHYI

Allah is the giver of life to things without life.

As Allah can make that which does not exist come to be, as Allah can give life to the one without life, Allah can kill a thing and restore its life. Allah is the one who has created life and who has created death: none else can do that. Think of yourself. Once you were nonexistent; you were not alive. Allah created us in our mothers' wombs and gave us life, brought us to this world to breathe, to eat, to grow. . . . He gave us strength, the ability to think, to seek, to find, to know, to hear, to talk, to build, to destroy, and to propagate. All this, and this life, does not belong to us. It is a gift, lent to us. The only thing that is ours is the choice we make in the testing-ground of this world: to be faithful or unfaithful, to obey or to revolt. That choice will qualify us for heaven or hell when we die and are brought back to life again.

The faithful are thankful for the life they have received. They put their thankfulness into action by serving Allah's creatures for Allah's sake, working hard continuously as if they were never going to die. Yet we should also remember death continuously, and work for the Hereafter, for our salvation, as if we were going to die at the next moment.

'Abd al-Muhyi is the one who brings his heart to life. A heart filled with the beasts of this world is dead. A heart that is cleansed of this world and contains nothing but Allah is alive, and becomes the house of Allah. To such a servant, Allah may even give permission, as He did for Jesus (ﷺ), to restore the dead to life.

If someone who suffers from being a slave to his ego continues to recite this Name until he falls asleep from fatigue, he may be able to control his evil desires.

If people recite this Name daily 68 times, Allah will beautify their hearts with the light of faith and wisdom, and will give them the wish to help others in need.

If a believer suffering from a chronic sickness recites this Name 68 times after each of the obligatory prayers, he may be restored to health.

AL-MUMIT

Allah is the creator of death.

All who are alive will certainly die. Death may come at any moment. Allah Most High has destined a time for each being to come into existence, and a time for it to leave.

The human being is made of a combination of flesh and soul. The flesh is visible; the soul is hidden. The body is temporal; the soul is eternal. Thus there are two lives in each of us, the temporal and the eternal. The life of the material being starts with conception and ends in death, when the soul leaves the body. Although the soul continues to exist without the body, it has no physical feeling or movement, as if paralyzed. And as the one who is totally paralyzed knows his state, so do the dead know their state. Death is like a total paralysis, affecting the heart, the mind, the nerves, the circulation, everything.

In life, the body is under the orders of the soul. In death, the soul is like a king who has lost his kingdom. In life, the soul is like a merchant who buys and sells, gains and loses. In death, it is like a merchant who has lost his business: he cannot profit anymore. When we die, we are left with whatever we have gained or whatever we have lost, our debts. In our grave, we wait either bankrupt, hungry, cold, and in pain, or in the midst of plenty, joy, and peace—until the day of Last Judgment.

Believers are not afraid of death: they prepare for it.

Death is Allah's will. Whether you say that all is here, that there is nothing after this, or you believe that every day has a tomorrow and that this world has a Hereafter, you will leave here sooner or later. If you seek the pleasures of this world alone, when this life ends, your happiness will end. All your work, all your plans, all your hopes will end. But if you profit from this world, perfecting your faith, acquiring wisdom, gathering its fruits, and preparing for the Hereafter, when this short life is over you will find eternal bliss. Allah in His mercy and generosity gives what His servants ask for, regardless of faith or faithlessness. If you wish for this world, you will receive it. If you wish for the eternal life of the Hereafter, you will receive it.

'Abd al-Mumit is the servant in whose heart lust, love of this world, and negativity are killed by Allah. Thus that

143

heart has found true life. When the negative forces of the ego in one's heart are dead, one is illuminated with the divine light. Those who are granted that light enlighten others around them also. Such people continue living, breathing the air of a divine and eternal life.

The one who recites this Name often may be able to control the negative influences of his ego and his lust for the pleasures of this world. Recitation of this Name also helps one to find alliance with the faithful and to achieve the conquest of one's enemies.

AL-HAYY

Allah is the perfectly alive and ever-living one. He is the source of life in all that is alive.

That which is alive is cognizant and active. Allah is cognizant of all, and all actions are His. All that is known and will be known is within His knowledge; all existence is comprehended within His action at all times.

With the exception of Allah, the life of everything living is held within the limits of its action and its realization. That realization and activity are the signs of life: when they end, life ends. The value of each life is judged by the extent of the knowledge and the activity of the living one. Allah Most High has given lives of different degrees and different kinds to His creatures. The value of a created being is in accordance with the degree of the signs of life in it.

A plant, which is alive, is more valuable than soil or stone. Plants are born, eat, drink, grow, propagate, and die. They also possess knowledge, enabling them to differentiate that which is profitable from that which is harmful for them. They are also active. They seek and find what is needed for their growth and propagation in the air, in the water, and in the depths of the earth. They suck in what they need and they digest it and transform it into food, fruit, remedies, and thousands of things that are beneficial to higher forms of life. Yet they are unaware that there is a higher form of life than theirs.

Life in the animal is more highly developed because the animal sees, hears, and moves. The life of vegetation is inferior to the life of the animal; that is why the animal is the master of vegetation. It steps on it, grazes and eats it. There is also a degree of life superior to that of the animal. The Creator has honored humanity with that superiority.

Human life contains all the qualities of vegetal and animal life, only in perfected form. In addition, the human being has intellect. This intellect with which we have been honored analyzes, compares, concludes, figures out the end at the beginning, and takes action in accordance. We know and act upon our knowledge: that is why we are the masters of this world. The most elementary signs of life are birth, eating and drinking, breathing, growth, and propagation. The higher sign of the higher form of life is to know and to act consciously in accordance with that knowledge.

People also differ one from another in the degree of their aliveness, which is judged by the extent of their knowledge and their action. The lowest degree of knowledge for a human being is the awareness and knowledge of oneself. Whoever does not know himself and is not aware of his own existence might as well be dead. The words of the unconscious living dead are dead and deadly: run away from them. Within the sacred name *Hayy*, pronounced by people of *ma'rifah*, true knowledge of reality, to whom the mystery of the Ever-Living One has been divulged, there is life. Hear it from their mouths and let it penetrate into your soul so that you, too, may come alive.

'Abd al-Hayy is he in whom Allah has killed the worldly desires of his flesh, thus giving him the eternal life of knowing himself.

A believer who recites this Name constantly, if Allah so wills, will have a long and happy life.

If someone is excessively stressed or disturbed, to recite this Name 500 times every day before sunrise may bring peace.

AL-QAYYUM

Allah is the self-existing one upon whom the existence of all else depends.

Many of the wise agree that *al-Hayy al-Qayyum,* the Ever-Living, the Self-Existing is the greatest Name, which has the power, when recited by those upon whom it is manifested, even to raise the dead. The Messenger of Allah (ﷺ) said that Jesus (ﷺ) recited these names when he revived the dead.

When Moses (ﷺ) split the Red Sea in two, his people asked him how he prayed to his Lord. He said that he recited *Ahiyyan ya Hayy, Sharahiyyan ya Qayyum.*

Hadrat 'Ali (ﷺ) relates that during the battle of Badr, when he checked on the Messenger of Allah, he would find him prostrating and begging *Allahu, ya Hayyu, ya Qayyum* for the victory which Allah accorded to him.

Allah is self-existing. His existence depends upon nothing other than Himself, and is exalted over all other existences. He is the one who gives that which is necessary for the existence of everything. He has created the causes for the existence of each thing until its destined time. All exists because of Him.

146

If people can see how our being, our life, our body are dependent upon our soul, we may understand a little the dependence of all that exists upon the Ever Self-Existent One. The soul governs the whole of our being. When the soul leaves the body, although the body appears to be the same, it does not breathe, it does not see, it does not hear, it does not move, and eventually it disintegrates, because what governed it and held it together was the soul.

It is the soul which is responsible for life, existence, and order and harmony within the whole being. The being—its wisdom, its beauty, its strength, its very life down to the last cell, the last atom—is in need of the soul at every moment. When the soul leaves, all these qualities disappear.

In this way, every atom of the created universe is in need at every moment of the divine favor, the manifestation of *al-Qayyum*. This divine grace is a special will of Allah that is present always, in different forms and strengths, in accordance with the need of everything in the universe for the perpetuation and amelioration *al-Qayyum* alone grants. It is with this divine will that every atom obtains the cause for the satisfaction of its needs. If Allah cut off that favor for a split second, nothing would be left standing.

O heedless one, Allah, who has infinite numbers of good servants and the whole creation to take care of, nevertheless cares for you and maintains you as if you were His only creation. Although you have no one else but He who keeps you, you behave as if you do not need Him and have other protectors who could care for you. Worse still, you behave as if you are self-sufficient, self-existent. How great is Allah's favor, how infinite is His mercy, and how deep is your heedlessness!

'Abd al-Qayyum is the one who witnesses that all exists because of Allah, and becomes an instrument of the manifestation of *al-Qayyum* by meeting the needs of others in Allah's name.

147

If someone who spends a lot of his valuable time sleeping should recite before he is about to fall asleep, *Alif lam mim, Allahu la ilaha illahu al-Hayy ul Qayyum* ("Alif. Lam. Mim. Allah, there is no god but He, the Living, the Self-Existing"Surah Baqarah 255) he may stop sleeping his life away.

On the other hand, if someone is afflicted with insomnia and recites *wa tahsabuhum ayqazan wa hum ruqudun* ("You would have reckoned them awake, but they were asleep" Surah Kahf 18) *fa-darabna 'ala adhanihim fil-kahfi sinina 'adadan* (". . . so We sealed up their hearing in the Cave for a number of years"Surah Kahf 11) at bedtime, he may be able to sleep.

Someone who has difficulty in memorizing can make a habit of reciting this Name 16 times a day in a solitary place, and may then overcome that handicap.

AL-WAJID

Allah finds and obtains whatever He wishes whenever He wishes.

Allah is able to find any of His creatures instantly, especially when He wishes to exercise His will upon it. It is even superfluous to use the word "find," because all creation is in His presence at all times. Nothing can hide or retreat to a place that is out of His reach. Allah has all He needs to exercise His will. The servant must never consider himself separated from his Lord. His Lord is ever-present within and without him, and the servant is ever in the presence of his Lord. When the servant has a need, it suffices him to feel and say, "O Lord, I am in Your presence

148

and my state and my needs are better known to You than to myself."

One is always in need. There is always trouble for which one seeks relief. At times, we feel the need of other people like ourselves—a doctor, a lawyer, a judge. It is not possible to seek an audience with these people at any time of the day or night: such ceremony and difficulty one must go through to present one's case to them! Yet how often we submit ourselves to go through all that complication while the Lord of all these servants, the Curer, the just Judge, the rich Sustainer, the Merciful, the Best of Masters, the Loving One, the All-Powerful, the Ever-Present, invites us into His presence five times a day, at the appointed times of prayer, and we neglect to go to Him to present our needs! Not only five times a day, but wherever you are, at whatever time of the day or night, He is there to satisfy your needs with all His love and compassion and wisdom and treasure. All you need to say is *Ya Allah*.

'Abd al-Wajid is the servant who finds everything in the essence of the One. Such a person knows the place of everything and is able to find it. Because he can obtain whatever he wishes, he neither loses nor asks for anything. He finds that which Allah wishes him to find.

A believer who makes a habit of reciting this Name as often as possible may be given strength of heart which will help him to find what he wishes to find and keep what he has found.

AL-MAJID

Allah is the Most Glorious, who shows infinite generosity and munificence to those close to Him.

For example, He gives us much more than we need, as well as the gift of good character and good conduct, enabling us to do good deeds. But if we are miserly in sharing that which we have received, He abandons us. If we are generous, He loves us and glorifies us for the character He has given, and rewards us by forgiving our sins and our errors. He hides our sins and errors from others and even from ourselves. He accepts our excuses; He protects our rights. He relieves our difficulties. He prepares the causes for our peace, happiness, and salvation. The servant, remembering the munificence of the Glorious One, should love Him and obey His orders with joy, and fear Him through loving Him, fearing to lose the favor of the Beloved One.

'Abd al-Majid is the one who is praised and honored by Allah and given the strength to carry the responsibility of this honor.

The believer who recites this Name 465 times during the day and 465 times during the night has his words understood by others as he meant them to be understood. His character improves. He is loved and respected. He even may understand the language of the beasts and plants, and they may understand him.

AL-WAHID

Allah is One. He has no equal, none like Him, nor any partner in His essence, in His attributes, in His actions, in His orders, or in His beautiful Names.

He is One in His essence. All else is His creation. How could any of what He has made and maintained be compared to Him?

He is One in His attributes. Among His creatures, and especially in the human being, signs or symbols of His attributes may be shown in order that we might feel a sense of His qualities and strengthen our faith. Otherwise the manifestations of His attributes are not like our attributes at all.

He is One in His actions. He does not need any help in His act of creation, nor in doing what He wills with His creation. What appear as material and spiritual causes to us are unable to cause anything by themselves.

He is One in His orders and in His justice. He is the only source of reward, punishment, good deeds, or sin. None other than He has the right to say "This is right, this is wrong, this is lawful, this is unlawful."

He is One in His beautiful Names, none of which can be attributed to other than He. Anyone who in any way claims the resemblance of anything else to Him is guilty of the only unforgivable sin—that of attributing partners to Him. He is the only one worthy of worship. His oneness is indivisible. He is a whole without parts.

Among human beings, the sign of the Oneness is manifested in that person who has reached such a height in good morals, character, and manners that no one else is equally excellent. Yet the uniqueness of this individual is limited by the span of his or her lifetime. Similar people could have existed before, and may exist later. And such uniqueness is only in relation to the aspect of character and does not include all possible considerations.

'Abd al-Wahid is the servant who has penetrated into the oneness of his Lord and has come to know the mystery of this attribute, which becomes the key to understanding all the attributes of Allah. Thus *'Abd al-Wahid* sees everything within the beautiful Names. He understands everything through the attributes of Allah and does everything in accordance with them. He is the master of the age. He is the first of his time after Allah. He is the *qutb*, the Axis of the world.

151

If someone who is afflicted with maleficent imagination, unreasonable fear of everything, and a heavy heart takes an ablution and recites this Name 1000 times in a quiet place, he may find relief.

If a believer who is facing a danger from a very powerful tyrant recites *ya Wahid al-Baqi awwala kulli shay'in wa akhirahu* ("O Thou the One, who remains at the beginning of everything and its end") 500 times after his noon prayers, he may be safe.

AL-AHAD

He is the unity in which all Names, all attributes, and all their relations to anything are united. In this Name they disappear and become nonexistent in themselves.

This Unity is devoid of having been created, of existence and nonexistence, of being and nonbeing. It is the manifestation of the essence of Allah. This Unity is the highest form of the expression of Allah's essence, manifest when He descended as the all-pervasive first burst of light from the dark void in which Allah found Himself before the creation. Within that Unity, the essence is free from all attributes, names, signs, and relativity, yet all is hidden within it.

A wall is made out of stone, brick, pebbles, sand, and mortar, and covered with stucco. When you see the wall, you see it as a whole, not its materials one by one. The wall is the sum total of the ingredients from which it is made; but the wall is not the stone, the brick, the mortar. In the concept of the wall, the materials lose their identity.

In a way, you are like that. You identify yourself as "I," yet within that "I" there are many "I's." You contain many values, qualities, attributes, thoughts, judgments, some true, some imaginary, and you relate to others at one moment with this "I" and at the next with another "I." The identity of everything in creation is constructed the same way.

All this seemingly infinite multiplicity is within one Unity—nonexistent within it, like the images in one great mirror. The images shift and change and disappear: the mirror of Unity stays.

The manifestation of Unity, the expression of the essence of Allah in humanity, the created, is impossible. But, if you are able to immerse yourself in that one "I" which is your essence, forgetting the qualities which you attribute to yourself or are attributed to you by others, forgetting your considerations and your thoughts; if you can see yourself within that single identity, being the "you" within you, incomparable, not related to anything else within or without you then you will be one in whom unity is manifested to the extent that it is possible in a created being.

If one sat alone in a quiet place and recited this Name 1000 times, contemplating its meaning and trying to feel unity in one's being, some matters concerning the inner self might be manifested.

AS-SAMAD

Allah is the satisfier of all needs, and all is in need of Him.

He is the sole recourse, the only place of support where one may go to rid oneself of all trouble and pain and to receive all that one needs through the blessings of this Name. Through *as-Samad*, inexhaustible treasures open and are distributed to all creatures in accordance with their needs.

There are people and other creatures of Allah who serve as sources from whom we seek the cure for our troubles and the satisfaction of our needs. However as our needs are different, the sources corresponding to our needs are different. If one needs wisdom, one seeks a person of knowledge. If one needs money, one goes to someone rich. If one is sick, one finds a doctor. It is not always certain that the scholar is going to answer your question, nor that the rich one will pay the money you need, nor that the doctor will be able to cure you, and they are not so readily available. One must go to them and wait for them to have time for you. These sources are the signs, the reflections of the attribute *as-Samad*, and indeed are a great gift from Allah.

The Satisfier of all needs is ever-present, knowing your needs before you do, satisfying your needs in the way they should be satisfied, not in the way you think they should be satisfied. It is good that you realize your need, that you ask for its satisfaction, and that you accept and are thankful for whatever manner it is in which He sees fit to satisfy it. It is good only to make you aware of your Creator and to make you aware of yourself. Otherwise, strictly for the satisfaction of the need, neither your feeling the need or asking for its satisfaction, nor your being cognizant of having received the satisfaction, are necessary. For Allah is the All-Knowing, All-Powerful, Generous, Compassionate Satisfier of all needs.

However, He loves His servants who are heedful more than those who are heedless. He loves His servants who are grateful more than those who are ungrateful.

'Abd as-Samad has received from Allah the duty of the maintenance and education of His creation. His hand, his tongue, his whole being are a means through which Allah satisfies the needs of the creation. That is why all seek him for the elimination of their troubles, for receiving good, for acceptance of their repentance, to escape from God's anger. He is the intercessor.

154

A believer who recites this Name 125 times after morning prayers and before sunrise, in a state of prostration, will be protected from lying and unlawful behavior as well as the hostility of others, and will find improvement in character and faith.

If one cares for someone who is under the influence of a bad person and is performing sinful acts, one may fast for a consecutive Thursday, Friday, and Saturday, breaking one's fast without touching meat or dairy products, and then recite *ya Samad* 100 times over food or drink. If one then feeds this to the person in trouble, it may help him to repent for his wrong ways and save him from bad influences.

AL-QADIR

Allah is the All-Powerful who does what He wills, as He wills.

Allah has created the universe as a mirror to reflect His power. He created the universe by Himself, without needing the help of anything, from nothing, with neither materials nor model. He said "Be!" and it became. If He wills, He can destroy everything and send all back to nothingness. If a thing has not happened, it is not because He does not have the power to make it happen: it is because He has not willed it.

Al-Qadir has infinite ability. His capacity for causing things to happen, His powers of invention and creation, are conditioned by only one thing: His will.

It befits the good servant of Allah to look into the mirror of the universe. See the billions of suns and galaxies within the immeasurable depths of the heavens above, defying mind and imagination! We should also observe how, just

155

as these galaxies swim in their allotted paths, innumerable creatures swim in a drop of water; how from two cells Allah creates a human being who becomes a microcosm containing all that exists; how He gives a tiny piece of bone in the ear the ability to hear and a piece of meat in the mouth the ability to speak. Isn't a believer going to prostrate in awe and respect? Such recognition of the immensity of divine power is our greatest honor.

'Abd al-Qadir is the one who is a witness to everything made by the Hand of Power of Allah. The manifestation of Allah's power is spoken of as "Allah's hand." Nothing can stop that which is made by Allah's hand.

If a believer recites this Name while washing each member in the course of making his ablution, it will give strength to his members.

If someone who is suffering from unrequited love keeps reciting this Name, 305 repetitions at a time, either the beloved will respond, or the suffering will cease.

AL-MUQTADIR

Allah is the one who creates all power and has total control over all power.

Because He has total power, He is able to create what He wills and put into His creation whatever power He wills. Without this energy that comes from its Creator, everything is lacking in itself, unable, in need. But if Allah gives it the power and enables it, an ant can move a mountain. Allah bestows power upon things on earth and in heaven, and uses them in accordance with His all-pervasive wisdom and will. If He wills, He strengthens the weak and weakens the strong, makes peace between them, makes them love each other; or if He wills, He makes them fight each other.

Allah is the helper of the well-intentioned who serve for His sake, and He is the enemy of tyrants. He gives ease, wisdom, patience, perseverance, and strength to His good servants. He increases the heedlessness, ambition, pleasures, and self-confidence in tyrants. Allah manifests His name *al-Muqtadir*, along with *al-Qahhar*, the one supreme over all forces, and *ash-Shadid*, the one who is severe in punishment, when He destroys His enemies in defense of the righteous.

All creation is allotted a certain power by *al-Muqtadir*. These powers are limited and controlled by the Giver of power. It seems to us that the powers of humanity are great, enabling us to do great deeds. We even say that we can invent, we can create. Human beings can neither invent nor create. Allah causes a thing to happen and leads people to discover something that has already been created. It is always Allah who creates, even if sometimes it appears to come about through His creatures.

The faithful person should know that all power comes from *al-Muqtadir*, and by submission to His will, by obeying Him, by loving and fearing Him, one should try to obtain that power. No force can overcome that power. All love the one who loves Allah: all fear the one who fears Allah.

When one receives the help of Allah and is victorious through it, one should not be spoiled and become self-confident. On the contrary, one should show one's thankfulness actively by repenting for one's mistakes, by being just, forgiving, generous, and compassionate, even to one's enemies.

'Abd al-Muqtadir is the one upon whom Allah has bestowed the knowledge of the secret of His first act of creation, the creation of the causal primary intelligence, *an-nur al-Muhammadi*, the Light of Muhammad (ﷺ) from which all other created existence was generated.

157

A believer who makes a habit of reciting this Name up to 744 times when he wakes up in the morning will be heedful during the day: his memory will be sharp. His affairs of the day will be solved in the best manner by the help of Allah.

AL-MUQADDIM

Allah brings forward whomever He wills.

Allah advances the chosen among His creation, bringing some above and ahead of others. For instance, He invites the whole of humanity to truth, but leads some to respond to the invitation, while others are left behind. He creates all human beings as Muslims: some realize their Islam, their submission, while others are left behind. Allah has made things lawful and unlawful for all people. To some, he has given discrimination: these abide by His law and advance, while others are trampled upon.

Allah favors some of his servants by the quiet love He creates in the hearts of people for them, and others by loud cheers and applause. There are great kings whose deaths are celebrated by their people with joy. There are poor men whose departures are mourned by the world.

The believer knows that although Allah is the one who advances whom He wills, He has also set laws of action for us. If we do not do anything and are lazy, the end is poverty, constriction, trouble, and pain. If we work for money and fame, that money will be spent on drinking, gambling, and debauchery. The end of that will again be poverty, constriction, and pain.

We must learn to be in harmony with Allah *al-Muqaddim* and work in accordance with His laws if we wish to advance. If the goal is to obtain the good of this world in a lawful manner, and if Allah does not permit the servant to become rich, although he tries very hard, still Allah knows best. Perhaps such acceptance is a greater advancement than being ahead in riches for the measure of true advancement is the degree of one's closeness to Allah.

'Abd al-Muqaddim is the one whom Allah keeps in the first rank in every respect. Allah also gives such a person control over the ones who are going to advance and the ones who have moved ahead.

Someone who is aware of the demands of his ego and the state of his soul, and who knows that his ego pulls him down toward the earth because it was created from it, while his soul pulls him up toward the heavens because it came from that direction, may make a habit of reciting this Name 184 times a day. That person will be given the wisdom to choose his or her priorities in this life as well as the will to perform our duties for the Hereafter at their proper times, and will be successful in both.

AL-MU'AKHKHIR

Allah is He who leaves whomever He wills behind, and delays advancement.

As He leads some into advancement, He leads others into regression. As He rewards some whose efforts are in harmony with His will by bringing them to the first rank, He leaves others behind who are making the same effort. There is always a reason. If a believer is left behind in spite of his efforts, there may be some wrong, some impurity, some hypocrisy in his intentions. Or it may be that advancement for him should necessitate more difficulty and pain, so that he will value the reward more and guard his station better when he reaches it.

Advancement and being left behind are also relative. The one in the first rank surely is ahead, but the one in the second rank, although behind the first, is ahead of the third. Allah in His wisdom advances and keeps back whomever He wills. The good servant accepts his station and state, continuing his efforts but also trying to understand the reasons for his condition.

The good servant should know that what is most important is our closeness to Allah. The means of closeness to Him are *'ibadah* and *'ubudiyyah*. *'Ibadah*, worship, is to do things to please Allah, and *'ubudiyyah*, servanthood, is to be pleased with what Allah does.

'Abd al-Mu'akhkhir is the servant who becomes instrumental in postponing the punishment of people who revolt against the *shari'ah*, who go astray, who tyrannize themselves and others. He also becomes an instrument for stopping these sinners at a certain point.

Believers who make a habit of reciting this Name 100 times a day become able to see their faults and repent. When they repent, if they recite it 1000 times, their repentance will be accepted, if Allah wills. The sign of the acceptance of the repentance will be an increase in their desire to perform their prayers.

If someone wishes to prevent a tyrant from gaining a high position, he should recite this Name 1446 times before sunrise for seven consecutive days. With Allah's will he may be able to prevent it.

Allah Muqaddim, Ya Mu'akhkhir,
Ya Awwal, Ya Akhir, Ya Zahir

AL-AWWAL

Allah is the First.

Even when we say that He is before the before, the first "before" precedes the second and is comparable to it. His being first is not at all related to that which comes after Him which is all existence, seen and unseen. We should not think that while He is the First, there is still a second. There is none like Him. His firstness means that there is nothing prior to Him, that He is self-existent, that all arises from Him and that He is the cause of all that becomes. By the grace of this attribute, the good servant should be the first in devotion, worship, and good deeds.

'Abd al-Awwal is the servant who has been given the secret of the beginning and the end of everything. Such a person is aware of eternity and endlessness.

Whoever remembers to recite this Name 37 times before starting an important task may suceed more fully.

A couple who cannot have a child, someone who has a beloved person missing, or people with any kind of over-whelming problem should recite *ya Awwal* 1000 times for 40 consecutive Fridays. They may then have their wish fulfilled.

AL-AKHIR

Allah is the Last.

We cannot say that He is after the after, because He cannot be compared to that which would then precede Him. As

He has no beginning, He also has no end. He is eternal. All existence has two ends: a beginning when it is created, born; and an end when it dies and disappears. Allah is the First because He has created the first existence from nothing: He is the Last because when all disappears, only He will exist.

Everyone upon it passes away and there endures forever the face of thy Lord, the Lord of Glory and Honor (Surah Rahman 26–27).

All existence will return to Allah. The circle of being begins and ends with Him. There is nothing before Him and there is nothing after Him.

The faithful know that all they have, material and spiritual, belongs to Allah and will return to Him. We ourselves will return to Him and will have to give an accounting of how we used and cared for that which was lent to us temporarily. Therefore the actions of the good servant from beginning to end are performed for Allah's sake, for His good pleasure, and in the name of good servantship.

It is proper to read, recite, and consider the attributes "The First" and "The Last" together, because the meaning is like a circle where the first and the last are one.

'Abd al-Akhir is the servant who knows that everything has an end except Allah Most High, who is the only Eternal One. Such a person works to lose the temporal self in the eternity of the Lord.

Believers who recite this Name 100 times a day will eventually stop fooling themselves and see the Truth, the real Reality. If one is being attacked by an enemy and one recites *ya Akhir* 800 times, the aggressor will withdraw. One who recites it 1000 times will have his heart filled with the love of God. Recitation of this Name 1000 times on Fridays will help to increase one's sustenance.

AZ-ZAHIR

Allah is the Manifest One.

A thing is apparent to some and hidden from others in accordance with their abilities to see and to realize. Allah Most High is hidden from those who seek to see by means of their senses or their imagination, but He is apparent to those who seek to know Him by the inference of that treasure of wisdom and reason that Allah has bestowed upon them.

Allah is hidden in the endlessness of His infinite power and existence. He is like a light that makes all visible, yet His Light itself becomes a veil to His Light. That which has no bounds seems not to have a shape, therefore becoming invisible. But He is apparent in everything: everything our eyes see, every sound we hear, everything we touch, everything we taste. The meaning of everything we think, everything without and everything within us, is not He but is from Him. Everything is a proof of His existence. Everything says, "I am nothing on my own. The one who made me, who keeps and maintains me, is my Creator. I am in need of Him every moment of my existence. Every shape, every color, every taste, every perfume, every movement, every force, every quality that appears in me is from Him. It is His making, His gift, His bounty, His work."

Allah is manifest in His attributes. One can know an artist from his artwork. If one does not see the setting sun, but sees its reflection in distant windows and says that one has seen the sunset, that is not lying. If certain people see the perfect attributes of Allah in His creation, within and without themselves, and say, "I have seen Allah," they are not lying.

We are able to see only what is closest to us, and that which is closest to you is yourself. The human being is Allah's best creation. All creation is within the human being. If you see His perfect attributes in the perfect creation that you are, you will see Allah the Manifest One, and your faith will be complete.

The apparent and the hidden are also in the human being. Our form, our words, our actions, and our work are manifest. Our feelings and thoughts are hidden: People are not what they are only because of what is manifest in us. We may grow fat or thin, we may even lose a limb but our essence, our identity, that which is "us", that which is constant, is hidden in us. Yet our identity becomes manifest only through our actions, through the evaluation of the quality of our actions.

'Abd az-Zahir is the one to whom the inner meaning of things becomes outwardly manifest, like the prophet Moses (عليه السلام), upon whom the secret of the Manifest One was bestowed. He saw the manifestation of the divine light in the flames of the Burning Bush, and invited the Children of Israel to faith with a huge Torah revealed to him in golden script, ordering worldly law, salvation from the hand of the tyrant, and the benefits of Paradise.

If a believer has a sincere wish and is trying hard to realize it, he may make two cycles of extra prayer and then recite *Huwal-Awwalu wal-Akhiru waz-Zahiru wal-Batinu wa huwa bi kulli shay'in 'Alim* ("He is the First and the Last, the Manifest and the Hidden, and He is the Knower of all things"Surah Hadid 3) 145 times. He may have a better chance of obtaining that which he desires.

Recitation of this Name enables one to see things which were previously hidden. If someone has a difficulty and has no idea how to find a solution, he may, after his obligatory night prayer, do an extra two cycles of prayer and then recite *ya Zahir* 1006 times, asking God to show him the solution

165

of his problem. The solution may then be shown to him in his dreams.

AL-BATIN

Allah is the Hidden One.

His existence is both manifest and hidden. He is apparent because the signs of His existence are visible even to the blind, but His essence remains hidden from us. If there is an artwork, there is certainly an artist who created it. If there is a creation, there certainly is a Creator. If you exist, He exists. But to truly know the Creator is not possible for the creature because the knowledge, the mind, the understanding of the created one are limited. Therefore their comprehension has only a limited range. Allah Most High is eternal, infinite, without a beginning or an end, inexhaustible in His knowledge and power. To expect a temporal, limited existence to understand and encompass an eternal and infinite concept is absurd. Is it possible to fit an ocean into a bucket? Yet although a bucketful of water from the ocean is not the ocean, it is from the ocean. The manifestation of Allah's attributes in His creation is like that bucket of water: not He, but from Him. His hidden essence is like the ocean whose depth and breadth are infinite, unfathomable.

To know the essence of anything, no matter how small— to know it in totality, outwardly and inwardly, to penetrate all its secrets is practically impossible in every case. Science in its advanced state today, and in what we imagine it will become tomorrow, always ends and always will end in impotence and awe. Of everything in creation, we are closest to ourselves. Has humanity been able to know and understand itself?

166

That is why the Messenger of Allah (ﷺ) ordered us to contemplate Allah in His attributes and forbade us to speculate further than that. Only Allah knows His own essence: we have no power to conceive of it. Those who have pushed their minds to go further have either lost their wits or fallen into the chasm of disbelief, faithlessness, and attributing partners to Allah.

To open one's heart to receive the manifestation of this divine Name, a believer's inner state and outer appearance should be the same. One should avoid sinning whether the sin is visible to others or not, and one should at the same time avoid trying to discover the sins of other people.

The hypocrite is like a used chamber pot. The outside of it looks clean but the inside is foul. The Messenger of Allah says: "Allah does not judge you by your appearance: He looks into your hidden deeds and into your hearts."

'Abd al-Batin is the good servant upon whom Allah bestows the knowledge of the heart, whose inner self is purified, in whom spirituality surpasses material being. For such people the veils part, the secret becomes manifest, the future is known. They become instruments inviting people to cleanse their inner world with the divine light, encouraging them to reach spiritual perfection. Allah the Hidden One manifested His attribute *al-Batin* in the prophet Adam (ﷺ), and taught him not only the manifestation of His attributes but their inner meanings. Until Adam, even the angels knew Allah only through the manifestation of His attributes. That is the difference between Adam and the angels in the degree of perfection of faith. It is why Allah ordered the angels to prostrate themselves in front of Adam, and why Adam became the teacher of the angels.

If believers made a habit of reciting this Name 33 times a day, their inner world would become enlightened, the eyes of their hearts would open, they would start seeing the real Reality and understanding the meaning of things, by Allah's

167

will. They would find peace, their words would become sweet and effective. They would be loved and appreciated by others.

AL-WALI

Allah is the sole manager and governor of the whole creation.

His government is of such might that the whole creation from beginning to end (even before it was created!) is under its will and power. With the single order "Be!" all came into existence from nonexistence. Everything appears in this way: managed, developed, and when its time comes, dying, disappearing from sight. Even after death, everything stays under His government, and finally will be brought back to life again. In His managing of the creation, Allah knows at all times what has happened, what is happening, and what will happen, as all is planned, predestined. He is the one who wills and He is the one who executes.

Prior to your creation, He prepared a program for you: at what moment and place and from which mother you would be born, and all that would happen to you, all that you would do every minute of your life, up to the number of breaths you would inhale, up to the morsels of food that you would consume. Every syllable you will pronounce, every sound you will hear, all that you will see and all that you will do, is planned.

In the whole of creation, He has given will only to human beings. You think you can change your destiny with this will. In reality, your willing only serves your realizing, receiving, benefiting from, and enjoying that which is written for you.

When you think you revolt, what would have happened to you still happens to you, only you are unaware, unconscious, resentful ,and in disharmony with what happens. Your will is your ability either to open your eyes to see the creation of Allah in which His beautiful Names are manifested, and to receive the light of faith and knowledge or to revolt and sin, closing your eyes and remaining in darkness. Yet that which exists still exists, whether you see it or you are blind to it.

The whole of creation is governed by Allah's knowledge and power: not a leaf moves without His will. Neither is the movement of the leaf disconnected from other things moved by the same wind, by the same will.

Do not think you are left on your own. Know and see that you are part of a divine order under a just, compassionate, beneficent Governor. All is measured, all is registered, all moves swiftly. Use your will to be aware of it, to have faith in it, and to be in harmony with it.

'Abd al-Wali is the servant who governs himself and those who are entrusted to his care according to Allah's rules. He is just, he is good, and he dispenses justice and goodness. In return for his services he receives bounties and wisdom from Allah with which he further perfects his management and his generosity toward other people.

When such a servant teaches others to be just and generous like him, each time those he teaches act justly and generously, he receives twice the reward they receive. The good ruler is the one whose good deeds will surpass his wrongdoings on the scale of the Day of Judgment. Allah keeps such rulers under the shade of His throne. Allah is the helper of all those who help others.

If a believer who holds a responsible position of power recites this Name 1000 times on Fridays for the good of the people under his management, his words will benefit them. They will also be more thankful, respectful, and obedient toward him.

If one fears an oncoming natural disaster may endanger one's home, if one writes this Name on a vessel filled with water and sprinkles the water around the house, it may be protected.

AL-MUTA'ALI

Allah is the Supreme One.

His greatness grows. As He gives from His inexhaustible treasures, His riches increase. As the needs of His creation increase, His bounties increase. Yet if all the forces, the conniving minds, and the armies of the entire universe united, they could not by force take anything from Him, even a thing the size of a mustard seed, without His permission and His will.

You might be strong, young, and handsome today, but you may be sick, decrepit, and crippled tomorrow. You might be wise and intelligent today, but you may lose your wits tomorrow. You might be rich, and become bankrupt. Think of the nations that were supreme on the face of this earth, but then were trampled and dishonored and have disappeared from the maps.

Allah the Supreme One is exempt from all such failures and defects.

The true servant, who sincerely says *amantu bi-Llahi*, "I believe in Allah," believes in that One whose attributes, qualities, and beautiful Names are described in the Holy Qur'an and the hadiths. There are also those who believe in nothing other than themselves, in this world, and in the joys, pleasures, and riches of this world. There are yet others who believe in gods who walk in the gardens of Eden in the cool of the day or walk upon the clouds or sit on thrones, who have wives and children, who regret having created some among their creations and some among human beings.

Allah the Supreme One is free from such attributions. Those who lower Him to the level of their imagination are lowering themselves from the high state of servantship to the lowest state of their evil-commanding egos.

'Abd al-Muta'ali is that exalted servant of Allah who climbs from one height to another in the comprehension of things within and without himself. He witnesses limitless divine heights, soaring to this level through Allah's generosity and reward for his continuous consciousness, remembrance and devotion. His whole purpose, intention, effort, and attention are focused on knowing, finding, and being with Allah.

Allah Most High, in Surah Ta Ha (114), addressing Muhammad (ﷺ), the highest being in the entire creation, says:

(O My beloved) Say: My Lord, increase me in knowledge.

Even he was ordered to wish to know more about his Lord.

If a believer, demoted through no fault of his own, recites this Name 540 times, he may regain his position, or be raised to a position above others who have the same qualifications. Recitation of this Name the same number of times before an interview may help one to be more effective.

AL-BARR

Allah is the perfect Doer of Good.

All good and bounty come from Him. He loves for His servants only good, comfort, and ease. He does not like hardships for them, neither does He like those who create hardships. Yet in His mercy He forgives the ones who do no good. He hides meanness. If, in His justice, He chooses to punish, His punishment never exceeds the sin committed, while His reward for good deeds is tenfold their value. He delays His punishment so that perhaps the erring servant will realize a wrongdoing and repair it with a good act. Then He transforms the sin that has been repented for into a good deed itself. If His servant intends to do a good deed but is unable to actualize it, He rewards the intention as if it were actualized. But if His servant intends to sin and is unable to actualize it, He forgives the intention.

When you do good to Allah's creation, even if it is by a kind word or a smile, you see the reflection of Allah, the Perfect Doer of Good, in you. When the prophet Moses (ﷺ) talked to his Lord on Mount Sinai, he saw a man standing on the highest point of Allah's Throne. He asked, "O Lord, how did this servant reach such heights?" Allah Most High answered, "He was never envious of the good that I bestowed upon my servants, and he was especially good to his mother and father."

The Messenger of Allah (ﷺ) says, "Someone who reads the Qur'an and does not act upon what he reads is like someone who has not looked upon the Qur'an. Someone who looks upon the faces of his parents in anger, even if he serves them loyally, has not cared for them. Neither have I anything to do with these kinds of people, nor do they have anything to do with me."

'Abd al-Barr is the one in whom all the qualities of good, both material and spiritual, are manifest. Allah has given the possibility of wishing to do good to all believers. It becomes active in those who submerge themselves in the sea of mystery of Allah's beautiful name *al-Barr.*

People who are paralyzed and continue reciting this Name 202 times daily will find either a cure, or relief, or the courage to endure their sickness.

People who are alcoholic, if they recite this Name 700 times a day, may be cured.

People at sea when a storm erupts may find safety if they keep reciting this Name.

AT-TAWWAB

Allah is He who constantly turns people to repentance.

Tawbah, repentance, means literally to return: to return from revolt and sin to the straight path of virtue. Allah awakens the hearts of believers from the sleep of heedlessness through love of Him, with the manifestation of His existence around them, with the words of good advice of those who are close to Him, with the promise of His rewards and Paradise, and with the fear of His punishment and Hellfire.

Allah has servants whose hearts catch fire with a single spark. He also has servants whose hearts have turned to cold stone. If one poured heaps of fire upon them, they would still not become warm. Some have hearts like iron, which softens a bit from the fire and turns immediately back into iron again. That is why one has to be awakened frequently by listening to Allah's commands in the Qur'an. The whole universe, everything, including you, is the Qur'an. If you take lessons from what you see, inside and outside yourself, you will wake up and return from the sinful state of unconsciousness and disharmony to the state of being in harmony with Allah's will. That is repentance acceptable to Allah, with which His anger is transformed into mercy, compassion, and love.

The repentance that is acceptable to Allah is not simply seeing the wrong and ugliness of one's actions, regretting having done bad things and wishing not to repeat them, fearing Allah's punishment and hoping for Allah's mercy. This is like cutting off the crabgrass and leaving the root. One has to dig out all the roots. The repentance acceptable to Allah is the effort of inner cleaning, trying to eliminate the cause of the sins. Allah promises not only His mercy and forgiveness, but His love, to such purified ones.

Allah says of the punishment due for sin:

. . . save him who repents, and believes, and does righteous work—those, Allah will change their evil deeds into good deeds, for Allah is Oft-Forgiving, Most Merciful (Surah Furqan 70).

and

For Allah loves those who turn to Him and He loves those who seek to make themselves pure and clean (Surah Baqarah 222).

When you are able to forgive and keep forgiving those who hurt you, you will see the manifestation of *at-Tawwab* in yourself. Allah forgives the ones who forgive others. No matter how sinful they are, no matter how often they forget their repentance, they must never doubt the mercy of Allah and the acceptance of their repentance.

174

Many a misfortune that falls upon people is a result of their unrepented sins. If you complain about these difficulties, they will only increase. But if you accept them, look upon them as Allah's will, and submit, Allah will consider your submission as payment for your sins and as a true repentance, and the difficulties will cease. If you are able to go beyond this, welcoming your difficulties and feeling thankful for receiving a temporal punishment in this life rather than eternal fire in the Hereafter, your faith and spiritual state may reach new heights. To show thankfulness in adversity is the attitude of saints.

'Abd at-Tawwab is the blessed servant who has been made to return from the desires of the flesh and from the lies and imagination of this world to the Truth. By repeated repentance for his wrongdoings he has come to know the multiplicity in himself, and shedding it with his repentance, has achieved unity and oneness.

A believer who cannot stop doing wrong, is aware of it, and is crushed under the feeling of being sinful, may recite this Name 409 times in the mornings. One day he will feel that his repentance is accepted. The sign of the acceptance of one's repentance is that one cannot commit that sin again, and the recollection of it leaves one's memory.

AL-MUNTAQIM

Allah is the Great Avenger.

Allah punishes those who persist in revolting, raving in their unconsciousness and egotism, creating disharmony, tyrannizing Allah's servants and His creation. These are the ones who are faithless and attribute partners to Allah.

He gives them time and occasions to realize and repent for their wrongdoing. He warns them with repeated warnings. He accepts their excuses; He delays their punishment. In forgiving the faithless, in delaying their punishment, His eventual revenge becomes more terrible for the persistent sinner has had further chances to sin, thus making himself deserving of severer punishment. Those who become the servants of their egos instead of becoming Allah's servants risk a terrible fall when they feel they are not punished for what they are doing. They are spoiled by Allah's mercy, soaring higher and higher in their arrogance. Suddenly, one day, Allah brings them down. The fall becomes greater from such heights. Many tyrants were brought to great heights before they were smashed. Allah makes those upon whom He takes vengeance a lesson to those whom He wishes to save.

People who know how to take revenge upon the enemies of Allah, the greatest being their own egos, reflect Allah's attribute *al-Muntaqim*. Hadrat Bayazid al-Bistami says, "One night I felt too tired and lazy to perform some of my devotions. I punished myself by not drinking water for a whole year."

'Abd al-Muntaqim is he whose vengeance upon the enemies of Allah is terrible, and who is most vengeful toward his own ego, which is his greatest enemy.

If a faithful person is tyrannized by an enemy of Allah who deserves punishment, reciting *ya Muntaqimu ya Qahhar* 1000 times a day will remove the tyrant's power.

AL-'AFU

Allah is the forgiver, the eliminator of sins.

Al-'Afu is the opposite of al-Muntaqim, the Avenger. Its meaning is close to that of al-Ghafur, the All-Forgiving One, only here the sense is more intensive. The root of the word Ghafur means to overlook sins, while the root of the word 'Afu means to destroy sins, eliminate them altogether. In the first instance the overlooked sins still exist; in the second, the eliminated sins disappear.

Allah loves to forgive, to erase sins. He does not often punish the ones who deny, the ones who revolt. He accepts their recognition of their sins as repentance. He erases their sins. Instead of punishment, He bestows His bounties upon them.

There is a secret in His delaying punishment and forgiving sins. In teaching us that Hellfire is there, He is teaching us that there are ways to salvation. It is like an announcement by a rich, generous, compassionate host, declaring, "Our doors are open, our tables are set. The one who accepts this invitation is welcome, and we do not reproach those who do not come to our feast."

Allah's bounties in this world, which are temporal, are nothing in comparison to those promised in Paradise. The forgiving of sins is an encouragement to deniers to change their ways, to come to the straight path, to reach Paradise. Allah's infinite mercy is certainly more than the sins of His servants. His doors are always open to the ones who choose to enter.

But those who are blind and deaf to the warning that is in the compassion, mercy, and forgiveness of Allah, who persist in their infidelity and denial, who find justification for their denial in their being repeatedly forgiven, who are spoiled, who take pleasure in sinning, who try to lead others astray, they will finally be punished in this world by drowning in the gold they have accumulated, and in the Hereafter by Hellfire. That punishment does not negate the attribute of the Forgiving One, the Eliminator of sins, but it is a manifestation of His beautiful Name, the Just. Good and bad are not the same. If it were made to appear so, it might cause confusion in the mind of the good servant.

'Abd al-'Afu is the one who truly believes, who fears Allah, not so much Allah's punishment, but the loss of Allah's love. He is the one who has conscience, who has shame. And for him, the good and the bad that come to him from Allah are equal. He reflects the attribute *al-'Afu* by forgiving the one who tyrannizes him, by feeding the one who causes him hunger, by giving to the one who forcibly takes from him. Allah treats His servants the way they treat others.

A believer who recites this Name 166 times a day will be better able to control the wrong demands of his ego. His character will ameliorate and people will overlook his faults.

To remember to recite this Name when on the verge of getting uncontrollably angry and to follow it by a salutation to the Prophet (ﷺ) will help to keep one calm.

Someone who is facing a judge about to condemn him for a wrong action he has committed may recite this Name 166 times. He may have his punishment cancelled or reduced.

AR-RA'UF الرَّؤُوف

Allah is All-Clement.

He has created all with His hand of power, and He can extinguish all, for He is not in need of His creation. This power and independence do not prevent Him from exercising His mercy and clemency nor does His ability to see all, including the revolt and denial in some of His creatures. On the contrary, the fact that He chooses to forgive in spite of His ability to see our sins, of His being just, of His being able to punish, proves His mercy and clemency are infinite.

Even someone who lacks faith, whose arrogance is boundless, who believes that we obtain our livelihood by ourselves and are the masters of our own destiny, can reflect upon the animals and plants. They are without language, understanding, or intellect. How do they care for their offspring? How do birds build nests? Why are they not excessive in any direction that might cause their destruction, while human beings are? What is the mystery in that factory which is the silkworm, which builds its cocoon and produces the most beautiful and soft clothing, or in the little bee who builds her hive and produces the sweetest of all foods?

These and all else are the signs of the clemency, mercy, and generosity around you. But for human beings, the manifestation of Allah's clemency is greater. He has ". . . created everything for you and you for Himself." He created you as the best of creatures, perfect, as His deputy to govern, to guide, to use His kingdom. He has given you the means to think, to talk, to read and write. He has taught you what is best for you, what is bad for you, the right and the wrong, the lawful and the unlawful. If you try to count His bounties and blessings upon you, you will be unable. For believer

179

and unbeliever alike, His generosity, mercy, and clemency are boundless.

The one in whom the clemency of Allah is reflected is the one who remembers his sins and realizes that all these bounties of Allah arrive in spite of them. He tries to serve Allah's creation with his mind, his body, and his property.

'Abd ar-Ra'uf is the servant in whom Allah's mercy and compassion are manifest. He is clement in every way except regarding punishment in accordance with the *shari'ah*. Although the justice of the religious law seems to be punishment, in reality it is mercy, because the fault for which one has paid is eliminated.

The believer who recites this Name 286 times a day will have a heart filled with compassion and care for others, and this feeling will be mutual. That person will also be given the means to help those who are in need.

MALIK AL-MULK

Allah is the eternal owner of His kingdom.

He shares neither the ownership nor the power, government, or guardianship of the universe with anyone. Indeed, the whole universe is one kingdom because all creation is interconnected. In this way it resembles the human being, whose hands, feet, eyes, mind, heart, and all organs are individual units, yet connected, forming a single totality.

The universe is a whole with harmonious parts, created for a purpose, realizing and fulfilling this purpose. Allah says, "I was a hidden treasure, I wished to be known; therefore I created creation." Thus the purpose and function of the creation is to know, to find, and to be with the Creator.

The human being is the universe in microcosm: whatever exists in it, exists in us. Humanity is also the supreme creation and the deputy of Allah. That is why Allah bestows upon some of His servants, for a prescribed time, kingdoms, land, property, wealth, and lets them rule over them. Allah also gives certain servants the knowledge of how to govern so that their kingdoms grow, their profits grow. He forbids them to follow their egos, their selfishness, which can only lead them to perdition. If they become servants of their egos and use the wealth left in their care for themselves, all will be lost upon their deaths. They will be bankrupt, imprisoned in the dungeons of Hell. If people apply Allah's law to His kingdom which is lent to them and apply it to themselves as well, and if they govern for His pleasure and spend for His sake, the true Owner of the Kingdom will exchange the temporal kingdom He has bestowed upon them here for the eternal kingdom of the Hereafter.

'Abd Malik al-Mulk becomes a witness to Allah's power over His kingdom. He therefore realizes that Allah uses him as His deputy in governing the universe and himself. That realization makes him a perfect servant, and Allah's rewards to him may increase to the greatest worldly heights.Such a person depends on nothing except Allah, knowing that He is the only true King, and himself tries only to be a true servant, the highest level any human being can hope to reach.

The faithful who recite this Name 212 times daily will have their sustenance increased by unexpected means. The doubts they may have in their minds will turn into assurances. People under their care will respect and obey them with pleasure.

DHUL-JALALI WAL-IKRAM وَذِالْجَلَالِ وَالْإِكْرَامِ

Allah is Lord of Majesty and Bounty.

There is no perfection that does not belong to Him, no blessing or honor that comes from other than He. Allah is the owner of all majesty. Nothing else can even exist by itself, nothing can sustain itself. In His majesty, He can destroy all instantly, just as he created it. On what power are you depending when you revolt against Him? To show His generosity, He has bestowed His bounty and honor upon you. Do not attribute this to yourself and glorify yourself! The honor He gave you is to make you see the Giver of the honor, the truly Honorable One. All is in need of Him; all comes from Him. Yet to tie every person to other people, to tie every creature to the rest of creation, Allah uses an invisible rope called need. He uses each person, each creature, as a means, as a vehicle to give to another what it needs. One must be grateful to the vehicle through which Allah's blessing comes, but one must know the true source and not forget to give all thanks to Him. All thanks are due to Him who not only provides for our worldly needs, but has also promised us and taught us how to obtain His eternal blessings. These we can achieve by spending upon others, for His sake, that which He gave to us through others' hands.

The Lord of Majesty and Bounty is one of those beautiful Names that cannot be attributed to anyone but Allah. Some of the ones who know have even claimed it to be al-ism al-a'zam, the greatest Name of Allah.

'Abd Dhul-Jalali wal-Ikram is the servant who fears only Allah, bows his head only to Him, and hopes to receive only from Him. This is the sign of the sincere believer's faith in the oneness of Allah. He expects nothing from

182

people, neither does he fear their condemnation. For him, a sword held to his throat is no different from gold poured at his feet. He is neither worried by the one nor overjoyed by the other. Allah is enough.

The Messenger of Allah (ﷺ) says, "Recite *Dhul-Jalali wal-Ikram* when you are begging for something from Allah."

If a believer recites this Name 100 times a day for a week, all the burden of his troubles, doubts, and problems will leave his heart, which will be free of maleficent imagination, worries, and expectations. Evil will not touch him, and he will find peace.

AL-MUQSIT

Allah is the one who acts and distributes in justice and fairness.

How harmonious and balanced is the creation: all the beauties in heaven and earth; mountains, seas, sunsets, flowers, and also eyes to see! If there were none to see, wouldn't the creation of all these beauties be without sense? If the earth were closer to the sun all of us on its face would have burned to ashes. If it were further, we would have frozen. How right is its place. If the oxygen in the air had been more or less, it would have harmed us. Allah the Equitable One gives riches to some and poverty to others. He gives power to some, weakness to others, valor to some, fear to others. He gives what He gives to the right ones, although some may use it one way and others another way, making us doubt. We do not know what He knows, for we can see only what is in front of us, while He sees and knows the whole.

When we see laws, order, and harmony in an institution, in a town, in a country, we attribute it to the existence of a just and intelligent leader. If we could see the cosmic order or the order in ourselves, who are microcosms, we would see the proof of Allah the Equitable One.

Allah treats His servants equitably. Not a single good deed goes unnoticed. Each receives a reward. Mistakes, errors, injustices are corrected. When people tyrannize each other, He takes from the tyrant and gives to the tyrannized one. Yet in doing this, He renders them both content. Only Allah can do that.

It is reported in a hadith that the Prophet (ﷺ) smiled. Hadrat 'Umar (﵁) asked, "What is it that amuses you, O Messenger of Allah?"

The Messenger of Allah answered, "I see two men among my people who are in front of Allah Most High. One says, 'O Lord, take from this man that which is rightfully mine!' Allah Most High tells the other man, 'Give to your brother what belongs to him.' The usurper responds, 'O Lord, I have no good deeds with which to repay this man.' Allah turns to the wronged one and says, "What should I do to your brother? He has nothing left to give you.' The wronged one says, 'O Lord, let him take some of my sins.'"

With tears in his eyes, the Messenger of Allah said, "That day is the Day of Judgment; that day is a day when each man will wish others to carry his sins."

Then he continued to relate: "After the wronged one has wished the usurper to take over some of his sins, Allah asks him to lift his head and look at Paradise. He says, 'O Lord, I see cities of silver and palaces of gold bedecked with pearls. For which prophet, which saint, which martyr are these palaces?' Allah Most High says, 'They are for those who can pay their price.' The man who was wronged says, 'Who could possibly pay the prices of these?' Allah said, 'Perhaps you could.' The man says, 'How, O Lord? I have

nothing. What could I do to gain the price of Paradise?'
Allah *al-Muqsit* says, 'By forgiving your brother, by giving
up your claim in that which he took from you.' The
wronged man says, 'I forgive him, my Lord. I do not want
my right.' Allah the Most Merciful, the Most Generous,
says, 'Then hold your brother's hand and enter My Paradise
together.'"

Then the Messenger of Allah said, "Fear Allah and fear
doing harm to each other and make peace among yourselves, for Allah Most High will make peace between the
believers on the Day of Judgment."

'Abd al-Muqsit is one who has a perfect sense of measure, who sees things justly and demands justice. Above all,
he demands justice from himself. He does not demand justice from another for himself, yet he seeks justice for another from the one who has been unjust. He protects the one
who should be protected. He helps the one who should be
helped. He raises to the heights the ones who deserve to be
elevated. The Prophet (ﷺ) says, "The just will stand in pul-
pits of divine light in Paradise."

If one's mind wanders constantly while doing one's
prayers, reciting this Name 239 times before starting one's
worship may help. The same recitation also helps to calm
people down when they are angry or depressed.

AL-JAMI'

Allah is the Gatherer of whatever He wishes, wherever He
wishes.

Jama'a means gathering things that are dispersed. Allah
gathers things together whether they are alike or different or

even opposite. Allah has gathered together within this universe spaces, galaxies, stars, earths, seas, plants and animals, things whose nature, size, shape, and color are different.

In the bodies of the creatures He has created, Allah has gathered opposing entities, such as fire and water, air and earth, heat and cold, dry and wet. He has gathered six million cells in a drop of blood. The body has incalculable cells, each moving, seeking, finding, rejecting, growing, dividing, dying, each a life, an entity unto itself. He has combined all those cells in the body by means of His knowledge and His power. He can scatter them to the far corners of the universe and then gather them again. That is how our bodies, decomposed, spread in earth, water, and air at death, will be gathered on the Day of Resurrection. So will the bodies of billions and billions of people. Their lives, their minds, their souls returned to them, they will be gathered in the field of 'Arafat on the Day of Judgment. Allah will gather the sinner and the pure one, the tyrant and the tyrannized, the good and the bad face to face, and judge them all. Then He will gather His friends into His Paradise and His enemies into His Hell.

As Allah combines the cells of a human body, He puts each person together with his or her actions on the path to eternity. Our only comrades are our deeds. In our heedlessness we do not see the flesh, the heart, the mind, the soul gathered together, and the thousands of "me's" and "I's" and "mines" living together within us, any more than we see the billions of units combined in our bodies. We do not see our deeds, which are always with us, nor the Hell or the Paradise that are around us.

Your preoccupation with this world—eating, drinking, seeking more and more to eat, to have, to enjoy; your slavery at the hands of your flesh and your ego have made you inattentive to everything else. Only when the bird of the soul flies from the cage of the flesh will this dream evaporate, and you

186

will find yourself alone with your deeds. Then you will see that single companion whom you hug and press to your chest. Is it something warm and friendly, or is it full of snakes and scorpions and poisonous thorns? Then you will know that what you presumed to be good was Hell, and what you thought was suffering was Paradise.

'Abd al-Jami' is the servant in whose being visible character and morals and hidden truths of the heart are combined into one. Both his exterior and interior are beautiful. The manifestations of all the beautiful Names of Allah are gathered in him. He is able to bring together all that which is dissimilar, different, and opposite inside and outside of himself.

Our father, the Prophet Adam (﷌), found our mother Eve(﷐) on the plain of 'Arafat after they had been separated and sent from the Garden to Earth by reciting this Name. If someone has lost something, or is separated from someone dear, recitation of *ya Jami'* 114 times, followed by *ya Jami' an-nasi li-yawmin la rayba fiyhi ijma' 'alayya dalati* ("O Gatherer of humanity for a Day about which there is no doubt, bring what I have lost together with me!") helps to find that which was lost.

AL-GHANI

Allah is the Rich One who is sufficient unto Himself.

His essence and attributes have no relationship to anything else. Someone whose existence and perfection depend on another needs to earn that existence from the other. Only Allah has no needs and does not earn. His riches are independent of others, yet all else is dependent on Him.

Allah says in Surah Muhammad (38):

Allah is the Rich and you are the poor.

Some people who see themselves as superior to the rest of creation fall into the pitiable state of arrogance and conceit. They cannot see and be thankful for the honor of being created as the supreme creation and for being given the function of being Allah's *khalifah,* His deputy in the universe.

True human supremacy depends on being thankful and humble, serving Allah's servants and that which Allah has placed in our charge. The arrogant, by contrast, push their conceit to the point of denying their Creator, their Lord. In their arrogance, they cannot accept to be servants of Allah. Yet they see nothing wrong with being slaves to each other!

Such people cannot see that even to live they need Allah's air, water, and food; as food for their souls, they need worship. In fact, in all creation, there are no creatures whose needs are greater than ours. Nothing but Allah is rich enough to satisfy all those needs. If Allah has sent His books and His prophets and established religions to teach us what to do and what not to do, it is not for His need, it is for ours—to enable us to exist in this world and in the Hereafter as we were meant to exist. Even the scientists, sociologists, and economists of today say that the prescriptions, canons, and religious laws of Allah lead people to the best of physical, moral, and economic existence. Indeed, all that Allah has created and ordered is beneficent.

To be a servant of Allah is the highest level to which a human being can aspire. When we praise our Prophet, the Beloved of Allah (ﷺ), we say *'abduhu wa rasuluhu,* His servant and His messenger. The good servant of Allah knows that Allah does not need a servant, nor does He need to be served. He needs nothing. He also knows that his own duty is to serve Allah's servants and Allah's creation, including himself. Though in reality Allah has no need of servants to serve His servants, for as the Satisfier of needs, He Himself serves them. He honors whomever He chooses to appear as a means, as a tool of His service to His servants.

In reality, the good servant serves only himself in serving Allah. He obtains the greatest of gifts, coming close to Allah in knowing Him, in finding Him and in being with Him. Service and faithfulness (the quality of being a *mu'min*, faithful) become a common denominator, a common name and attribute, and thus are the only means for servants to know their Lord. When Allah addresses us in His Qur'an as "O you who believe," or "O you faithful," He calls upon us with His own attributes, with His own Name, *al-Mu'min*, one of His 99 beautiful Names.

Faith is a treasure from the treasury of Allah. The faithful person is the richest among people, for such a one knows that there is no need of anything from anyone else except from Allah, the only true Rich One.

'Abd al-Ghani is the rich one who is provided with the satisfaction of all needs without having to ask from Allah. This servant performs all the duties of servantship not in order to receive benefits from Allah, but only because they have been ordered by Allah.

If the ones who are in material need recite this Name 1060 times on Saturdays, they will not need the help of others, for Allah will satisfy their need from most unexpected places.

Allah Jami, Al-Ghani, Al-Mughni, Al-Mani, Al-Hadi

AL-MUGHNI

المُغْنِي

Allah is the Enricher.

Allah renders whomever He wishes rich and whomever He wishes poor. Then He may render the rich, poor, and the poor, rich. Some rejoice in their riches and others suffer in their poverty. Some become conceited in their riches, some become doubtful and claim injustice in their poverty. We do not know, only He knows what is best for us. One must consider that poverty and riches, like other aspects of our lives, are but a touchstone that shows the degree of our purity. One sees in some, faithfulness, trust, and submission; in others, objection and revolt.

This life is a testing ground. One and all, we come here to show our true colors. Who we are and what we are is not measured by our bank account. There are greater riches than all the riches of this world, which may be spent, lost, or taken away by others, and which will certainly be left behind when we meet our Lord. But the true riches are knowledge and faith, which do not decrease by spending, nor devaluate with time. They are our companions in the grave and in the Hereafter. Which do we prefer? How do we behave with what we have? The purpose of our lives is to pass this test.

Allah tests some with riches and others with poverty. Neither condition is important: what matters is submission to Allah's will. The riches of this world tempt people to revolt and to be arrogant. Poverty tempts us to doubt and complain. It is difficult for the rich to be humble, while the poor are humble easily. It is difficult for the poor to accept their status and to be generous, but easier for them to be devout.

The Prophet (ﷺ) said, "My poverty is my pride." The test is not a simple test. It is not sufficient for the rich to be humble to pass the test, nor for the poor to trust in Allah and be accepting of their condition. The rich have to know thankfulness and to consider that their riches are not theirs, and to show their thankfulness by their generosity. The poor have to work hard to better their situation and accept the poverty that persists in spite of their efforts. That is the true meaning of trust in Allah, who says:

Allah does not change the lot of people who do not change what is in themselves (Surah Ra'd 7).

The poor who accept their state, who are content with what they have, who are not envious, in reality are rich. The rich who are miserly, ambitious, who want more, in reality are poor. The patient poor are bound for Paradise, as are the thankful, generous rich.

Once a pure man asked a man of knowledge what should be the attitude of the one upon whom Allah has bestowed riches and the one whom Allah has given poverty. The wise man replied that a rich person should show thankfulness and a poor person should be patient. The pure believer exclaimed that the dogs in his village behaved that way! The wise man, annoyed, asked him what he, then, thought they should do. The pure one answered, "The poor one should be thankful and the rich one should give away all his riches."

'Abd al-Mughni is the servant of Allah who has been rendered totally rich, both materially and spiritually, so that he becomes an instrument of satisfying the needs of the needy. He also becomes an example for other rich people to do the same. He becomes a means of distributing the riches of this world and of the Hereafter to the ones chosen by Allah.

To recite this Name 1121 times each Friday for 10 consecutive Fridays may help eliminate nervous tension. If one recites it towards open palms and caresses the parts of one's body which are afflicted with some sickness, one may recover. This may also help people who are imprisoned unjustly to be released.

AL-MANI‘

Allah is the one who averts harm from His creation.

People are unable to *do*, yet we do not understand this. We wish, we will . . . and we try to obtain that which we wish and will. Our wishes are endless and our plans, calculations, and efforts to obtain what we wish are boundless. But our fulfillment of those wishes depends on many circumstances. We do not obtain everything that we wish and work for. The causes that produce the things we desire and bring them into being for us depend on the manifestation of Allah's attribute *al-Wahhab*, the Bestower. When our wishes are not fulfilled, it is a manifestation of Allah's attribute *al-Mani‘*, the Preventer. In both cases, what happens is what was bound to happen in accordance with Allah's destiny: one knows one's destiny only after it is actualized.

Allah *al-Khabir* is aware of our wishes. Allah *al-Ghani* has infinite treasuries containing what we wish. Allah *al-Karim* does not withhold what we wish. Allah *al-Qadir* is able to procure it instantly. Allah is the Richest, Most Beneficent, Most Powerful, Most Just. If we do not receive what we wish, it is not because He does not know of it, because He does not have it, because He cannot afford to give it, or because He is unable to hand it to us. He is perfect, free from all defect. Though the reason may be unknown to us, we must believe that if we do not receive what we will and wish, it is because that is best for us.

It is as if there were a perfect father who is most loving and protective to his children. He is wise, rich, generous, and kind, not only to his children and his family, but to everyone. If he prevents one of his children from eating too much, or from eating an unripe fruit, or from playing with a dangerous toy, can we call him lacking in compassion? Certainly he prevented the child from having or doing something with the thought of what was best for the child. Indeed, Allah's compassion is infinitely superior to that of the most compassionate of fathers.

Allah says in Surah Baqarah (216):

> ... and it may be that you dislike a thing while it is good for you, and it may be that you love a thing while it is evil for you; and Allah knows while you know not.

'Abd al-Mani' is the one who has been rendered safe by Allah from things harmful to him. He in turn protects those around him from harmful things, even though they may appear in such attractive forms as wealth, fame, beauty, or joy.

Recitation of this Name 161 times in the mornings and evenings helps relieve pain and fear. When a husband and wife feel lack of affection between them, to recite it silently in bed may rekindle love between them. To recite it during a voyage may help avoid dangers and difficulties.

AD-DARR

Allah is the creator of the harmful and evil just as He is the creator of the good and beneficial.

The attribute *ad-Darr*, the Creator of Evil, is usually conceived together with the attribute *an-Nafi'*, the Creator of Good. Neither name appears in the Qur'an. They belong to the attributes of Allah on the authority of the Prophet (ﷺ).

Sometimes the two attributes are inseparable. What is poison to one is medicine to another, what is sweet to one is bitter to another. We think that food feeds by itself and poison kills by itself. We think that the one responsible for good and evil is a human being, or an angel, or the Devil, while all that happens is by the will of the Eternal Power. Although Allah has created evil as well as good, He has also taught us to opt for the good and escape the evil. He has given us the power of discrimination, given us a will and freedom to choose. In the whole creation, only the human being has a will. Through this will, Allah has separated humanity into two parts: the good doing good and being led toward good, and the bad doing evil and being led toward evil. This, knowingly and willingly, people do themselves.

Allah Most High is *Halim*, gentle, and He is *Sabur*, patient. He does not destroy those who have opted for evil. He keeps feeding them, letting them have time so that possibly they will change. And sometimes they do: the good for the worse and the evil for the better. This is all a test. The final exam does not come until the moment one inhales one's last breath.

Indeed, if a wall is cracked and leaning to the right, as time passes it will lean further, and finally collapse on the right side. But, rarely, just as the wall is about to collapse to the side toward which it is leaning, does an unusual thing happen. A hurricane, an earthquake, will either straighten the wall or make it collapse on the other side. Likewise some people who revolt, who disbelieve, who become toys in the hands of their egos and the claws of the Devil, may one day feel the pang of the fear of Allah and take to the right path. Other people may resemble those who follow the straight path devout, compassionate, and generous but then become pleased with themselves, turn arrogant, think themselves better than others . . . and may be rejected from Allah's mercy, as was the arrogant Devil.

Indeed the suffering we go through, the harm that comes to us, is only our own fault. Although Allah created evil and ordered us to shun it, forbade it to us, we run after the things that are forbidden. That is the test. We think of the Devil as an ugly creature. The Devil shows his ugliness only to the ones who detect him. When he comes to tempt even the saints, he makes himself very attractive, as when he appeared to Jesus Christ (عليه السلام) as a beautiful woman.

Allah has manifested His attribute of the Creator of the Harmful in the Devil and the ones who follow him: He created hellfire for them. But although Allah has created evil, the cause of its coming upon you is only yourself. If bankruptcy comes upon you, it is through your dishonesty or overambitiousness or incapability. If sickness comes upon you, usually it is because of your carelessness or your negligence of your body. Although Allah has created evil, the one who wants it, works for it, and gains it is always the servant.

Some of us serve as lessons to others, others learn from their own lessons. There is practically no one who does not slip into sinning at one time or another: those who suffer in consequence are the ones who learn from their mistakes, and that is the best of repentance.

Allah says in a divine tradition,

> The ones who do not submit and accept My justice and My punishment, and the ones who are not thankful for My bounty upon them . . . let them seek a Lord other than me.

In another tradition He says,

196

There is no remedy for the sickness of a person
who does not accept his destiny and My judgment.

However, sin and error are not the only reasons for suffering. Sometimes Allah Most High puts a veil of pain and distress over the ones whom He loves and the ones who love
Him to hide them from the eyes of others. This is a blessing
of Allah given through misery. Allah uses difficulty and
pain as a means of educating His servants. If there were
nothing negative, disturbing, or painful in the world, and if
people were not afflicted by these things, how could they
have gained such beneficial states as patience, perseverance,
bravery, and steadfastness?

When you are afflicted with grief, fear, sickness, or
poverty, know that only Allah can dispel it. When you are
blessed with happiness, health, success, or riches, again
only Allah can sustain it. Therefore, whether in health or
sickness, joy or sorrow, you are bound to submit and turn
only to Him, because both good and evil come from the
same source. They are both true and right.

Yet this does not mean that one should leave everything in
the hands of Allah. One should seek the causes created by oneself or others and try to put things right in a lawful manner. To
act thus does not mean lack of faith in the Creator of good and
evil. It is the best form of worship under the circumstances.

'Abd ad-Darr is the servant who bears witness to the
only One who does what He wills to do when He wills to do
it. Such a person is taught the mystery of the unity of all that
happens, and knows that evil as well as good comes from
Allah and that evil as well as good is welcome.

Someone who has been forced to a lower position than
he or she had previously held may recite *ya Darr, ya Nafi'*
100 times during the nights of Fridays, or better still on the
13th, 14th and 15th of the lunar months. Such people may then
regain their position.

To recite this Name 1001 times may save one from the tyranny of a powerful enemy.

AN-NAFI'

Allah is the creator of good.

Allah has created the human being as the best of His creatures and has bestowed upon us gifts which render us unique and superior to the rest of creation. The highest of the gifts He has given to humanity are intellect, conscience, and faith. These are the means by which He has taught us to discriminate, to choose for ourselves what is best. The human being is also unique in having a will—the only one in the universe, with the exception of Allah. Our small will can only be checked by the greater will of Allah. This limitation means that we are not free and left on our own.

Allah has given us freedom only so that we may find out for ourselves whether we will submit to the will of Allah, govern in His name, be the best of creation, and have the best of creation, or whether we will revolt, cause our own downfall, and be rejected from Allah's mercy, as was the Devil. Our ability to choose between good and evil is not a test for Allah to see how His servant will behave. Allah created our fates before He created us: therefore He already knows what we will do. Only the person who believes in fate may be saved from it!

Allah's mercy is sent down upon us continually, as is all the good He has created. Our will cannot bring anything to us that is due to someone else, nor can it prevent anything from coming to us that is our destiny. Neither are we able to

198

choose what we would prefer, for often what we choose slips from our hands, while what we never wanted seeks us out. And even if we have what we choose, it would have come to us in any case.

When we look at the universe, what we see is Allah's will, what we see with is Allah's will, what we understand of what we see is Allah's will, what we seem to have chosen is Allah's will. Our small will consists of being able to open our eyes to receive all the good that Allah has willed for us, or to close our eyes and receive nothing. It is as if the treasures of Allah are pouring continuously like a blessed rain. We have to be present to receive it. If we are not there, it will go to waste. To be present, we have to open our eyes, our minds, our hearts, and our hands. We have to be aware, awake, conscious. That is how we see and receive the good that Allah has created.

'Abd an-Nafi' is the one who sees and receives the good Allah has created and is charged with distributing the blessings of Allah, the greatest of which are knowledge and faith, to the ones worthy to receive. He is like Khidr, the ever-present materialized spirit who helps believers in need, and follows his path and example.

Recitation of this Name relieves sadness, depression, and stress. A person who remembers to recite this Name silently during intercourse will find his or her partner more responsive.

AN-NUR

Allah is the Light shed upon the whole creation, making it apparent.

Just as this Light is responsible for making the percep-
tible seen, it also makes the conceivable known. The Light
that shows the conceivable is the light of faith and wisdom,
and the eye that sees it is the *basirah*, the eye of the heart.
That Light is the light of existence: nonexistence is darkness. That Light is the light that brought existence out of
the darkness. That Light makes itself visible as well as
making all else visible. There is not one atom among all the
things that exist in the heavens and on earth and in that
which is between them that does not point to the existence
of its Creator

> . . . *the Light of the heavens and the earth* (Surah
> Nur 35).

The sun sheds light upon the sky and the earth, enabling us
to see things around us, large and small, of different shapes
and colors, enabling us to identify that from which we may
profit and that which may harm us. In its light we find our
way and see the pits and swamps. In the same way, Allah
has bestowed upon us the light of faith, which shows us the
straight path of salvation and the pits and swamps of infidelity, sin, and revolt. That sun of faith in the heart of
believers renders them beautiful of face and beautiful in
character. The light of faith eliminates the darknesses of
infidelity and sin within and without, bringing us to the light
of truth and salvation and serenity.

The Devil, and one's own devil, the ego, are thieves who
like to operate in darkness and enter dark houses. They will
not enter that divine house, the heart illuminated by the light
of faith. The gate to the heart is the mind; the light of that
gate is knowledge. That light blocks out the evils of ignorance, imagination, hypocrisy, and arrogance. The soul
needs light and detests darkness. As the light of the soul is
consciousness, its darkness is heedlessness.

200

You who spend so much effort and wealth to illuminate your material life with chandeliers, sparkling jewels, and bright ostentation, why do you turn off the light of your heart? Don't you see that you may cause it to become used to darkness, and go blind like the bat? If the eye of your head goes blind, someone may lead you by the hand on the road; but the one whose heart is blind cannot be led, and will be lost for eternity.

'Abd an-Nur is the servant of Allah who has received the blessing of a response to the prayer of the Prophet Muhammad (ﷺ) "O My Lord, render me light!" and who has come to know the secret of the verse of the Qur'an

Allah is the Light of the heavens and the earth (Surah Nur 35).

Such a one knows that all existence, knowledge, thought, and feeling come from that Light, and that all existence and knowledge in the universe are nothing but that Light.

If believers who find their hearts darkened with doubt and sadness reads Surah Nur (the Qur'anic chapter of Divine Light) seven times and recite this Name 1000 times, they will find their doubts eliminated and their hearts enlightened.

If a person who has lost his way recites this Name 256 times, he will find his way.

AL-HADI

Allah is the One who creates guidance, leading His servants to good, benefit, and the satisfaction of their needs.

His highest guidance is that which leads His best servants to knowledge of His essence. He guides His other good servants to see His attributes manifest in His creation. He guides every creature to that which is needed for its existence.

Allah says in Surah Ta Ha (50):

Our Lord is He who gives to each thing its nature then guides it (to knowledge to satisfy its needs).

The result of this guidance is faith. The opposite of guidance is to be led astray, the result of which is infidelity. Human beings are made like a pair of scales. We have the potential to incline one way or the other. Therefore, for us to turn either to the side of faith or to the side of infidelity there must be some weight placed on one side of the scale or the other. Allah is the only one who creates guidance and misguidance. He is the creator of the causes of faith, which delights the heart, and of faithlessness, which delights the ego. He guides whomever He wishes and leads astray whomever He wishes.

Whomever Allah has guided well, none can lead astray. Whomever Allah has misguided, none can lead to the straight path. But Allah does not forcibly and without reason lead His servant astray. He leads people astray only when we misuse our will and turn our potential towards infidelity. Yet in human beings, faith is essential, fundamental. Faithlessness is nonessential and accidental.

Faith is intrinsic to human beings. Allah gathered the souls prior to creation in the realm of the spirits and asked,

Am I not your Lord?

and we all answered

Indeed! (Surah A'raf 172).

So our souls made a covenant with Allah before we were even born. We may not remember the promise of our souls, but that does not invalidate the pact. It is this covenant with Allah before our creation that is the reason for Allah's guidance and bounty for each of us. He has granted each soul a perfect body to live in, sustenance for the maintenance of that body, a mind to perceive things that will remind it of His existence and of our covenant with Him. He has given the Books, the Messengers, prophets and saints and people of knowledge all to remind us, to teach us, to confirm the covenant. All this is a part of Allah's guidance. As people wish it, will it, and abide with it, Allah's guidance will ever increase.

The one who is well guided knows the truth, respects the truth, and accepts the truth. Such people will prefer death to the application of untruth, which is injustice and tyranny. Even if they had the interest, strength, and support to oppose the truth, they would not do it. They tell only the truth, listen to the truth, live by the truth, and die for the truth. Such are the well-guided ones.

'Abd al-Hadi is the servant of Allah who has received the response to his prayer

Guide us on the right path (Surah Fatihah 5).

He knows the secret of the beautiful name *al-Hadi*, and thus becomes an instrument for human salvation. He has been charged with enforcing truth: that which Allah ordains, and that which Allah forbids.

Recitation of this Name 200 times each day may lead one to success. If you are not sure of your purpose, this may lead you to the right choice. If one writes this Name on a cup, puts rain water in it, recites *ya Hadi* 200 times upon it, and lets one's child who has difficulty in remembering things and is disobedient drink from it, it may ameliorate the condition.

AL-BADI'

Allah is the originator of the creation, having created it without model or material.

He does not need previous knowledge to think, to investigate, to figure things out. He invents the original of everything in the creation. There was nothing before Him, so He is unlike anything, and everything after Him is made by Him— unique, matchless, unequalled by anything else, and in no way similar to Him. Everything He creates is a wonder, a marvel, since He originated it from nothing. Like the original creations, all the continuously created things are different from one another. Although they resemble each other, they are also diverse. There are no two people exactly alike.

A man marveled to the caliph, Hadrat 'Umar (ﷺ), about the chess game. "Look at this board, not bigger than a foot square," he said. "A man can play thousands of games on it, none like any other!"

Hadrat 'Umar (ﷺ) said, "Why don't you look at a man's face, which is smaller than the chessboard? Although the eyes, the nose, the mouth are always in the same place, if you look at millions of men, you will not find two alike. And when you add the variety of expressions, there is no end to the differences, as there is no end to the power and wisdom and the originality of Allah Most High."

Attention and curiosity are two of the greatest gifts to humanity. All knowledge, science, industry, are consequences of these qualities. Human beings cannot invent or originate; all we can do is discover things that Allah has previously created. As people observe phenomena with their attention and investigate with their curiosity, seeing the model of the bird and the fish, using the minerals and materials available to them, they discover airplanes and submarines. Some stop there, profiting from the material gains and fame, and become arrogant, thinking that they have invented, that they have created. Blessed are those scientists and inventors who use their success as an introduction to the greater success of receiving the love of Allah in their hearts: they see the Hand of Power of Allah the Originator and Allah the All-Powerful, who has used them as tools to bring about their discoveries.

How well have the wise ones said, "The ones who work with divine wisdom are lights, the ones who practice knowledge are guides, the ones who give good advice are lamps, the ones who think and know are alive, the ones who are ignorant are dead."

'Abd al-Badi' is the witness that Allah Most High is the creator of everything in its essence, attributes, and actions. Such a person is given the ability to know, to discover, and to build things that others cannot.

If believers recite this Name 86 times after each of their daily obligatory prayers, their understanding will expand, their inner eye will open and penetrate into the inner meanings of knowledge, they will be able to do difficult tasks better than others, and their speech will be words of wisdom.

To recite *ya Badi'as-samawati wal-ard* ("O Originator of the heavens and the earth!") 70 times when one encounters a situation difficult to solve may make its solution easier.

To recite the same prayer 1000 times may help ease depression and stress.

AL-BAQI

Allah is the Everlasting One whose existence in the future is forever.

Time only exists for the changing creation. It started with Allah's word of creation and will end on Doomsday. There was no time before the creation, but Allah existed. The creation will end, and time with it, but Allah the Everlasting One will still exist.

This world is but a guesthouse where the visitor stays for a while, then leaves. Over millennia, how many visitors have come and gone! Who were they? Where are they? Where did they go? Nations and civilizations have come and gone. Humanity and everything else in the universe is like this but for human beings, this world is also a field where we labor to grow wheat or thorns, and whose harvest we will find in the Hereafter. This life is like a parade ground: everyone passes as his turn comes, all in different groups, under different banners, with different uniforms, marching to different music. No one is left in this world, nor is this world left with anyone. All is material, temporal, including the world itself, the whole universe, except Allah the Everlasting One.

Yet there is a way to gain an eternal life during this short visit here. It is achieved by not tying one's heart to this world. It is by not working only for profit in this world, by not working for one's own immediate benefit. If one works for Allah's sake, for Allah's pleasure, for the benefit of Allah's creation now and in the future, when all is ended and this body has returned to dust one's work will carry one to eternity.

If you are a doctor or an architect, when you go to that realm where there is no one who is sick and nothing to build, both your being and your knowledge will disappear. But if you discovered penicillin, which will keep curing the sick long after you are gone, or if you built a bridge that people will cross for a long time, and if your intention in doing these things was to serve rather than to gain, you will earn eternity in the Hereafter for what you have done in this temporal life.

'Abd al-Baqi is the good servant of Allah who is given the knowledge of eternity, whom Allah has rendered eternal within His eternity in the state of *baqa' bi-Llah*. In that state, his worship is his servantship: the servant and the Lord have become one, and there is nothing left of the servant himself.

The faithful who recite this Name 113 times daily will find health and prosperity, their work and property will be safe, and it is to be hoped that they will receive Allah's mercy and compassion on the Day of Judgment.

If someone who is afflicted with chronic fear recites this Name 113 times each night when going to bed, relief may come.

AL-WARITH

Allah is the ultimate Inheritor, to whom everything is left after its temporal possessors are gone.

It is He who exists after all existence disappears; it is He to whom all existence returns. It is He who will ask:

To whom belongs the kingdom this day?

And it is He who will answer:

To Allah, the One, the Ever-Dominating One
(Surah Mu'minun 16).

The heedless are unaware that what they possess, including themselves, is only lent to them. Those who are ungrateful for the infinite bounties of Allah, the Most Generous One, are arrogant, thinking that what they have is theirs. They use it for their own pleasure. When they disappear, they and all else return to Allah the Everlasting One, who is before the before and after the after, who is the only Owner, the Inheritor of all. Then they will be asked:

To whom belongs the kingdom this day?

And they will know the truth, only too late.

But the ones whose eyes of the heart see and whose ears of the heart hear, remember and hear continuously:

To Allah, the One, the Ever-Dominating One.

They know that they are but temporal keepers of what is in their hands. They are like honored tellers in Allah's bank, who do not follow the desires of their flesh nor the commands of their egos, but do what Allah wills for His sake and for His pleasure. In doing so, they become one with Allah, and in that way become eternal and everlasting.

'Abd al-Warith is the servant who attains the secret of the name the Inheritor and enters the state of *baqa' bi-Llah,* "everlastingness with Allah," thus receiving his share of divine wisdom and of the station of the prophets. *'Abd al-Warith* is the inheritor of the prophets in knowledge, wisdom, and guidance.

Couples who are having difficulty producing a child may conceive if they recite together as often as they can *Rabbiy la tadharni fardan wa anta khayr ul-warithin* ("My

208

Lord, do not leave me without offspring, though you are the best of inheritors"Surah Anbiya' 89).

Someone who cannot decide among various alternatives may find the right choice by reciting *ya Warith* 1000 times between the sunset and night prayers.

AR-RASHID

Allah is the Righteous Teacher who ordains righteousness for all creatures.

In His wisdom He leads all matters to their conclusion perfectly and in perfect order. He is the ultimate teacher who guides us to the straight path and salvation, who never fails in His wisdom or His actions. Everything done by Him has a clear and beneficial purpose. His teaching is so effective that it becomes the nature of everything in the universe that follows His will.

To humanity He has taught bliss, prosperity, and salvation in His Qur'an. Although He is All-Powerful, He does not enforce what He teaches, but leaves it for human will to act upon. He shows the way to peace as a reward for acting upon what we learn. He chooses to let us gain our rewards by our own decision through practicing what we are taught.

Every person, as a student, first has to be aware and conscious of what is being taught. Then we must use the intelligence that has been given to us by our Teacher to discipline and educate ourselves, our egos. Then we must learn Allah's divine laws, and in accordance with them, drive the machine of our material being.

Islam is the religion in which learning is obligatory for all men and women. As we learn from Allah the ultimate Righteous Teacher, we see the perfect order within and

Allah Al-Warith, As-Sabur, Ar-Rashid

outside ourselves. The Greatest Teacher makes His students see His Will, His Power, His Generosity, His Love, His Compassion. He makes the student love Him, live to do what He says, love to work for His pleasure and to become righteous.

'Abd ar-Rashid is the righteous one who has arrived at the right path that leads to Allah's will and His Messenger's orders. This is the station of the *murshid*, the great teacher who has come to know, to find, and to become close to Allah. Since he is on the straight path, he also has the license to lead others on the straight path.

Many blessed saints of Islam including Hadrat Hasan al-Basri, Ja'far as-Sadiq, Shibli and others have claimed *ar Rashid* as the greatest Name, the recitation of which makes prayers come true.

A faithful teacher who recites this Name 504 times will be safe both from passing on erroneous information and from being misunderstood.

Reciting this Name 152 times a day will improve both one's wordly and inner life. The reciter's words will be effective, his actions will be right.

AS-SABUR

Allah is the Most Patient One.

In everything He is in perfect measure and in perfect time. He is patient, and He loves and . . .

is with the patient ones (Surah Anfal 46).

In His creation as in His actions, in His dealings with His creatures, nothing is either bigger or smaller, better or worse, earlier or later than He has determined it must be. He does not delay things beyond their appointed times or fail to finish them as a lazy person might do, nor does He hasten and imperfectly finish things as an impatient person might do. Rather He does everything in its proper time and in just the manner that it ought to be done.

Allah does not hasten the punishment of the sinful. He sends them their sustenance, protects them from harm, and lets them live in health and prosperity, for He has set a particular time for everything. All things must run their course. His patience with sinners is in order to give them time to be heedful, to realize their wrong and come to repent. Allah is Merciful; His Mercy is in giving time for repentance and accepting repentance.

Patience is in Allah's divine disposition; therefore, patient people reflect this honored disposition. A patient person refuses things that his flesh and ego desire but that are unacceptable to reason and to the religion. He applies himself to things that are acceptable to reason and to the religion, yet hateful for his ego, as he knows how to put a bridle on the wild horse of his lower being.

Patience is a very high state for the faithful, because the affairs both of this world and of the Hereafter are resolved by it. No success, no perfection, can be achieved easily and without pain. That pain is the pain of the flesh, which is hasty in things that it wants, lazy in working for what it wants, does not know measure, and always wants more than it needs.

The Prophet (ﷺ) says that "Paradise is surrounded by things that the flesh does not want." Allah promises infinite rewards for those who can be patient with the turbulence of the desires of their flesh and of their egos. There are even greater rewards for patience in supporting misfortunes, poverty, accidents, and sickness, which are unavoidable and come from Allah. Indeed calamities come from Allah, but rewards for being patient and accepting them accompany them. If people show patience, they receive rewards that far surpass the pain. If they are impatient, the misfortune doubles—first the initial calamity and then the greater misfortune of having lost the reward.

The meaning of Islam is submission: to forego one's appetites, desires, and will in favor of the will of Allah. To be able to submit, one has to be patient. In Islam, patience is a sign of faith: abasement and humiliation are sins. Do not confuse humiliation caused by fear and laziness with patience and endurance. To give up one's property, one's honor, one's dignity to a tyrant may lead one to give up one's religion and faith for fear, or to sell one's soul for this world. The believer who fears Allah fears no one, and is one whom others fear. For the faithful to abase themselves before anyone except Allah is not lawful.

'Abd as-Sabur is the blessed servant who has perfect equilibrium and moderation in himself and in all that he does, who neither delays nor hastens, but acts in a determined time. He is patient in his continuous battle with his ego and in the opposition of his desires and appetites. He perseveres in keeping Allah's ordinances and in his worship.

If a faithful person is in difficulty or pain or unjustly accused or tyrannized, reciting *ya Sabur* 298 times will bring relief, by Allah's will and his heart will be flooded with Allah's love.

O Lord, for the sake of Your beautiful Names,
and for the sake of the ones
in whom Your names are manifest,
lead us on their path. Let us see
your attributes everywhere without,
and cleanse the mirror of our hearts
that perchance we may see Your Beauty reflected within.

Amin bi hurmati sayyid al-mursalin.

213

THE DIVINE NAMES
OF THE PROPHET

BISMILLAH AR-RAHMAN AR-RAHIM

O Allah, for as long as day turns to night and night recedes into day, for as long as the ages succeed one another, as day and night unceasingly follow upon each other and as the glowing stars remain suspended in the firmament, we beg that You bestow Your grace and favors upon our Master Muhammad and that You transmit unto his blessed soul and unto the souls of the people of his house our greetings and our respect, and that You bestow upon him Your peace and blessings in great abundance.

So may Allah bestow His peace and blessings upon our Master Muhammad and upon all the prophets and messengers; upon the saints and the righteous servants; upon the angels and upon those who reside by the Throne of Grace; and upon the obedient and vigilant servants among the people of the earth and those of the heavens. And may Allah Most High be pleased with His Prophet and with all His companions and people. *Amin.*

Muhammad (ﷺ) is the one who is "sent as a mercy upon the universe" (Surah Anbiya' 107). The light of his soul was the first creation to issue from the Light of Allah, and everything else is created from his light. He said, "O Jabir, the first creation that Allah created is the soul of your prophet." When he was asked at what point he became a prophet, he answered, "I was a prophet when Adam was between water and clay." He said, "Whoever sees me sees the truth."

Allah says:

And whoever obeys Allah and His Messenger, He will cause him to enter gardens wherein rivers flow (Surah Fath 17).

And he has said, "As long as you do not love me more than anything else you have, your faith is not complete." For Allah says:

Certainly a Messenger has come to you from amongst yourselves; grievous to him is your falling into distress; most solicitous for you, to the believers he is merciful (Surah Bara'at 128).

He upon whom Allah has bestowed

A tremendous nature (Surah Qalam 4).

is sent to teach us to be noble in behavior, morals, and character. "Whoever prays to Allah to bestow upon His Messenger His peace and blessings, receives Allah's blessings tenfold, and may hope for the intercession of His Prophet on the Day of Judgment, and to enter Paradise."

We are presenting 201 beautiful names of our beloved Prophet (ﷺ) as mentioned in the *Dala'il al-khayrat* of Shaykh 'Imran az-Zannati, may his soul be sanctified. Allah praises His Prophet with most of these names in the Holy Qur'an, and announces his coming by certain names in the other Holy Books: the Torah, the Zabur (Psalms of David),

218

and the Gospel. They also appear in the Hadith, or traditions of the Prophet (ﷺ).

Shaykh Ibn al-Faris reports from Hadrat Ibn al-'Arabi that he had counted 2,020 beautiful attributes of our Prophet (ﷺ). Imam al-Kastalani, the author of the interpretation of the great hadith collection Bukhari al-Sharif, has counted 1,000 beautiful names.

May the ones who read the beautiful names of the Beloved of Allah (ﷺ) contemplate the meaning, properties, and effects of these names and feel the love, the respect, and the consideration with which we hope their hearts will be inspired. We must realize that to love is not within our will, but within the greater will of Allah. He is the one who inspires the heart with love. By ourselves we cannot love Allah and His Prophet; by ourselves a man cannot even love a woman, or a woman, a man. In Islam it is unlawful for a man to insist that his wife love him or for a wife to insist upon the affection of her husband, for that is considered equivalent to forcing someone to lie. As a person cannot be forced to love, and we cannot force ourselves to love someone, how then should we understand the hadith, "If you do not love me more than anything else you have, your faith is not complete?" First comes the wish to love him, which can only be obtained through knowing him, through knowing his beautiful names, through finding a trace of these attributes in our own selves, through praying for him and for his blessings, through following his path and his example. Then, if Allah wills, you will be blessed with His love, and in return, you will love Him and find Paradise in this world and in the Hereafter.

'Ali ibn Abi Talib (رضي الله عنه) said in describing the Prophet (ﷺ):

He was neither tall and lanky nor short and stocky, but of medium height. His hair was neither crisply curled nor straight but moderately wavy. He was not overweight, and his face was not plump. He had a round face. His complexion was white tinged with reddishness. He had big black eyes with long lashes. His bones were heavy and his shoulders broad. He had soft skin, with fine hair covering the line from mid chest to navel. The palms of his hands and the soles of his feet were firmly padded. He walked with a firm gait, as if striding downhill. On his back between his shoulders lay the Seal of Prophethood, for he was the last of the prophets.

He was the most generous of men in feeling, the most truthful in speech, the gentlest in disposition, and the noblest in lineage. At first encounter people were awestruck by him, but on closer acquaintance they would come to love him. One who sought to describe him could only say, "Neither before him nor after him did I ever see the like of him."

O Allah, bless and salute the Prophet of Mercy, the intercessor of the community, Muhammad, and all his family and all the prophets and messengers.

His being was of light; he had no shadow. His beautiful face shone like the sun and radiated light around him. At night people saw by this light. It is written in the Holy Qur'an that in the darkness of the Day of Judgment the light of faith of the believers is going to illuminate the space around them, and the hypocrites, envious, will come close to them to profit from this light.

Allah, addressing His Beloved, whose name is written with His upon the firmament as *La ilaha illallah, Muhammadun rasulullah*—"There is no god worthy of worship except Allah, and Muhammad is His Messenger"

—says,"If it were not for you, I would not have created the creation." Therefore the greatest gift bestowed by Allah upon the universe is His Beloved. He says in the Holy Qur'an:

And if you count Allah's favors, you will not be able to number them (Surah Ibrahim 34).

Thus if we try to count the beautiful attributes of our beloved Prophet (ﷺ), the best of Allah's favors, we will be unable to number them.

1. *Muhammad* The most praised one.

He is praised upon earth and in the heavens, from the beginning to the end, by men and jinn and angels, rocks and trees and animals, by prophets before him since Adam, by saints until Doomsday. As all of this cannot give him due praise, we beg Allah to praise him. He is the only one who truly knows the value and the mystery of His Muhammad (ﷺ), and He is the only one who can truly praise him.

2. *Ahmad* The most praiseworthy of those who praise Allah.

This is the celestial name of the Prophet (ﷺ). Allah, the Ever-Existing, the All-Powerful, created a sacred light from His divine Light 360,000 years before He created the rest of creation. That light upon light praised Allah before and during the creation of heaven and the heavenly and earth and the earthly. The inhabitants of the heavens named that light *Ahmad*. As his praise of Allah is greater than the praise of all that is created, he is called *ahmad al-hamidin*—the greatest of givers of praise.

Ahmad is the name by which he is mentioned in the Gospel.

221

And when Jesus son of Mary said, "O Children of Israel, surely I am the Messenger of Allah to you, verifying that which is before me of the Torah and giving good news of a Messenger who will come after me, his name being Ahmad (Surah Saff 6).

In the Bible, Jesus (ﷺ) says:

I have yet many things to say unto you, but ye cannot bear them now. Howbeit when he, the Spirit of Truth, is come, he will guide you unto all truth, for he shall not speak of himself, but whatsoever he shall hear, that shall he speak; and he will show you things to come. He shall glorify me (John 14:17).

That Spirit of Truth who speaks only Allah's words is *Ahmad*.

3. **Hamid** The only one who is given the ability to praise and give thanks to Allah.

He is the one who will praise Allah on the Day of Judgment, just as he praised Allah as the first created light. On that Day he will put his blessed face on the ground in prostration, praise the Lord, and beg mercy for us. *Hamid* (ﷺ) says, "On that day my Lord will enable me to praise Him as I never did before, and I will praise Him more than I did ever before. Then He will tell me, 'Lift your head, My Beloved. I promised that

I will give to thee so that thou wilt be well pleased (Surah Duha 5)

and I accept your intercession for your people until you are satisfied. Your praises are accepted, your intercession is accepted.'"

222

4. *Mahmud* The praised one.

He is praised by all who are raised on the Day of Judgment, for he will be the only one who will intercede for the faithful and whose intercession will be valid. He is the one who has been raised to the station of great glory—*al-maqam al-mahmud.* Allah asked His Beloved

> *During a part of the night keep awake and pray, beyond what is incumbent on thee. Maybe thy Lord will raise thee to* maqaman mahmudan *(a station of glory)* (Surah Bani Isra'il 79).

Mahmud is the name with which he is mentioned in the Psalms of David.

5. *Ahid* The only one who will protect his people from Hellfire.

On the day when sinners will be thrown into Hellfire, Allah will address *Ahid* (ﷺ) and say, "O My Beloved, these are the ones who have denied Us and revolted against Us because they have denied you, disobeyed you, and not followed you. You can use the Hellfire as you wish upon them. And these are the ones who said they believed in and obeyed you, but succumbed to the temptation of the accursed Devil and the desires of their flesh, and sinned. You can use My Hellfire upon them or free them." He is the key that locks the seven doors of Hell, he is the key that opens the eight doors of Paradise; he is the mercy of Allah upon the universe.

When Allah willed to take His Beloved to Himself, He sent the angel Gabriel (ﷺ) who said, "Allah Most High asks you: when He takes your soul, where in His Paradise do you wish your body to rest?"

At this the heavens, in great pride and joy, declared, "The suns are within us, the moons and the stars are within us, the Throne and Canopy and the Celestial Ka'bah in the seventh heaven and Paradise are within us, and Muhammad will be within us!"

The Mercy Upon the Universe asked, "O my brother Gabriel, where will my people be buried?"

Gabriel answered, "Surely under this earth, O Messenger of Allah."

The Beloved of Allah said, "In that case, I ask to be buried here with them, so that I will be with them when we are raised."

Then this world with joy declared, "O heavens! The suns the moons, the stars, the Throne, the Ka'bah of the seventh heaven, and Paradise may be within you, but the Beloved of Allah is within me!"

6. *Wahid* The unique one.

He is unique among men. He has come among us as a human being like ourselves, most beautiful in form and character, the gentlest, the highest in knowledge and wisdom. But his uniqueness is in the station bestowed upon him by the Creator. As Allah embued Adam with the knowledge of all the Names, so He gave the Last of the Prophets the knowledge of all the Names, all the Attributes, and the Essence. These he had received at the first creation of his light. He saw them with his own eyes upon his Ascension. He saw even his Lord, who is free of all dimensions.

7. *Mahi* The annihilator of the darkness of faithlessness and heedlessness.

He is the one who came to a world immersed in darkness, filled with tyranny, idolatry, denial, depravity, and disorder. He was sent as the mercy of the Creator upon the whole universe, and with the light of his message the tyranny turned into peace, the darkness into light, denial into faith, depravity

224

into purity, and disorder into harmony. With his teaching, the darkness and depravity were annihilated and the world was enlightened with the light of faith, knowledge, and wisdom. The sins and revolts of the believers disappeared with the love, respect, and obedience which he inspired for Allah and for himself, and the love and care which he inspired in human beings for one another.

8. *Hashir* The gatherer, the unifier, under whom all will reassemble here and on the Day of Judgment

He is the one who foretold that all people—who are all created Muslims, submissive to Allah, but then with their worldly environment assume false identities—will soon realize and gather under one God and the final message brought by His Messenger. On the Day of Judgment, also, all believers will gather around him under the shade of his banner of grace, hoping for his intercession.

9. *'Aqib* The successor of all the prophets; the final prophet.

Allah says:

> *Muhammad . . . is the Messenger of Allah and the Seal of the prophets. . . .* (Surah Ahzab 40).

No other Messenger will come after him until Doomsday, as his message will stay intact and unchanged until the end of time. He is called *'Aqib* because the totality of good character, morals, and deeds is complete within him. Neither the degree of perfection of other human beings nor their closeness to their Creator can ever surpass his.

This name will be remembered and mentioned by the inhabitants of Hell, as the sinners among his followers will be thrown into Hell, and after their punishment, their state will be made known to him. Then he will intercede and beg for mercy for them. When he does so, that place in Hell where the Muslims met their temporary punishment will lose its fire and be closed.

10. *Ta Ha* The pure purifier and the guide to true faith.

Ta Ha is the name of a chapter of the Holy Qur'an and one of the Names of Allah. Allah honors His Beloved Prophet by some of His own names and attributes.

The ones who know say that the letters "T" and "A" of *Ta* stand for *Tahir*, the pure and purified. The letter "H" and "A" of Ha stand for *Hadi*, the guide. He is the pure one who has helped purify humanity from faithlessness, sin, and error, and who has led us from heedlessness and ignorance into the straight path to the truth.

"T" also stands for *tuba* of *tuba li-man hudiya bihi*— "blessings upon those who have been guided by him"— while "H" stands for *Hadi*, the guide. Good tidings to those who have found the true path to Allah's pleasure and Paradise through believing in, loving, and obeying the Messenger of Allah.

In the system that assigns numerical values to Arabic letters, "T" equals 9 and "H" equals 5, totaling 14, the number of the day of the lunar cycle when the moon is full. This indicates that his light is like the full moon, eliminating the darkness of unconsciousness, faithlessness, and ignorance.

11. *Ya Sin* The Perfect Man, who is master of all humanity.

Ya Sin is the name of a chapter in the Qur'an that is considered to be the heart of the Holy Book. It is also one of the Names of Allah. It is said that the letters "Y" and "S" stand for *ya insan*, "O Human Being"—the best of all human beings, past, present, and future. It also means the master of all humanity. Allah has given him a name from among His own Names because the truth of Muhammad can be truly known to Him alone.

12. *Tahir* Pure and clean.

He is not only cleansed from moral and spiritual stains but also from material dirt. He is clean in this world and in the other—in his faith, in his worship, in everything he did, in everything he said. His breath, his spittle, his blood were pure. At the battle of Uhud, when his blessed cheek was wounded, Malik ibn Sinan (ﷺ), one of the Companions, pressed his mouth to the wound and swallowed the blood. The Prophet (ﷺ) did not stop him from doing this, but said, "O Malik, that blood you swallowed will bring you health in this world, and will protect you against Hellfire in the Hereafter."

13. *Mutahhar* The one who is rendered pure by Allah.

As *Mutahhar*, he purifies those who follow him from disbelief, sin, the dirt of the world and the desires of the flesh. He polishes them with the light of Allah's unity and perfumes them with the love of their Lord and their Prophet. On the Day of Judgment he will cleanse us of all the afflictions of this world and the Hereafter, and save us from purification by Hellfire.

14. *Tayyib* The pleasant and beautifully fragrant one.

His blessed body smelled more beautiful than the pink roses of May. When he caressed the head of a child or held someone's hand, his fragrance remained for a long time. People knew where he had passed because his fragrance lingered in the air. His wives put his perspiration upon themselves as the best of perfumes.

227

15. *Sayyid* The Prince of the Universe, the highest of the prophets.

Many among the wise have interpreted this name in different ways.

"*Sayyid* is he who is gracious in the opinion of Allah" ('Abdullah ibn Abbas [ﷺ]).

"*Sayyid* is he whose worship is complete, who is pious and chaste, who does not take revenge against injustice and tyranny but forgives, who deals gently even with his enemies" (Qatadah [ﷺ]).

"*Sayyid* is he whose state is equal, whether he is pleased or angry" ('Ikrimah [ﷺ]).

The Prophet himself has said, "I am the *sayyid*, master, of all men on the Day of Judgment," as Allah calls Himself

. . . *maliki yawm ad-din* (Surah Fatihah 3).

"I am the Owner, the Judge on the Day of Judgment."

Can you think of the awe and dread of that Day whose judge is Allah, and the grandeur and majesty of the one who is master of all humanity on that day? On that day, when all people are raised, when a thousand feet will stand on one foot, when men are trembling with fear, immersed in their own sweat, brains boiling in their skulls, all hoping for each others' aid—mothers, fathers, priests, popes, saints, even all the prophets thinking of their own salvation, and unable to help. The Beloved of Allah, the Master of the Day of Judgment, will be the only one to turn to for help.

16. *Rasul* The Messenger of Allah.

Allah says:

Certainly you have in the Messenger of Allah an excellent example (Surah Ahzab 26).

17. *Nabi* The Prophet who speaks Allah's words.

Allah describes His Prophet Muhammad, saying,

> *O Prophet, surely We have sent thee as a witness and a bearer of good news and a warner. And as an inviter to Allah by His permission, and as a light-giving lamp* (Surah Ahzab 45–46).

18. *Rasul ar-rahmah* The Messenger of the Most Compassionate.

Allah the Merciful, the Forgiver, addresses us through His Messenger:

> *Say: O My servants who have transgressed against their souls, despair not of the mercy of Allah, for Allah forgives all sins. For He is the Oft-Forgiving, Most Merciful* (Surah Zumar 53).

And Allah also says of His Prophet:

> *And We sent thee not but as a mercy upon the universe* (Surah Anbiya' 107).

Allah does not punish the sins of the believers, and delays the punishment also of the nonbeliever until his death, for the sake of this Messenger whom He has sent as His mercy upon the whole of creation.

19. *Qayyim* The right and good one who loves and is generous to all people.

He also teaches his followers brotherhood and love for each other, gives to them, and teaches them to give to each other what is needed in this world and in the Hereafter.

20. *Jami'* The one in whom all knowledge is gathered.

Allah taught Hadrat Adam (عليه السلام) all the words, and the names of all that exists from the beginning to the end, and He taught Hadrat Ibrahim (عليه السلام) all the attributes. In His last prophet He gathered all the knowledge of all the Names, all the attributes, and the Essence. Muhammad (ﷺ) not only knew them, but saw them and lived them during his ascension in the Night Journey, when he visited all the heavens, met the souls of all the prophets, saw the hundred levels of eight paradises and seven hells, and spoke 90,000 words with his Lord.

21. *Muqtafi* The last one, who follows and contains all the prophets.

The Last of the Prophets has said: "The resemblance between me and the other prophets is like a beautiful house which is complete except for a last brick. All who see this marvel at its beauty, but are also shocked by the missing brick. With me, that building of prophethood is completed."

He is the mercy upon the universe. Allah has wished to seal His messages with a Messenger who is His Mercy. Allah has honored the followers of His last prophet by making them the last community, so that their sins and errors are hidden from the previous Messengers. Allah has made their punishment light, His rewards for them greater, and their time of waiting until the Day of Judgment shorter.

22. *Muqaffi* The one behind whom are all the other prophets, who follow him and are confirmed in him.

The Blessed Prophet has said: "Allah Most High has honored me to be at the head of all. No prophet has reached to my level of closeness with Allah. They are all behind me, and they all follow me in all their natural and spiritual actions and merits in this world and in the Hereafter."

23. *Rasul al-malahim* Messenger to the warriors of truth.

Those who are honored to follow the most merciful, compassionate, and gentlest of prophets are the fiercest warriors against the tyranny of the unfaithful over the faithful. This jihad is ordered by Allah and helped by Allah. One of the miracles of Islam is the repeated victory of a handful of Muslim warriors during the short period of 25 years over the then greatest powers of the world, the Sassanids of Persia and the Byzantines.

Within the first 40 years of the Islamic era, the whole of the Arabian Peninsula, Egypt and North Africa, Persia and Asia Minor, and the Caucasus were in Muslim hands.

That which rendered the believers victorious was Allah's help and their faith in Him. But the Prophet (ﷺ) has said that the greater battle is the war with one's own ego and one's own devil, and the greatest victory is won over one's own faithlessness.

24. *Rasul ar-rahah* The Messenger of appeasement and quietude.

25. *Kamil* The perfect one.

26. *Iklil* The crown of the believers.

27. *Muddaththir* The one who shows patience towards those who tyrannize him.

Because he was patient toward those who were hostile, he has been addressed in the Qur'an as:

O thou wrapped up [in a mantle] . . . for thy Lord's cause be patient and constant (Surah Muddaththir 1,7).

28. *Muzammil* The one who wraps himself up in his cloak as he did in the awe of the first revelation.

29. *'Abdullah* Allah's ultimate servant.

With this name he received the highest honor, as to be the true servant of Allah is the highest level to which any human being may aspire.

30. *Habibullah* The Beloved of Allah.

This name is proper only to him.

31. *Safiyullah* The chosen of Allah out of the whole creation.

He was purified, sustained, brought up, and educated by Allah Himself. From him all that is lacking was taken away, and to him all perfection was given.

32. *Naji'ullah* The deliverer who leads to salvation.

33. *Kalimullah* The one who converses with Allah.

He spoke 90,000 words with Allah in his ascension during the Night Journey.

34. *Khatim al-anbiya'* The Seal of the Prophets, with whom all prophethood is fulfilled.

Allah declares:

Muhammad . . . is the apostle of Allah and the seal of the prophets (Surah Ahzab 40).

35. *Khatim ar-rusul* The Seal of the Messengers.

36. **Muhyi** The vivifier of dead hearts with the light of faith.

37. **Munji** The one who delivers from sin.

38. **Mudhakkir** The one who reminds us of the Creator and of the Day of Judgment.

39. **Nasir** The helper of humanity, the ally of the righteous.

40. **Mansur** The one made triumphant in this world and in the Hereafter.

He is the one fortified by the assistance of Gabriel and other angels, and by Allah Himself.

41. **Nabi ar-rahmah** The prophet who was sent as Allah's mercy upon the universe.

42. **Nabi at-tawbah** The prophet of repentance, striving for human welfare.

43. **Haris 'alaykum** The one filled with solicitude for you.

Mentioned in the Qur'an as the one zealous for your salvation. Allah says:

> . . . It grieves him that ye should perish; ardently anxious is he over you; to the believers is he most kind and merciful (Surah Tawbah 128).

44. **Ma'lum** The well-known.

45. **Shahir** The celebrated one.

46. **Shāhid** The witness.

47. *Shahid* The martyr.

48. *Mashshud* The witnessed.

49. *Bashir* The sender of good news to the believers.

50. *Mubashshir* The bringer of good news of blessings and Paradise.

51. *Nazir* The one who calls humanity to virtue with warnings of Allah's wrath.

52. *Munzir* The one who warns and dissuades from sin.

53. *Nur* The sacred light.

54. *Siraj* The torch of the right path.
The one illuminated with the light of faith and Islam.

55. *Misbah* The lamp which contains the light of faith and Islam which lights the realms of worship, submission, and salvation.

56. *Huda* The guidance to Truth and Paradise.

57. *Mahdi* The rightly guided one, guide to the path of knowledge, obedience, and worship.

58. *Munir* The illuminator of the universe.

59. *Da'i* The one who calls to faith and Islam.

60. *Mad'u* The one who heard and accepted the divine call.

61. *Mujib* The one who accepts prayers.

He brought humanity Allah's ordinances and warned us against sins. He became an example of acting in accordance with divine teaching, and he interceded for the good and the sinner alike.

62. *Mujab* The answered one, the answer to our prayers.

63. *Hafi* The true answerer of all questions.

64. *'Afu* The clement.

He is the example of forgiving the wrong done to him; Allah forgives the one who forgives.

65. *Wali* The friend of Allah and of all who believe.

66. *Haqq* The Truth.

67. *Qawi* The powerful.

68. *Amin* The trustworthy.

He was called *Muhammad al-amin*—"Muhammad the Trustworthy"—by the Meccans before he received the divine order to declare his prophethood at the age of 40.

69. *Ma'mun* The one in whom people confide.

70. *Karim* The generous one.

Allah bestows upon him the attribute of one of his beautiful names, the All-Generous One.

71. *Mukarram* The ennobled one.

72. *Makin* The authoritative one.

73. *Matin* The firm and consistent one.

74. *Mubin* The distinguisher and the explainer.

75. *Mu'ammil* The hopeful one.

76. *Wasul* The uniter.

77. *Dhu quwwah* The source of strength.

78. *Dhu hurmah* The source of sacredness.

79. *Dhu makanah* The source of integrity.

80. *Dhu 'izz* The source of might.

81. *Dhu fadl* The source of virtue.

82. *Muta'* The one whom the faithful obey.

83. *Muti'* The one who is obedient to Allah.

84. *Qidam as-sidq* The one constantly sincere.

85. *Rahmah* Compassion.

86. *Bushra* Good news.

87. *Ghawth* Savior.

88. *Ghayth* The benevolent one who brings dead hearts to life just as rain gives life to to the earth.

89. *Ghiyath* The helper.

90. *Ni'matullah* The blessing of Allah.

91. *Hadiyatullah* The gift of Allah to the universe.

92. *'Urwah wuthqa* The firm tie that binds humanity to its Creator.

93. *Siratullah* The path leading to Allah and the Truth.

94. *Sirat mustaqim* The straight and shortest way leading to Allah.

95. *Dhikrullah* The remembrance of Allah

96. *Sayfullah* The sword of Allah.

97. *Hizbullah* Allah's partisan, destroyer of the enemies of Allah.

98. *Al-najm al-thaqib* The Star whose fire burns devils.

99. *Mustafa* The divinely elected.

100. *Mujtaba* The chosen one.

101. *Muntaqa* The one chosen for his purity.

102. *Ummi* The unlettered one who has no teacher among men, who is divinely taught.

103. *Mukhtar* The chosen one who is autonomous.

104. *Ajir* The reward of the believers.

105. *Jabbar* The all-compelling one.

106. *Abul-Qasim* The father of Qasim.

107. *Abul-Tahir* The father of Tahir.

108. *Abul-Tayyib* The father of Tayyib.

109. *Abu Ibrahim* The father of Ibrahim.

110. *Mushaffa'* The one given the right of intercession.

111. *Shafi'* The intercessor.

112. *Salih* The righteous.

113. *Muslih* The conciliator.

114. *Muhaymin* The protector and guardian.

115. *Sadiq* The truthful.

116. *Musaddaq* The one proved true by the Truth that comes through him.

117. *Sidq* The essence of truthfulness.

118. *Sayyid al-mursalin* The master and best of all Messengers.

119. *Imam al-muttaqin* The leader of the pious who fear Allah.

120. *Qa'id al-ghurri al-muhajjalin* Protector and guide of the believers.

121. *Khalil al-Rahman* The close friend of the All-Merciful Allah.

122. *Barr* The good and beneficent one.

123. *Mabarr* The essence of piety and beneficence.

124. *Wajih* The one distinguished from all else.

125. *Nasīh* The true counsellor.

126. *Nāsih* Transformer of men's souls.

127. *Wakil* The faithful trustee.

128. *Mutawakkil* The one who puts all his trust in Allah.

129. *Kafil* The guarantor.

130. *Shafiq* The compassionate, kind, and benevolent one.

131. *Muqim as-sunnah* The one who holds the ordinances of Allah.

132. *Muqaddas* The sanctified one.

133. *Ruh al-quddus* Essence of the divine.

134. *Ruh al-haqq* The essence of truth.

135. *Ruh al-qist* The essence of justice.

136. *Kafi* The one who suffices for the believers.

137. *Muktafi* The one sufficient unto himself.

138. *Baligh* The one who has arrived at spiritual perfection.

139. *Muballigh* The bearer of news.

140. *Shafi* The curer of sick hearts.

141. *Wasil* The one who has attained the divine.

142. *Mawsul* The one who has been attained.

143. *Sabiq* The one who precedes everything.

144. *Sa'iq* The impelling motive for the faith of the faithful.

145. *Hadi* The guide.

146. *Muhdi* The one who gives guidance.

147. *Muqaddam* The premise of Islam.

148. *'Aziz* The highly esteemed beloved with no equal among men.

149. *Fadil* The one superior in virtue and generosity.

150. *Mufaddal* The favored of Allah made superior to all beings.

151. *Fatih* The conqueror of hearts, who opens them to faith and truth.

152. *Miftah* The key that opens the doors of Paradise and locks the doors of Hell.

153. *Miftah ar-rahmah* The key to Allah's mercy.

154. *Miftah al-jannah* The key of Paradise.

155. *'Alam al-iman* The symbol of faith that leads one to faith.

156. *'Alam al-yaqin* The symbol of certitude that leads one to certitude.

157. *Dalil al-khayrat* The guide to good deeds.

158. *Musahhih al-hasanat* The one who renders the wrong, right and the ugly, beautiful.

159. *Muqil al-atharat* The foreseer and warner of errors.

160. *Safuh 'an az-zallat* The one who deters errors.

161. *Sahib ash-shafa'ah* The one endowed with intercession.

162. *Sahib al-makan* The one embued with the highest degree of morals and character.

163. *Sahib al qidam* The one endued with the highest station.

164. *Makhsus bil-'izz* The one to whom all might and honor are proper.

165. *Makhsus bil-majd* The one to whom all that is noble, sublime, and majestic is proper.

166. *Makhsus bish-sharaf* The one to whom all excellence is proper.

241

167. *Sahib al-wasilah* The possessor of the means to Allah's mercy.

168. *Sahib al-sayf* The owner of the sword against Allah's enemies.

169. *Sahib al-fadilah* The source of Allah's grace.

170. *Sahib al-izar* The owner of the cloak of prophethood who is mentioned by this name in holy books.

171. *Sahib al-hujjah* The possessor of the proof.

172. *Sahib as-sultan* The owner of the sovereignty of kings.

173. *Sahib al-rida'* The owner of the woolen cloak.

174. *Sahib ad-darajat ar-rafi'ah* The one endowed with the exalted station.

175. *Sahib at-taj* The crowned one, crowned with the crown of Paradise on the night of his Ascension.

176. *Sahib al-mighfar* The one who wears the helmet of the holy knight.

177. *Sahib al-liwa'* Holder of the Banner of Praise under which all prophets and believers will gather on the Day of Judgment.

178. *Sahib al-mi'raj* The master of ascension who was brought, during his lifetime, above the seven heavens, to the divine realms close to Allah.

179. *Sahib al-qadib* The holder of the rod with which he

broke the 360 idols around the Ka'bah on the day of the conquest of Mecca.

180. *Sahib al-Buraq* The rider of Buraq, the heavenly carrier which brought him from the city of Mecca to Jerusalem on the night of the Ascension.

181. *Sahib al-khatam* The carrier of the Seal of Prophethood, which was between his shoulder blades.

182. *Sahib al-'alamah* The one endowed with the distinct signs of prophethood.

183. *Sahib al-burhan* The one endowed with the miracles proving his prophethood.

184. *Sahib al-bayan* The one endowed with the greatest expression of prophethood, which is the Holy Qur'an.

185. *Fasih al-lisan* The one whose speech is rendered most eloquent and effective.

186. *Mutahhir al-janan* The source of knowledge, wisdom, and gentleness, whose heart is purified and who purifies hearts.

187. *Ra'uf* The clement one on whom Allah has bestowed His own Name, by which he is mentioned in the Qur'an.

188. *Rahim* The merciful one, upon whom Allah the Most Merciful bestowed His own Name.

189. *Udhn khayr* The hearer of good.

190. **Sahih al-Islam** The truth of Islam which corrects and cancels human distortions of divine truths previously revealed, and reestablishes the true message of Allah.

191. **Sayyid al-kawnayn** The master of all created beings in this world and the Hereafter.

192. **'Ayn al-na'im** The source through which Allah's blessings come in this world and the Hereafter.

193. **'Ayn al-qurr** The source of light and splendor.

194. **Sa'd Allah** The joy of Allah who as the first created intelligence, contains the salvation, the victory, peace, and blessing of all creation.

195. **Sa'd al-khalq** The joy of all created beings, being the best and the most generous and closest to Allah among them.

196. **Khatib al-umam** The preacher to humanity.

197. **'Alam al-huda** The sign of guidance to truth, Allah's pleasure, and Paradise.

198. **Kashif al-karb** The one who lifts the pain, afflictions, and difficulties from humanity.

199. **Rafi' al-rutab** The one who raises the levels of those who believe and obey him.

200. **'Izz al-a'rab** The glory of the Arabs.

201. **Sahib al-faraj** The source of consolation, who gives bliss and comfort to those who believe in his prophethood and follow his commands.

BISMILLAH AR-RAHMAN AR-RAHIM

O Allah, we pray that You bestow Your mercy, grace, and blessings upon our Master Muhammad so that by this prayer You will deliver us from all fears and from our lowliness; that You will cleanse us of all our impurities, and that You will send to us the ultimate of all good in this life and in the Hereafter.

O most loving Allah, the Benefactor of all things. O Unique Creator of the heavens and the earth. O Living, Self-Sufficient Allah. O Master of all greatness, majesty and graciousness—In the name of Your exalted Essence, we beg that You change our nature from the nature of mortal man and that You raise our station to that of the most elevated of Your angels. O Transformer and Keeper of our condition and our power, transform our state into the best of states. Glorified and praised be You, O Allah. I bear witness that there is no god besides You: from You do I seek forgiveness, and unto You do I turn repentant. O Allah, bestow Your blessings and grace upon our Master Muhammad and upon his Family and Companions.

Amin

THE NOBLEST OF AIMS IN THE EXPLANATION OF GOD'S FAIREST NAMES

Al-Maqṣad al-Asnā fī Sharḥ Ma ͨānī Asmāʾ Allāh al-Ḥusnā[1]

I present here some selections from this very interesting work, among them the whole of the passage to which Ghazālī refers in the *Munqidh*.[2] I have also included my translation of Ghazālī's comments on a few of the ninety-nine Names. R. C. Stade [cf. Annotated Bibliography] has translated fully Chapter One of Section Two [Shehkdi, pp. 63–171], and the interested reader will find there much that will give him a deeper insight into Ghazālī's religious and spiritual doctrine. A summary of this chapter will be found in Appendix III of *El justo medio* by Asín Palácios, pp. 437–47; in the same work, pp. 458–71, there is a translation of the passage referred to in the *Munqidh*.

---

1. Should the reader be interested in the references mentioned, please consult Al-Ghazālī, *Deliverence from Error*, trans. R. J. McCarthy, Fons Vitae, 1999.

2. I have used the text edited by Professor Fadlou A. Shehādi—cf. Annotated Bibliography.

[The Introduction: Khuṭba]

In the Name of God, Merciful and Kind!

Praise be to God, matchless in His majesty and His might, solely sublime and sempiternal, Who clipped the wings of intellects [so as to keep them, restrain them] from the glow of His glory, and Who has made the way to know Him to consist solely in powerlessness to know Him, and Who rendered the tongues of the eloquent incapable of the [due] praise of His majestic high beauty save by the employ of His own praise of Himself and His own enumeration of His Names and His Attributes. And blessings upon Muḥammad, the best of His creatures, and upon his Companions and his family!

Now then: A brother in God—Mighty and Glorious!— to answer whom it is a religious duty asked me to explain the meanings of God's most beautiful Names. His requests kept coming to me one after another, and on my part I kept putting one foot forward and withdrawing the other, vacillating between complying with his demand so as to fulfill the duty of brotherliness and seeking an excuse from his solicitation so as to take the path of caution [the way of wariness] and to abstain from mounting the back of danger, and because I deemed human power inadequate to accomplish this aim.

How could it be otherwise? For there are two things which deter the man of discernment from plunging into such an abyss as this. One of them is that in itself the thing is an extraordinary desire hard to attain and difficult to comprehend. For in sublimity it is the acme and the most distant goal: minds are baffled [bewildered, perplexed] by it, and the sight [perceptive powers] of intellect falls far short of its beginnings [starting points], to say nothing of its farthest reaches. Whence, then, can human powers [essay to] follow the path of study and investigation of the Attributes of Divinity? [It is like asking] How can the eyes of bats endure the light of the sun?

[p. 12] The second deterrent is that in speaking clearly about the essence [true nature, essential being] of the True [the Truth, God] one must almost directly contradict the a priori notions of the masses of men. But weaning men from their habitual usage and familiar beliefs is difficult. And the abode [excellence] of the Truth is far above being a thoroughfare for every comer [a common thoroughfare, or market], and too sublime for men to gaze at save one by one [one after another]. And the greater the thing sought, the fewer the helpers. One who associates with men deserves to be shunned, but it is difficult for one who sees the True to pretend not to see [to shut his eyes]. For one who knows not God—Mighty and Glorious!—silence is imperative, and for one who knows God Most High silence is prescribed. For that reason it has been said: "The tongue of him who knows God is weak [blunted, languid, dull, expressionless]." But the sincerity of the demand, along with its persistence, have outstripped these excuses. So I ask God—Mighty and Glorious!—to make easy [supply, provide] that which is right and to enhance the recompense by His largesse and benevolence and lavish liberality: truly He is the Munificent, the Magnanimous, the Indulgent to His servants!

[p. 13]   *The Beginning of the Book*

We think it good to divide the discourse in this book into three Sections: the First Section on the Antecedents and the Preambles, the Second Section on the Aims and Goals, the Third Section on the Consequents and Complements. The chapters of the First Section address the Aims by way of preface and introduction; and the chapters of the Third Section are attached to them by way of completion and complement [supplement]. But the quintessential object is what the middle [chapters] contain.

The First Section explains (1) the true meaning of what is affirmed about the name and the named and naming, and discloses the error which has befallen such affirmtion in the case of most of the sects; (2) whether any name the meaning of which approximates the Name of God Most High, such as ʿal-ʿaẓīm and al-jalīl and al-kabīr, is to be predicated univocally, so that such names are synonyms, or [whether] their meanings must differ; (3) whether a single name with two meanings is "common" [shared: *mushtarak*] by [its] relation to the two meanings [and to be] predicated of them as the general is of its particulars [the things it names], or [is to be] predicated particularly of one of the two; (4) that the creature has a share in the meaning of each of the Names of God—Mighty and Glorious!

The Second Section explains (1) the meanings of the ninety-nine Names of God; (2) how all of them come down to an Essence and seven Attributes in view of the People of the Sunna; (3) how, according to the doctrine of the Muʿtazilites and the Philosophers, they come down to a simple Essence containing no multiplicity.

[p. 14] The Third Section explains (1) that the Names of God Most High are more than ninety-nine by positive tradition [*tawqīfan*]; (2) the permission to describe God Most High by whatever He is qualified by [can be described by], even though there has come no positive tradition regarding it, providing it is not [explicitly] prohibited; (3) the advantage of the enumeration and specification by one hundred minus one.

[p. 15]   SECTION ONE
*On the Antecedents and Preambles
It Contains Four Chapters*

[p. 17]　　　　　　　　Chapter One
Explanation of the Meaning of "Name,"
"Named," "Naming"

Many have plunged into the [meaning of] the *name* and
the *named,* and have gone different ways. Most of the sects
have deviated from the truth. Some say: The *name* is identified with the *named,* but different [distinct] from the *naming.* Another view is that the *name* is different [distinct]
from the *named,* but identified with the *naming.* A third
group, known for skill in the art of dialectic and polemic,
alleges that the *name* may be identified with the *named,* as
[in] our saying of God Most High: He is an essence and
existent [being]; and it may be distinct from the *named,* as
[in] our saying [of God]: He is creating, sustaining—for this
indicates sustaining and creating, and these are distinct from
Him; and it may be such that one cannot say it is identified
with the *named,* or that it is distinct from it, as [in] our saying: Knowing and powerful—for these indicate knowledge
and power, and one cannot say of God's Attributes that they
are God or that they are other than God.
1　The dispute comes down to two points: one is whether
or not the *name* is the *naming,* and the second is whether or
not the *name* is the *named.* The truth is that the *name* is
other than the *naming* and other than the *named,* and that
these three names are different and not synonymous. The
only way to lay bare the truth in this matter is to explain
individually the meaning of each of these three words
[terms], then to explain the meaning of our saying "it is [the
same]" and the meaning of our saying "it is distinct
[diverse]"—[i.e. of identity and diversity]. This is the
method of disclosing realities [truths, facts], and one who
deviates from this method will in no wise succeed.
　　Every judgmental [propositional: *taṣdīqī*] cognition
[knowledge: *ʿilm*], i.e. one susceptible of being declared true

or false, is undoubtedly a proposition containing a subject and a predicate [*mawṣūf wa ṣifa*: something described or qualified, and something describing or qualifying, quality, attribute], and the relation of that predicate to the subject. So it must be preceded by the knowledge of the subject and its definition by way of conceiving [representing; *al-taṣawwur,* also: concept] [p. 18] its definition and its reality [true meaning, essence: *ḥaqīqa*], then by the knowledge of the predicate and its definition by way of conceiving its definition and its reality, then by the consideration of the relation of that predicate to the subject—whether it exists [as] belonging to it or is denied of it. For example, if one wishes to know whether an angel is eternal or incipient, he must first know the meaning of the term [word] "angel," then the meaning of "eternal" and 'incipient," then he must consider the affirmation or denial of one of the two descriptions of the angel. Similarly one must have knowledge of the meaning of "name" and of "named" and knowledge of the meaning of identity [*al-huwiyya*] and "diversity" [*al-ghayriyya*] so that he may conceivably know thereafter whether it [name] is it [named; is identified with it] or different from [other than] it.

In explanation of the definition and reality of *name* we say: Things base an existence in individuals [*al-aᶜyān;* or, essences; individual, or essential, existence], and an existence in the tongue [linguistic, or, verbal existence], and an existence in minds [mental existence]. The existence in individuals is the basic [fundamental], real [actual] existence; and the existence in minds is the cognitional, formal existence; and the existence in the tongue is the verbal, indicative existence. For example, "the heaven" [*al-samā'*] has an existence in its essence and itself; then it has an existence in our minds and our souls, because the representation [form] of the heaven is impressed in our eyes [sights] and then in our imagination [*khayāl*], so that, were the heaven to cease to exist and we were to continue [existing], the representation of the heaven would be present in our imagination. And this representation is what we express by "knowledge" [cognition], and it is the likeness of the cognoscible, for it imitates the cognoscible and corresponds to it, and it is like the form impressed in the mirror, for it imitates the form outside and confronting it.

The existence in the tongue is the word composed of sounds divided into three [p. 19] syllables, the first of which is expressed by the *sīn* [s] and the second by the *mīm* [m] and the third by the *alif* [with the *hamza*]—and they are like our saying *samā'*. So this saying is an indication of what is in the mind, and what is in the mind is a representation of what is in [individual] existence and is conformed to it. If there were no existence in individuals, no form [image, representation] would be impressed in minds, and if it were not impressed in the form [image] of the minds and a man were unaware of it, he would not express it by the tongue. So the word and the cognition and the cognoscible are three different things, but they are mutually corresponding and comparable, though they may be confused for a stupid person and one of them may not be distinguished from another.

And how can these existents not be different, and how can there not attach to each of them properties [*khawāṣṣ*— special qualities] which do not attach to the other? For a man, for example, insofar as he exists in individuals, there attaches to him that he is asleep and awake, living and dead, standing, walking, and sitting, etc.; and insofar as he exists in minds, there attaches to him that he is an inchoative and a predicate, and general and specific, and universal and particular, and a proposition, etc.; and insofar as he exists in the tongue, there attaches to him that he is Arabic and Persian and Turkish, and having many letters and having few letters, and that he is a noun and verb and particle, etc. This latter existence is something which may differ in [different] ages and be diverse in the usage of [different] countries. But the

253

existence in individuals and in minds in no wise differs in [different] ages and nations.

Now that you know this, set aside the existence which is in individuals and in minds and consider [reflect on] verbal [linguistic] existence—for our aim concerns the latter. We say, then: Words are an expression of the separate [syllabified] letters which have been posited by human choice to indicate the individuals [essences] of things. They are divided into what is posited primarily and what is posited secondarily. [The use of "posited," *mawḍūᶜ*, indicates a "conventional" origin of language.]

[p. 20] What is posited primarily is like your saying: heaven, tree, man, etc. As for what is posited secondarily, it is like your saying: noun, verb, particle, command, prohibition and imperfect [aorist]. We say that it is posited secondarily simply because the words posited to indicate things are divided into what indicates a meaning in something else, and it is called a particle, and what indicates a meaning in itself. The latter is divided into what indicates the time of the existence of that meaning, and it is called a verb, e.g. your saying "he struck, he strikes or will strike," and what does not indicate the time, and it is called a noun, e.g. your saying "heaven, earth." Words were first posited as indications of individuals [essences], and thereafter the noun, verb and particle were posited as indications of the divisions of words, because the words, once they were posited, also became existents in individuals and their forms were impressed in minds, and [so] were also suited to be indicated by the movements of the tongue.

Conceivably there are words which have been posited thirdly and fourthly, so that when the noun is divided into [several] divisions, and each division is known by a name, that name is the third rank [degree], as one says, for example: The noun is divided into indefinite and definite, etc. The purpose of all this is that you know that the noun comes

254

down to the word posited secondarily. So if one says to us: "What is the definition of the noun?" we say: It is the word posited for indication; and perhaps we add to that what distinguishes it from the particle and the verb. But the formulation of the definition is not our present purpose; the purpose is simply that what is meant by the name is the meaning which is in the third rank, i.e. which is in the tongue, not what is in individuals and minds.

Once you know that by the name is meant simply the word posited for indication, then know [p. 21] that everything posited for indication has a positor and a positing and an object of the positing [that for which it is posited]. The latter is called "the named," i.e. the indicated qua [as] indicated. The positor is called "the namer," and the positing is called "the naming." One says: So-and-so named his son—when he posits a word to indicate him, and his positing is called "naming." The term "naming" may also be applied to the mention of the posited name, as when one calls out to a person and says "O Zayd!"—and it is said that he named him; and if he says "O Abū Bakr!" it is said that he used his agnomen [*kannāhu:* the *kunya* is a name formed by combining the prefix *Abū* (father) or *Umm* (mother) with the name of the child]. The term "naming" is common to the positing of the name and the mention of the name, though the likelier is that it is worthier [truer] of the positing than of the mention.

Name and naming and named are analogous to motion and moving and mover and moved, and these are four different names indicating different notions [meanings, things]. "Motion" indicates a moving from a place to a place; and "moving" indicates the production [causing] of this motion; and "mover" indicates the agent of the motion; and "moved" indicates the thing in which the motion is along with its proceeding [issuing] from an agent—and not like "that which is in motion" [*al-mutaḥarrik*], which indicates only the place [*maḥall:* substrate] in which the motion is, without indicating the agent [i.e. that there is an agent]. If the meanings of these words are now clear, one should consider whether it can be said of them that one of them is identified with another, or it must be said that it is other than [distinct from] it.

This will be understood only through knowledge of "the other" [diversity] and of "it is it" [identity]. Our saying "it is it" is used in three ways. *One way* is like one's saying: *"al-khamr* [wine] is *al-ʿuqār* [wine]," and *"al-layth* [lion] is *al-ʾasad* [lion]." This takes place in the case of everything which is one in itself, but has two synonymous names the meaning of which does not differ at all, nor it is dissimilar by any addition or lack, but only their letters are different. The likes of these names are called "synonymous."

[p. 22] *The second way* is like one's saying "The *ṣārim* [sharp sword] is the sword [*al-sayf*]," and "The *muhannad* [sword made of Indian steel] is the sword [*al-sayf*]"—and this differs from the previous case [Para. 20]. For these names have different meanings and are not synonymous, because *al-ṣārim* indicates the sword in so far as it is cutting, while *al-muhannad* indicates the sword in so far as it has a relation to India, and the sword [*al-sayf*] indicates sword in an absolute way without any allusion to anything else. But the synonymous differ only in their letters and are not dissimilar by any addition or lack. So let us call this kind [genus] "interpenetrating" since "the sword" enters into the meaning of the three words, though some of them indicate along with it an addition.

The third way is that one say "Snow is white [and] cold; so the white and the cold are one, and the white is the cold—and this is the most improbable [farfetched, farthest out] of the ways. That comes down to the oneness of the posited qualified by two qualities and means that a single individual [essence] is qualified by whiteness and coldness.

In general, our saying "It is it" indicates a plurality which in some way has a oneness. For if there were no oneness, one could not say "It is it, one [that is, identically]," and so long as there were no plurality, there would be no "It is it" [identity], for the latter is an allusion [a pointing to] two things.

The name cannot be the named in the first way [synonyms—Para. 20]. For the meaning of the named is other than the meaning of the name, since we have shown that the name is an indicating word and the named is something indicated and may be other than a word; and because the name is Arabic and Persian and Turkish, and the named may not be such; and in asking about the name one says: "What is it?" whereas in asking about the named one may say: "Who is it?" . . . [p. 23] . . . and the name may be a figure of speech, but not the named; and the name may be changed, but not the named.

The name cannot be the named in the second way [Para. 21] . . . because this would necessitate that the naming and the namer and the named and the name all be one and the same—a foolhardy statement example of motion, moving, etc. . . . [p. 24] . . . each of the terms has a proper and distinct meaning.

The third way [Para. 22] not applicable to the name and the named, or to the name and the naming . . . [p. 25]. . . .

The third view [Para. 9—"a third group"] is the farthest from the right and the most confused unless it be interpreted in a certain way—but then the name and the named are clearly different . . . long discussion [Paras. 29–48; pp. 26–35] on the use of certain of God's Names; and answers to difficulties drawn from the Qurʾān.

This is enough, really too much, but given to show the way to deal with such problems.

[pp. 36–38] Chapter Two

Explanation of Names Close to One Another in Meaning: Are They Synonyms Indicating Only One Meaning, or Must Their Meanings Differ?

In the case of God's Names such names are not synonyms. Examples: difference between al-Ghāfir, al-Ghafūr and al-Ghaffār: must be considered as three Names. The first indicates only "pardoning"; the second indicates "multiplicity of pardoning in relation to multiplicity of sins"; the third indicates multiplicity by way of repeated pardoning. Other examples: al-Ghanī and al-Malik; al-ʿAlim and al-Khabīr; alʿAẓīm and al-Kabīr. In general there is no synonymity in the Names included in the Ninety-Nine, because the latter are intended, not for their letters or pronunciation, but for their semantic contents and meanings.

[pp. 39–41] Chapter Three

On the One Name Which Has Different Meanings

It is common in relation to them, e.g. *muʾmin* [believing, and, affording security or protection]. But it is not predicated of each of its "objects named" as the general is of its objects named. Difference possible in legal and linguistic usages.

Case of *al-Salām*. . . . The meaning more indicative of perfection and praise is the one to be preferred.

[pp. 42–59]   Chapter Four

Explanation of the Fact That the Servant's
Perfection and Happiness Lie in Putting on
the Moral Qualities of God Most High
and Adorning Himself with the Meanings of
His Attributes and His Names as
Far as He Conceivably Can

Know that one whose only portion [lot] of the meanings of the Names of God—Great and Glorious!—is that
he hears the words and understands its linguistic explanation and positing, and believes with his heart that the
meaning exists in God Most High, is luckless in his lot and
of low rank and cannot rightly boast of what he has
acquired. For such things are shared by many, and while
they possess a certain relative excellence, are still a clear
defect in relation to the acme of perfection. For the good
deeds of the righteous are the bad deeds of the intimates
[close friends of God, Saints]. The lots [portions] of the
intimate respecting the Names of God Most High are three
[kinds].

The first lot is the knowledge of these meanings by way
of revelation and direct vision [*al-mukāshafa wa l-
mushāhada* [cf. Notes 55 and 183 to my Translation of the
Munqidh] so that their realities become manifest to them by
proof in which error cannot be and God's being qualified by
them is disclosed to them in a manner which, in clarity and
distinctness [plainness], is analogous to the certainty a man
has of his interior qualities which he perceives by direct
experience of his interior, not by any exterior sensation.
How great a difference there is between this and the belief
acquired from parents and teachers by servile conformism
and persistence in it, even though it be accompanied by
dialectical and *kalām* proofs!

THE NAME AND THE NAMED

The second lot is their high regard for [thinking great] what is disclosed to them regarding the Attributes of splendor in a way such that their high regard gives rise to their desire [*shawq*] to be qualified by these Attributes so far as they can be, in order thereby to draw close to the True [God] qualitatively, not spatially, and so to acquire from that qualification a likeness to the Angels brought close to God—Great and Glorious! It is inconceivable that the heart be filled with high regard for an Attribute and esteeming it radiant without an ensuing yearning for that Attribute and a passionate love of that perfection and splendor and an avid desire of being adorned by that quality, if that be possible for the one who has a high regard for its perfection. And if it cannot be [attained] in its perfection, there arises the yearning for the amount possible of it—no doubt about it!

One will be devoid of this yearning only for one of two reasons: either because of the weakness of the knowledge and certainty that the quality known belongs to the qualities of splendor and perfection, or because the heart is filled with and absorbed in another yearning. Thus when a disciple sees the perfection of his master in knowledge there is aroused in him a yearning to resemble and imitate him—unless, for example, he is filled with [totally preoccupied with] hunger: for his interior's absorption with the yearning for food may prevent the arousing of the yearning for knowledge. [p. 44] Therefore one who contemplates [looks into] the Attributes of God Most High ought in his heart to be devoid of the desire for anything other than God—Great and Glorious! For knowledge is the seed of yearning, but [only] so long as it encounters a heart free of the thorny growths of the passions: so if it be not free, the seed will not flourish [be productive].

The third lot is striving to acquire what is possible of those qualities, and to be changed [molded] by them and to be adorned with their beauties. By this the servant becomes "divine" [Lordly], i.e. close to the Lord Most High, and by this he becomes a companion [associate] of the heavenly host of the Angels, for they are on the carpet of proximity [to God]. So one who inclines to a likeness respecting their qualities obtains something of their proximity commensurate with what he obtains of their qualities which bring them close to the True—Exalted He!

If you say: Seeking proximity to God—Great and Glorious!—by quality [attribute] is something obscure and hearts almost recoil from accepting it or believing it. So give a fuller explanation to break [down] the force [violence] of the rejection of those who reject it, for this would be like something disapproved of [rejected] by the majority unless you were to disclose its true meaning. *I say:* It is not unknown to you, or to one who has developed [grown, progressed] a little from the rank of the common ulema, that existents are divided into perfect and imperfect—and the perfect is nobler than the imperfect. However much [whenever] the degrees of perfection differ, and the ultimate perfection is restricted to one, so that only he possesses absolute perfection and the other existents do not possess an absolute perfection but rather possess perfections differing from each other in relation [relatively], then undoubtedly the most perfect of them is closer to Him Who possesses absolute perfection—I mean a closeness in rank and degree, not in perfection.

Furthermore, existents are divided into animate and inanimate. And you know that the animate is nobler and more perfect than the inanimate, and that the degrees of the animate are three: that of angels, that of men, [p. 45] and that of beasts. That of beasts is the lowest in that very life in which is its nobility, for the animate is the perceptive and the active—and the beast is imperfect in perception and action, since its perception is limited to sensation and its action is motivated only by passion [appetite] and anger [irascibility]. . . .

The degree of the angel is the highest, because closeness and distance have no effect on his perception and he is exempt from passion and anger, his only motive for action being to seek to draw near to God—Great and Glorious!

Man's degree is intermediate between those two, as though he is composed of "angelic-ness' and "beast-ness." The latter is dominant in him at first, until the light of reason [al-ᶜaql] illumines him and enables him to act freely in the kingdom of the heavens and the earth. At first, also, he is mastered by passion and anger, until there appears in him the desire to seek perfection . . . and by conquest of passion and anger he acquires a likeness to the angels. So, too, by weaning his soul from sensibles and "imaginables" he acquires another likeness to the angels . . . and his imitation of the angels in perception and actions brings him close to the angel, and the angel is close to God—and the close to the close is close.

If you say: The literal meaning of what you say points to the affirmation of a resemblance between the servant and God, but it is known of God by revelation and by reason that "there is nothing like Him" [42.9/11] and that nothing resembles Him, *I say:* Once you know the likeness [resemblance] denied of God, you know that He has no like, but it must not be thought that sharing in any Attribute [quality] entails likeness.

[p. 47] Do you not see that two contraries are like one another, yet between them is an extreme distance, while they share in many qualities. For example, black and white share in being an accident, and being a color, and being perceived by sight, etc.? Do you think that one who says that God is existing not in a substrate, and that He is hearing, seeing, knowing, willing, speaking, living, powerful, acting, and that man also is like that, has likened and affirmed a like? Not at all! The matter is not so. Were it so, all creatures would be

262

like [God], at least in the affirmation of existence, and this would suggest resemblance. On the contrary, likeness is an expression for sharing in species and essence [*al-māhiyya:* quiddity]. For even though the horse be very clever, it will not be "a like" of man, because it is opposed to him in species, but it will simply resemble him in cleverness, which is accidental [*ᶜāriḍa*] [and] outside the quiddity constituting the essence [*dhāt*] of "humanity" [man-ness].

The peculiar divine property is that God is a being [existent] necessarily existing of Himself, from Whom there exists everything the existence of which is possible according to the best ways [modes] of order and perfection. It is inconceivable that there can be any sharing at all in this peculiar property, but likeness to it occurs. The servant's being compassionate [and] patient [and] grateful does not entail likeness, as his being hearing, seeing, knowing, powerful, living [and] acting. On the contrary [Nay more], I say: The peculiar divine property belongs only to God and only God knows it, and it is inconceivable that anyone know it save Him or one who is His like; but since He has no like, no other knows it. The truth, therefore, is what al-Junayd—God's mercy upon him!—said when he remarked: "Only God knows God." Therefore He gave His greatest [most exalted] creatures only a Name by which He veiled him [Himself] and said: "Praise [glorify] the name of thy Lord Most High" [87.1]. [This may all be in the citation from Junayd] So, by God, no other than God knows God in this life and the next. And it was said to Dhū l-Nūn when he was at death's door: "What do you crave [desire]?" He said: "To know Him before I die, if only for an instant." Now this confuses [would muddle] the hearts of most of the weak and makes [would make] them think [suggest to them] the doctrine [assertion] of negation and "divesting" [God of His Attributes: *al-taᶜṭīl*]—and that because of their inability to understand this discourse [to understand what you say].

I also say: Were one to say "I know only God," he would be truthful; and were he to say "I do not know God," he would be truthful. Of course negation and affirmation cannot be true simultaneously—but when the mode [way] of speaking differs, truth in both is conceivable. It is like one's saying to another "Do you know The Upright [al-Ṣiddīq], Abū Bakr?" And the other replies: "Can he be someone unknown, or can there conceivably be in the world one who does not know him, given the fame and renown of his name?"—and he is truthful. And were it said to another: "Do you know him [Abū Bakr]?" and he were to reply: "And who am I that I should know al-Ṣiddīq? Far from it! Only al-Ṣiddīq knows al-Ṣiddīq. . . ," [p. 49] he would also be truthful. . . . Thus must be understood the assertion of him who says "I know God" and that of him who says "I do not know God."

If you were to show some ordered [tidy] handwriting to an intelligent person and to say: "Do you know its writer?" and he were to say "No," he would be truthful. And were he to say "Yes. Its writer is a person living, powerful, hearing, seeing, with a sound hand and with a knowledge of the art of writing—and if I know all this about him, how do I not know him?" he would also be truthful. But the former answer would be truer and more correct, for he does not really know him, but simply knows that orderly writing requires such a writer. Similarly, all creatures know only that this ordered and well-made world requires a Maker-Manager [Planner, Director] Who is living, knowing and powerful.

This [latter] knowledge has two extremities [aspects, sides]. One of them pertains [refers] to the world and its meaning [maʿlūmihi: notion, semantic content] and its need for a manager [director, planner], and the other pertains to God—Great and Glorious!—and its semantic content is names derived from attributes which do not enter into the reality and essence [quiddity] of the essence. For we have shown that when one points to something and says "What is it?" the mention of the derived names is not at all an answer. . . . [p. 50] The knowledge of a thing is the knowledge of its reality and its essence, not the knowledge of its derived names. . . .

If you say: Our declaration that He [God] is the necessarily existent from Whom alone exists all that can possibly exist is an expression of His reality and His definition—and we indeed know this, *I say:* Not at all! It merely denies that He has a cause and relates actions to Him and is simply names and attributes and relationships.

If you say: What, then, is the way to knowledge of Him? *I say:* If a child or one impotent were to say to us: "What is the way to knowledge of the pleasure of sexual intercourse and the perception of its reality?" we would say: There are two ways. One is for us to describe it to you so that you may know it; the other is for you to be patient until the natural impulse of passion appears in you, then for you to practice sexual intercourse so that its pleasure may appear in you and you will know it—and this second way is the sure way leading to true knowledge.

The first way [description] can lead only to suggestion and comparison with pleasure he knows, e.g. food, drink, sweetmeats—and this is quite inadequate [p. 51]—eg. sweetness of sugar or sweetmeats—not a real likeness, but misleading. . . .

Similarly, there are two ways to the knowledge of God, one inadequate and the other closed. The inadequate is the mention of God's Names and Attributes and comparison with what we know of ourselves as living, knowing, powerful, etc. This is even more inadequate than the comparison of the pleasure of sexual intercourse with that of eating sweetmeats . . . and ends with saying "Nothing is like Him" [42.9/11] . . . [p. 52] . . . comparison of the divine Attributes with ours is insufficient, because the real likeness must be denied and only a sharing in names remains. . . .

The second way—and this is closed—is that the servant wait until he comes to have all the divine Attributes and becomes a "Lord"—[p. 53] and this is something impossible for a creature and closed to all save God.

Therefore it is impossible for anyone except God to truly know God.

Nay more, only the Prophet can know the Prophet, and furthermore, one can know the reality of death and of the Garden and the Fire [Heaven and Hell] only after death and entrance into the Garden or the Fire. It is impossible to make one understand in this life the pleasures of the Garden and the pains of the Fire. Comparisons are inadequate: we can only say "Eye has not seen nor ear heard [p. 54] nor has it occurred to the heart of a man" [cf. 1 Cor 2:9]. Likenesses must be denied—and this a fortiori regarding the knowledge of God. . . .

The ultimate knowledge of the "knowers" [al-ʿārifīn— Sufi overtone, "gnostics"] of God is that they are powerless to know Him, and that their knowledge really is that they do not know Him, and that they cannot know Him, and that only God can know God. . . . then they know Him, i.e. they have reached the limit of the creature regarding knowledge of God.

Abū Bakr alluded to this when he said: "Powerlessness to attain perception is a perception;" and this is what Muḥammad meant by his assertion: "I reckon no praise of You like Your own praise of Yourself."

[p. 55] *If you say:* By what, then, do the ranks of the Angels and the Prophets and the Friends [Saints] differ in knowledge of God, if knowledge of Him is inconceivable? *I say:* You indeed know that there are two ways to knowledge. One is the true way, but it is closed to all save God Himself. . . .

266

The second way—knowledge of His Attributes and His Names—is open to creatures, and in it their ranks differ. One who knows that God is, in general, knowing and powerful is not like one who sees the marvels of His signs in the kingdom of the heavens and the earth and the creation of spirits and bodies and becomes cognizant of the wonders of His domain and the marvels of His making in the details and fine points of His wisdom and governance and becomes qualified with the angelic qualities which bring one close to God: between them is a great and incalculable distance, and in details and quality the Prophets and the Saints differ.

You will understand this only by an example "while God's is the highest likeness [Blachère: la Représentation Auguste]" [16.62/60]. You know that a pious and perfect man like al-Shāficī, for example, was known by his own porter and by al-Muzanī [a disciple of al-Shāficī who propagated his doctrine; d. 878]. The porter knew him to be learned in the Law and a writer on it and a director of God's creatures in a general way. But al-Muzanī's knowledge of him was not like that of the porter, but rather a knowledge embracing the details of his qualities and his learning. Moreover, one learned in ten kinds of sciences is not really known by his disciple [p. 56] who has acquired only one kind, to say nothing of his servant who has learned nothing of his sciences. He who has learned one science really knows only a tenth of him, if he so equals him in that science that he does not fall short of him. If he does fall short of him, he really knows what he falls short in only by name and general suggestion, viz. he knows that his master knows something other than what *he* knows. Thus you should know that the difference of creatures in the knowledge of God is commensurate with what is revealed to them of the objects of His knowledge— Great and Glorious He!—and the marvels of His power and the wonders of His signs in this life [world] and the next.

The knowledge of God [possessed by] the Angels and Spirits [*malakūt:* kingdom ?] is greater and their knowledge approaches that of God Most High. *If you say:* If they do not know the reality of His Essence and the knowledge of it be impossible, do they know [His] Names and Attributes with a perfect, true knowledge? *We say:* Far from it! That also is known perfectly and really only by God—Great and Glorious! For if we know that an essence is knowing, we know something vague [ambiguous] the reality of which we do not know, but we know that it has the attribute of knowledge. And if the attribute of knowledge is known to us truly, our knowledge that He is knowing is a perfect knowledge of the reality of this attribute—otherwise no [it is not]. But no one knows the reality of the knowledge of God—Great and Glorious!—save one who possesses the like of His knowledge; but only He possesses that—so no one else knows Him. Another knows him simply by comparison with the knowledge of himself, as we adduced in the example of the comparison with sweetmeats [Paras. 75–76]. The knowledge of God—Great and Glorious!—does not at all resemble the knowledge of creatures, so the creatures' knowledge of Him is not perfect and true, but rather suggestive and comparative.

Do not be surprised at this, for I say: Only the sorcerer [magician] himself knows the sorcerer [p. 57], or a sorcerer like him or superior to him. One who does not know sorcery [magic] and its reality and essence [quiddity] knows of the sorcerer only his name, and knows that he has a knowledge and a special quality, without knowing what that knowledge is, since he does not know what the sorcerer knows, and without knowing what that special quality is. To be sure, he knows that that special property, though vague, belongs to the genus of the cognitions, and that its fruit is changing hearts and altering the qualities of individuals and scrutiny [detection of qualities] and the separation of spouses [introducing discord between the married]; but he is excluded from the knowledge of the reality of sorcery. And one who does not know the reality of sorcery does not know the reality of the sorcerer, because the latter is one who possesses the special quality of sorcery. The purport [meaning] of the name "sorcerer" is that it is a name derived from a quality [attribute]. If that quality be unknown, the name [the sorcerer] is unknown, and if it be known, it [he] is known. What is known of sorcery by someone other than the sorcerer is a general description far from the essence [quiddity], viz. that it belongs to the genus of the cognitions, for the name of knowledge is applied to it.

Similarly, the purport, in our view, of the power of God—Great and Glorious!—is that it is a quality [description] [and] its fruit and effect is the existence of things. The name "power" is applied to it because it resembles our power the way the pleasure of sexual intercourse resembles that of sweetmeats. But all this is apart from the reality of that power. To be sure, the more the servant comprehends the details of the objects of [God's] power and the marvels of [His] making in the kingdom of the heavens [and the earth], the ampler is his portion of the knowledge of the Attribute of power, because the fruit indicates the fruitful [producer of fruit], just as, the more the disciple comprehends the details of his master's lore and his writings, the more perfect is his knowledge of him and the greater his esteem of him.

To this comes down the difference of the knowledge of the "knowers." It is susceptible of an unending difference, because what a man cannot know of the objects of God's knowledge is infinite [limitless]. So also what God can do is infinite, though what enters into [actual] existence is finite. [p. 58] But man's power respecting knowledges has no limit. To be sure, what emerges into existence is different in multiplicity and paucity, and in it difference appears. It is like the difference among men in the power they

269

acquire by wealth through property. One man possesses a dānaq [or: *dāniq*—sixth of a dirham] and [or?] a dirham [drachma], and another thousands. So it is with knowledge [cognitions], nay but the difference in knowledge is greater, because cognoscibles are limitless whereas the chattels of property are bodies, and bodies are finite and limit cannot conceivably be denied of them.

Hence you indeed know how creatures differ in the seas of the knowledge of God—Great and Glorious!—and that that has no limit. You also know that he who said "No other than God knows God" was indeed truthful, and that he who said "I know only God" was also truthful. For there is in existence only God and His works—Great and Glorious He! So when one considers His works in so far as they are His works, and his consideration is limited to that [?], and he does not see that as heaven and earth and tree, but as His doing [making], his knowledge does not exceed [go beyond] the Presence [Majesty] of Divinity and he can say "I know only God, and I see only God—Great and Glorious!"

If one were to imagine a person who sees only the sun and its light diffused in the horizons [remote countries], it would be correct for him to say "I see only the sun," for the light emanating from it belongs to its totality [and] is not outside of it. Everything in existence is a light from the lights of the eternal Power and one of its effects. And as the sun is the source of the light emanating on everything illuminated, so also the meaning [notion] for which expression is inadequate [which is inexpressible], and it is of necessity expressed by "the eternal Power," is the source of the existence [being] emanating on [flooding] every existent. [p. 59] So in existence there is only God—Great and Glorious! And the "knower" can rightly say "I know only God."

One of the wonders is that a man say "I know only God" and be truthful, and also say "Only God knows God" and also be truthful—but the former in one way and the latter in

270

another. If contradictory things were false when the ways of consideration differ, the Most High's declaration would not be true: "And you did not cast, when you cast, but God cast [8.17]. But it is truthful because the casting has two regards: it is ascribed to the servant in one of them, and to the Lord Most High in the second—so there is no contradiction in it.

Let us grasp the bridle of explanation, for we have indeed waded into the depth [abyss] of a shoreless sea. The likes of these mysteries ought not to be vulgarized by depositing them in [entrusting them to] books. And since this has come about accidentally and unintentionally, let us desist from it and return to the explanation of the meanings of God's fairest Names in detail.

[p. 61]   SECTION TWO

On the Aims

[pp. 63–162]   Chapter One

On the Explanation of the
Meanings of the Ninety-nine Names of God

[This is the Chapter translated by R. C. Stade. It begins with a Tradition attributed to Abū Hurayra: "The Apostle of God—God's blessing and peace upon him!—said: God—Great and Glorious!—has nine and ninety Names, one hundred minus one: He is Odd [i.e. single, unique] and loves the odd; whoso enumerates them will enter the Garden." (Then follows the enumeration of the ninety-nine Names.) I shall give the list, and will translate Ghazālī's comments on the first few by way of example; all the comments will be found in Stade's work.]

1—As for his saying *Allāh* [God], it is the Name of the True Existent [Being], Who unites [combines, comprehends] the Attributes of Divinity, the qualified by the Qualities of Lordship, the unique possessor of true Existence [Being]. For every existent [being] other than He does not merit [claim, is not entitled to] existence by its essence [of itself], but simply derives existence from Him. So it, with respect to its essence [itself], is perishing [perishable], but from the aspect [side] adjacent to Him it is existent. So every existent [being] is perishable except His Face [Countenance: metonymy for "Him—cf. 28.88]. The more likely [explanation] is that it [Allāh], in indicating this meaning [explained above], is analogous to the proper names [nouns], and everything which has been said about its derivation and definition is arbitrariness [aberration, inaccuracy] and affectation [studiedness, forcing].

Note [*fā'ida*]: Know that this Name, of the nine and ninety, is the greatest of the Names of God—Great and Glorious! For it denotes the Essence combining [comprehending, uniting] all the Divine Attributes without exception, whereas all the other individual Names denote only individual meanings, such as [a] knowledge or [a] power or [an] action or something else. Also because it is the most proper [peculiar, specific] of the Names, since no one can apply it to another either truly [literally] or figuratively, whereas by the other Names another may be named [denominated], e.g. the Powerful and the Knowing and the Merciful etc. So for these two reasons it is likely [clear ?] that this Name is the greatest of these Names.

Precision [*daqīqa*: detail, particular, fine point]: It is conceivable that the creature may be qualified by something of all the other Names so that the Name may be applied to [predicated of] him, e.g. the Merciful and the Knowing and the Indulgent [Forbearing] and the Patient and the Very Grateful, etc.; but the Name is applied to it [creature] in another way different from its predication of God—Great and Glorious! As for the meaning of this Name, it is peculiar [proper: to God] in a special sense, [and] it is inconceivable that there be any sharing in it either figuratively or truly [literally]. Because of this specialness all the other Names are described as being "the Name of God [Allāh]"— Great and Glorious!—and are defined [explained] in relation to Him [It—Allāh]. So one says: the Patient and the Very Grateful and the King and the Compeller [Almighty] are among the Names of God [Allāh]—Great and Glorious! But one does not say: Allāh is among the Names of the Very Grateful and the Patient. For that [Allāh], inasmuch as it is more indicative of the Essence of the divine meanings and more peculiar to them, is [p. 65] better known [more celebrated, renowned] and more manifest [distinct]; hence there is no need to define it by something else, but others are defined in relation to it.

Remark [*tanbīh:* admonition, counsel, alerting]: The creature's [man's] portion [lot, share in] respecting this Name ought to be *al-taʾalluh* [becoming Godlike, deification, divinization, "putting on" God]. By this I mean that his heart and ardor [ambition] be wholly engaged by [immersed in, claimed completely by] God—Great and Glorious! He sees none but Him, attends to no other, hopes [in] and fears only Him. How could it be otherwise when it has been understood from this Name that He is the True, Real Existent [Being], and everything else is transient [ephemeral, evanescent] and perishing and null [nothing, worthless] except through Him. So man first of all sees himself as the first thing perishing and worthless, just as the Apostle of God—God's blessing and peace upon him!—saw himself when he said: "The truest verse uttered by the Arabs is the statement of Labid:

Sorely everything except God is worthless, And every happiness [comfort] without doubt is fleeting."

273

2 and 3—*The Merciful, the Compassionate* [al-rahmān, al-rahīm]: two Names derived from "mercy" [*al-rahma*]. Mercy requires [calls for] an object of mercy" [*marhūm:* a "mercified"], and there is no such object save that it is needy [in need, in want]. One because of whom the need of the needy is satisfied without any design [intent] and will [volition, desire] and concern [solicitude] for the needy is not called [named] "compassionate." And one who wishes to satisfy a needy man's need but does not satisfy it, if he be able to satisfy it, is not called "compassionate;" for if [his] wish were fulfilled, he would satisfy the need. But if he be powerless [to satisfy the need], he may be called "compassionate" with regard to the graciousness [sensitivity] which affects [influences] him, but it [he?] is imperfect [faulty, defective]. Perfect mercy [*al-rahma al-tāmma*] is simply the pouring forth of good upon the needs and one's [God's?] will for them out of concern for them. And general [inclusive, all-embracing] mercy [*al-rahma al-ʿāmma*] is that which includes [encompasses] the deserving and the undeserving. The mercy of God—Great and Glorious!—is perfect and all-embracing. It is perfect in so far as He wills to fulfill the needs of the needy and [actually] fulfills them. It is all-embracing in so far as it comprehends the deserving and the undeserving, and embraces this life and the afterlife, and includes necessities and needs and the advantages [privileges] outside of them. So He is in truth the Absolute Merciful [*al-rahīm al-mutlaq*].

Precision: Mercy is not devoid of a painful empathy [sympathy, sensitiveness] which befalls [afflicts] the merciful [compassionate] and moves him to satisfy the need of the object of mercy. But the Lord—Praised and Exalted He!—is deemed far above that. So perhaps you will think that to be a defect [an imperfection] is the meaning [notion, concept] of mercy. Know, then, that that is a perfection and not an imperfection in the meaning of mercy. That it is not an imperfection [is clear] from the fact [standpoint] that the perfection of mercy is by the perfection of its fruit. So long as the need of the needy is fulfilled perfectly, the object of mercy has no share in the suffering and affliction of the merciful, but the suffering of the merciful is simply due to the weakness and imperfection of his soul. And its weakness adds nothing respecting the aim of the needy after his need is perfectly satisfied. And that it is a perfection in the meaning of mercy is that one who is compassionate out of sensitiveness [sympathy] and suffering, almost as good as intends by his action the removal of the pain of sympathy from himself [his soul] and will have had a regard for himself and will have exerted himself for a personal end—and that diminishes [detracts from] the perfection of the meaning of mercy. Rather the perfection of mercy is that his regard be for [be directed toward] the object of mercy for the latter's sake, not for the sake of finding ease [repose, rest] from the pain of sympathy.

Note: Al-Raḥmān is more specific [particularized] than Al-Raḥīm, and for that reason no one other than God— Great and Glorious!—is named by it, whereas al-raḥīm may be applied to other than God. So from this viewpoint it [Al-Raḥmān] is close to the Name of God Most High which functions like a proper name [i.e. Allāh], though this [Al Raḥmān] is certainly derived from *al-raḥma* [mercy]. For that reason God—Great and Glorious!—united [joined] the two of them and said: "Pray to [call upon] God [Allāh], or pray to the Merciful [al-Raḥmān]: Whichever you pray to, He has [possesses] the Fairest Names" [17.110]. From this aspect, and inasmuch as we have forbidden [barred, declared impossible] synonymity in the enumerated Names, it follows necessarily that one must distinguish between the meanings of the two Names. To be exact, the meaning of Al-Raḥmān is a kind of mercy beyond creatures' objects of power, and it [this mercy] is connected with the beatitude of the afterlife. So Al-Raḥmān is He Who is compassionate toward servants [men] [p. 67], first by creation [of them], and secondly by guidance to the Faith and the causes of happiness, and thirdly by making [them] happy in the afterlife, and fourth by granting [them] the favor of looking at [beholding] His gracious [noble, eminent, precious] Face.

Remark: The servant's [man's] portion of the Name Al-Rahmān is that he be merciful to God's heedless servants and turn them from the way of heedlessness to God—Great and Glorious!—by admonition [preaching] and counsel, gently and not harshly, and that he look upon sinners [the disobedient] with the eye of mercy, not that of contempt, and that every sin taking place in the world be like his own personal sin so that he spares no effort to remove [do away with] it as far as he can out of mercy [compassion] for that sinner lest he be exposed to God's wrath and merit being far from God's presence [vicinity].

And his portion of the Name Al-Rahīm is that he leave no want of a needy person without trying to satisfy it to the best of his ability, and abandon no poor person in his neighborhood and his town without undertaking to care for him and to drive away his need either by his own wealth [property], or by his repute [rank], or by striving for him through intercession with another. If he is unable to do all that, then he will help him by [private] prayer [*duʿāʾ*], or by manifesting grief because of his need, out of compassion and sympathy for him, so that he is, as it were, a sharer of his in his hurt and his need.

A question and its Answer: [pp. 67–70; Paras. 105–10] Here Ghazālī attacks the perennial problem of evil: How can God be Merciful and Compassionate and "the most merciful of the merciful" [7.150/151; 12.64 and 92; 21.83]? One who is merciful tries to remove every pain, etc. which he can. God can remove all suffering, sickness, pain, grief, etc.—yet this world is full [brim-full] of such things.

Ghazālī answers this objection at some length. Basically his answer is that God allows evil for the sake of the good that results—and every evil has in it a good. A fond mother tries to spare her child the ordeal of cupping [bleeding], but the good father has it done because it will really benefit the child. A diseased hand is amputated to save the whole body. God Himself said: "My mercy outstrips [takes precedence over] My wrath" [cf. 9.15]. You may think of an evil in which there is no good, or that the good is possible without the evil. Your thinking is awry. No one can know such an evil: you are like the child who regards cupping as an unmitigated evil, or like a stupid person who does not realize that the just killing of a man, as punishment, promotes the general good. So also your thinking that the good is possible without the evil is faulty: this is a very abstruse matter incomprehensible to most men. So doubt not that God is truly "the most merciful of the merciful": herein there is a mystery which the Law forbids to be divulged: be content with prayer and seek not divulging.

You would have heard had you called out to one living:
But the one you called out to has no life!

Such is the status of the majority. But you, my brother for whom this explanation is intended, are, I think, seeking insight into [are aware of ?] God's mystery concerning predestination [*al-qadar*] and have no need of these adulterations [coatings] and remarks.

4—*The King* [*al-malik*]: This is He Who, in His Essence and His Attributes, has no need [is independent] of every existent, while every existent has need of Him. Nay more, nothing is independent of Him in anything: not in its essence, nor in its attributes, nor in its existence, nor in its duration. Rather the existence of everything is from Him, or from what is from Him. So everything other than He belongs to Him in its essence and attributes, and He is independent of everything [has no need of anything]. This, then, is the King absolutely.

Remark: The servant [a man] cannot conceivably be an absolute king, for he is not independent of anything. For he always is in need of God Most High, even though he be independent of others. And it is inconceivable that everything have need of him: on the contrary, most existents are independent of him. But when it is conceivable that he is independent of some things and that some things are not independent of him, he has a "touch" ["dash"] of the King.

The king, among servants [men], is he who is possessed [ruled] only by God Most High, nay but he is independent of everything save God—Great and Glorious! Along with that he rules his kingdom in such fashion that in it his soldiers [troops] and subjects obey him. But his proper [special] kingdom is his heart and his soul [*qālab, qālib:* form, mold]. His soldiers are his appetite and his anger and his desire, and his subjects are his tongue, his two eyes, his two hands and all his other members [organs]. When he rules them, not they him, and they obey him, not he them, he indeed attains the rank of king in his world. And if there be joined to him his independence of all men, and all men need him in their present and future life, he is the king in the world of the earth.

[p. 71] That [just mentioned] is the rank of the Prophets—God's blessings on them all! For, regarding guidance to the afterlife, they are independent of everyone save God—Great and Glorious!—and every one needs them. In this sovereignty they are followed by the ulema [learned, "doctors"], who are the heirs of the Prophets [a Tradition: cf. Wensinck, *Handbook,* p. 234]; and their [ulema] sovereignty [kingship] is commensurate with their power to guide men and their own independence of seeking guidance.

By these attributes the servant [a man] approximates the Angels in their attributes, and by them he draws close to

278

God Most High. This sovereignty [kingship] is a gift from the True King in Whose Kingship there is no "doubling" [*mathnawiyya:* reservation?; i.e. it is unique.] One of the "knowers" [Sufis] spoke the truth when one of the princes said to him: "Ask me your need [for what you need]." He replied: "Do you say this to me, when I have two servants who are your masters?" He said: "Who are they?" He replied: "Greed [covetousness] and passion [caprice, whim]: I have indeed mastered them, but they have mastered you; and I rule them, but they rule you." And someone said to one of the Shaykhs [Masters: of Sufism]: "Counsel me." He replied: "Be a king in this life [and] thou will be a king in the afterlife—i.e. cut off your need and your passion [appetite] from this life, for sovereignty [kingship] is in freedom and independence. [I now list the remaining Names of God, each followed by Stade's translation and that of Asín Palácios.]

5—al-Quddūs: The Most Holy One; Santísimo.

6—al-Salām: the Sound One; Salud.

7—al-Mu᾿min: The Author of Safety and Security; Protector.

8—al-Muhaymin: The Protector and Guardian; Vigilante.

9—al-ᶜAzīz: The Incomparable and Unparalleled One; Precioso.

10—al-Jabbār: The One Who Compels His Creatures to Do as He Wills; Enérgico.

11—al-Mutakabbir: The One Supreme in Pride and Greatness; Soberano.

12, 13, 14—al-Khāliq, al-Bāri᾿, al-Muṣawwir: The Creator, The Maker, The Fashioner; Inventor, Creador y Formador.

15—al-Ghaffār: The Very Forgiving One; Indulgente.

16—al-Qahhār: The Dominating One; Victorioso.

17—al-Wahhāb: The One Who Gives Freely, without Thoughts of Compensation; Donador.

18—al-Razzāq: The One Who Provides All Sustenance; Proveedor.

19—al-Fattāḥ: He Who Opens All Things; Revelador.

20—al-ʿAlīm: The Omniscient One; Conocedor.

21, 22—al Qābiḍ al-Bāsiṭ: The One Who Withholds and Provides the Means of Subsistence as He Wills; Entristecedor y Consolador.

23, 24—al-Khāfiḍ al-Rāfiʿ: The One who Abases the Unbeliever and Exalts the Believer; Humillador y Exaltador.

25, 26—al-Muʿizz al-Mudhill: The One Who Raises to Honor and Abases; Ennoblecedor y Envilecedor.

27—al-Samīʿ: The All-Hearing One; Oidor.

28—al-Baṣīr: The All-Seeing One; Vidente.

29—al-Ḥakam: The Arbiter; Providente.

30—al-ʿAdl: The Just One; Justo.

31—al-Laṭīf: The Subtle One; Bondadoso.

32—al-Khabīr: The All-Cognizant One; Sagaz.

33—al-Ḥalīm: The Nonprecipitate and Forbearing One; Manso.

34—al-ʿAẓīm: The Great One; Grande.

35—al-Ghafūr: The Most Forgiving One; Perdonador.

36—al-Shakūr: The One Who Expresses Thankfulness by Rewarding Bounteously; Agradecidor.

38—al-Kabīr: The Grand One; Magnifico.

39—al-Ḥafīz: The Preserver; Conservador.

40—al-Muqīt: He Who Is Cognizant and Capable of Providing His Creation with Everything It Needs; Alimentador.

41—al-Ḥasīb: He Who Satisfies the Needs of All Creation; Suficiente.

42—al-Jalīl: The Sublime One; Majestuoso.

43—al-Karīm: The Selflessly Generous One; Generoso.

44—al-Raqīb: The One Who Watches All; Guardián.

45—al-Mujīb: The One Who Responds to Every Need; Complaciente.

46—al-Wāsiᶜ: The One Whose Capacity Is Limitless; Inmenso.

47—al-Ḥakīm: The Ultimately Wise One; Sabio.

48—al-Wadūd: The Objectively Loving One; Amoroso.

49—al-Majīd: The Most Glorious One; Noble.

50—al-Bāᶜith: The Quickener; Resucitador.

51—al-Shahīd: The One Who Witnesses and Knows Everything Manifest; Testigo.

52—al-Ḥaqq: The Real One; Verdad.

53—al-Wakīl: The Ultimate and Faithful Trustee; Abogado.

54, 55—al-Qawī al-Matīn: The Perfectly Strong and Firm One; Fuerte y Robusto.

56—al-Walī: The Patron; Amigo.

57—al-Ḥamīd: The Ultimately Praiseworthy One; Alabado.

58—al-Muḥṣī: The Absolute Reckoner; Comprehendor.

59, 60—al-Mubdīʾ al-Muᶜīd: The Originator and Restorer; Productor y Reproductor.

61, 62—al Muḥyī al-Mumīt: The One Responsible for Both Life and Death; Vivificador y Mortificador.

63—al-Ḥayy: The Absolutely Percipient One; Vivo.

64—al-Qayyūm: The Self-Subsisting One; Subsistente.

65—al-Wājid: He Who Has No Needs; Perfecto.

66—al-Mājid: The Glorified One; Ilustre.

67—al-Wāḥid [Stade: al-Aḥad; cf. Shehadi, p. 63, n. (5)]; He Who is Uniquely One; Uno.

68—al-Ṣamad: He to Whom One Turns in Every Exigency; Fin.

69, 70—al-Qādir al-Muqtadir: He Who Acts, Or Does Not Act, as He Pleases; Libre y Poderoso.

71, 72—al-Muqaddim wa l-Muʾakhkhir: The One Who Causes Men to Be Both Near to and Distant from Him; Aproximador y Alejador.

73, 74—al-Awwal al-Ākhir: He Who Is Both First and Last; Primero y Ultimo.

75, 76—al-Ẓāhir al-Bāṭin: The Manifest and Hidden One; Manifesto y Oculto.

77—al-Barr: The Dutiful One; Bueno.

78—al-Tawwāb: He Who Constantly Turns Man to Repentance; Clemente.

79—al-Muntaqim: The Avenger; Vengador.

80—al-ᶜAfw [ᶜAfū]: The One Who Erases Sin; Absolvedor.

81—al-Raʾūf: The Very Indulgent One; Benévolo.

82—Mālik al-Mulk: The One Who Has Perfect Power over His Kingdom; Emperador.

83—Dhū l-Jalāl wa l-ʾIkrām: The One Possessed of Majesty and Honour; Digno de gloria y honor.

84—al-Wālī: He Who Has Charge over All; Gobernador.

85—al-Mutaᶜālī: The Highly Exalted One; Sublime.

86—al-Muqsiṭ: The Ultimately Equitable One; Juez equitativo.

87—al-Jāmiᶜ: He Who Combines All Things in the Universe to Accomplish His Purposes; Reunidor.

88, 89—al-Ghanī al-Mughnī: The Rich, the Enriching One; Rico y Enriquecedor.

90—al-Māniᶜ: He Who Repels Those Things Detrimental to His Creation; Defensor.

91, 92—al-Ḍārr al-Nāfiᶜ: He Who is Responsible for Both Good and Evil; Causa del bien y del mal.

93—al-Nūr: The Light; Luz.

94—al-Hādī: The Guide; Guía.

95—al-Badīᶜ: The Matchless, Unequaled One; Innovador.

96—al-Bāqī: The Everlasting One; Eterno.

97—al-Wārith: The Inheritor; Heredero.

98—al-Rashīd: The Absolutely Judicious Guide; Director.

99—al-Ṣabūr: He Who Times All Things Perfectly; Paciente.

A Conclusion to This Chapter and
a Disclaimer [Plea, Excuse]

Know that what has prompted me to give these remarks [admonitions, counsels, comments] following these Names and Attributes is the declaration of the Apostle of God— God's blessings and peace upon him!—"Put on [clothe yourself with, don] the virtues [the excellent qualities] of God Most High," as well as his saying: "God has nine and ninety virtues: whosoever puts on one of them will surely enter the Garden [Heaven]." Certain sayings [words] passed by the Sufis from tongue to tongue hint at what we have mentioned, but in a manner which would suggest to the uninitiated something of the notion of indwelling [inhabitation] and identification [union]. But that is not to be thought of in the case of an intelligent person, to say nothing of those distinguished [characterized] by [gifted with] the prerogatives of mystical visions [insights].

I actually heard the Master Abū ʿAlī al-Fārmadhī relate of his Master Abū l-Qāsim al-Kurkānī—God hallow his face!— that the latter said: "The nine and ninety Names become qualities of the servant who follows the path [of perfection, i.e. the Sufi] while he is still in the way and not yet arrived." This citation of his is true [correct] if by it Abūl-Qāsim meant something in accordance with what we have adduced—and nothing other than that is to be suspected of him. But the pronouncement smacks of figure and metaphor. For the meanings of the Names [the notions expressed by, or contained in, the Names] are the Attributes of God Most High—and His Attributes do not [cannot] become an attribute of another. Rather it means that one [the Sufi] acquires for himself something resembling those qualities, just as one says: So-and-so has acquired the knowledge of his master; but the actual knowledge of the master is not acquired by the disciple, but rather the like of the master's knowledge.

If anyone thinks that what is meant by it is not what we have mentioned, this is decidedly false. For I [would] say: The statement [claim, assertion] of one who declares that the meanings [notions] contained in the Names of God— Praised and Glorified He!—have become qualities of his admits of only two interpretations. Either he means by it those very Attributes themselves, or the like of them. If he means by it the like of them, then he must mean by it the like of them absolutely and in every respect, or he must mean by it the like of them regarding the name and the sharing in the general notion of the Attributes, but not in the intrinsic essences of the notions [contained in the Names]. These, then, are two divisions. Now if he means by them the very Attributes themselves, then it must come about either by way of the passage [transference] of the Attributes from the Lord to the creature, or not by such passage. If it be not by passage, then it must be either by the identification of the creature [servant, man, Sufi] with the essence of the Lord to the point [degree] that they are one and the same [identical] and His Attributes are his [creature's], or it must be by the way of indwelling [inhabitation]. And these are three divisions, viz, passage [transfer], identification, and indwelling.

So there are five divisions, of which one division is the correct one, viz. that the creature really possesses certain elements of the Attributes which resemble them in general and share the name with them, but they are not perfectly [totally, exactly] like them—as we have mentioned in the remarks.

As for *the second division,* viz. that the creature possesses the likes of the Attributes really and truly, it is impossible [absurd]. For in God's totality is that He possesses a comprehensive [all-embracing] knowledge of all the cognoscibles to the degree that "there does not escape Him an atom in the earth and in the heavens" [cf. 10.62/61], and a single [unique, individual] power which extends to all the created things to the point that He is truly the Creator "of the earth and the heavens and of what is between them" [a Qur°ānic phrase—cf. e.g. 5.20—21/17/18], And how can this conceivably be true of anyone other than God Most High? How can a creature be the Creator of the heavens and the earth and of what is between them, when he himself belongs to the totality of what is between them—so how could he be the Creator of himself? Furthermore, if these Attributes were possessed by two creatures, each of them would be the Creator of his fellow so that each would be the Creator of him who had created him. All that is a farcical collection of absurdities!

As for *the third division,* viz. the transfer of the divine Attributes themselves, it is also impossible. For attributes cannot separate themselves from [quit] their subjects. This is not peculiar to the eternal Essence: it is even inconceivable that the very knowledge of Zayd be transferred to °Amr; nay more, the only subsistence of attributes is in specific subjects. [That is so] because the transfer would entail the emptiness of what suffered the transfer, and hence it would entail the stripping of the Essence from Which the divine Attributes would be transferred so that the later would be stripped of divinity and of its Attributes: that is also patently impossible.

As for *the fourth division,* viz. identification, that is even more patently false, because a speaker's assertion that the creature becomes the Lord is a statement which is self-contradictory, nay but the Lord— Praised and Glorious He!—must be deemed too holy to have the tongue utter in His regard such absurdities. We say unequivocally that a speaker's assertion that one thing becomes another is absolutely impossible. For we declare that, if Zayd be understood [conceived] alone, and °Amr alone, then it be asserted that Zayd has become °Amr and has become identified with him, then, at the identification, either both of them must be existent, or both of them must be nonexistent, or Zayd must be existent and ᶜAmr nonexistent, or vice versa: no division beyond the four is possible.

If both are existent, then the essence [substance, individuality] of one of the two has not become the essence of the other, but the essence of each one of the two is existent: at most only their locus is identical, and this does not entail identification; for knowledge and volition and power may be united in one and the same essence and their substrates not be distinct without power being knowledge or volition and without part having become identified with part.

And if both are nonexistent, then they have not become identified but have ceased to exist [have vanished, disappeared] and the incipient may be a third thing. And if one of the two is nonexistent and the other existent, then there is no identification, since the existent cannot be identified with the nonexistent.

Identification of two things is absolutely impossible. This is true of essences which resemble one another, to say nothing of those which differ. For it is impossible that this black become that black, just as it is impossible that this black become that white or that knowledge. And the dissimilarity between the creature and the Lord is greater than that between black and knowledge.

So the principle of identification is false. Whenever one speaks of identification [identification is predicated] and declares "This is identified with this," it can only be by way of the extension and allowance proper to the usage of the Sufis and the poets. For in order to make what is said more pleasing to minds they follow the way of metaphorical usage, as the poet says: "I am the one I love, and the one I love is I." That is the poet's interpretation, for he does not mean thereby that he is really the beloved, but it is as though he were, because his interest is as absorbed by the beloved as it is by himself; so he expresses that state by "identifitation" through [poetic] license.

In the same way one ought to interpret the utterance of Abū Yazīd [al-Bisṭāmi, d. 261/875]—God have mercy upon him!—when he said: "I sloughed off [shed] myself as the snake sloughs off [sheds] its skin: then I looked, and behold, I was He!" It means that whenever one casts off his soul's passions [desires] and love of them and concern with them there remains in him no room for other than God and no eagerness for other than God—Praised and Exalted He! If only God's majesty and beauty dwell in a heart so that it is absorbed in Him, it becomes as though it were He, but it is not He in reality. There is a difference between our saying "as though it were He" and our saying "it is He." But by our saying "it is He" can be expressed our saying "as though it were He," just as the poet sometimes says "As though I were whom I love," and sometimes "I am whom I love." This is a slippery place, for one whose foot is not firmly planted in rational matters may not discern for himself one from the other. Then he will look at the perfection of his own essence, once it has been adorned by what gleams in it of the finery [ornament] of the Truth [God], and will consequently think that he is He, and so he will say 'I am the Truth" [famous utterance of al-Ḥallāj, d. 309/922—cf. Annotated Bibliography under Massignon].

Such a man commits the same error as that of the Christians: when the latter see that [the finery of the Truth] in the Christ, Jesus—God's peace upon him!—they say: "He is the true God!" Even more it is the same as the error of a man who looks at a mirror in which is impressed [reflected] an image colored with his own coloration and thinks that that image is the image of the mirror and that that color is the color of the mirror. Not at all! Rather the mirror has no color in itself. Its function is to receive the images of colors in such fashion that it appears to superficial observers that that is the image of the mirror, so much so that when a child sees a man in the mirror he thinks that the man [really] is in the mirror. Similarly, the heart is in itself empty of images and forms. Its forms are simply the receiving of the meanings [abstractions, ideas, notions, "las esencias ideales," "intentiones"] of the forms and images and realities. So what subsists [dwells] in it is as though identified with it—not that it is *really* identified with it. If one unfamiliar with glass and wine were to see a glass. containing wine, he would not comprehend their distinction and would say at one time "There is no wine," and at another time "There is no glass," as the poet put it when he said:

> Clear the glass and clear the wine
> So they are alike and the matter unclear;
> So it seems there is wine and no cup,
> And it seems there is a cup and no wine.

The utterance of the one of them who said: "I am the Truth" either has the same meaning as that of the poet's declaration "I am whom I love, and he whom I love is I," or he indeed erred in that, as the Christians erred in their supposition of the identification [union] of the divinity with the humanity. Abū Yazīd's utterance—God have mercy on him!—if he really said it, "Glory to me! How great is my dignity!" either was uttered by him in the form of a quotation from God—Mighty and Glorious!—as, had he been heard to say "There is no God but I: so worship me!" [20.14], it would have been interpreted as a quotation, or he would have seen the perfection of his share of the Attribute of holiness, according to what we have reported regarding the ascension by knowledge above things imagined and sensed and by zeal above passions and pleasures, and so he announced the holiness of his own soul and said: "Glory to me!" and he would have seen the greatness of his dignity in comparison with that of the generality of creatures and said: "How great is my dignity!" knowing all the while that his holiness and greatness in dignity were in comparison with

288

that of creatures and completely unproportioned to the holiness of the Lord—Exalted and All Holy!—and the greatness of His dignity.

And he may have uttered this phrase in his [mystical] intoxication and under the influence of his ecstatic rapture. For his return to sobriety and mental equilibrium would entail guarding his tongue from [such] suspect utterances, whereas the state of [mystical] intoxication may not suffer that. If you go beyond these two interpretations to "identification," that is decidedly impossible. One should not have such a high regard for the ranks of men as to believe in the impossible: rather men ought to be known by the truth, not the truth by men [ef. Para. 53 of my translation of the *Munqidh*].

As for *the fifth division,* viz. indwelling [inhabitation], it may conceivably [be affirmed in two ways]: that one affirms that the Lord— Blessed and Exalted!—dwells in [descends into] the creature, or that the creature dwells in [descends into] the Lord—Exalted the Lord of Lords above the claim of the unjust! Even if this were true, "identification" would not be entailed, nor that the creature be qualified by the Attributes of the Lord. For the attributes of the "indweller" do not become the attributes of the "dwelt in," but remain the attribute of the "indweller," as was the case [before the indwelling]. But just how indwelling is impossible can be understood only after the meaning [notion, concept] of indwelling is understood. For isolated [single, individual] meanings [notions], when they are not perceived by the process of simple apprehension [*al-taṣawwur*—concept, conception, representation], cannot understandably be denied and affirmed. So if one does not know the meaning of indwelling, whence can he know whether indwelling is existent or impossible?

We therefore say: Two things are understood by indwelling. *One of them* is the proportion [relationship]

289

between a body and its locus in which it is—and that can be only between two bodies: hence that is impossible regarding what is free of the notion of corporeality. *The second* is the proportion [relationship] between an accident and a substance. For the subsistence of the accident is in the substance, and this may be expressed by [saying] that it indwells [inheres] in it—and that is impossible for what has its subsistence in itself. So make no mention of the Lord—Exalted and Blessed!—in this connection, for it is impossible for anything which has its subsistence in itself to indwell [inhere] in what has its subsistence in itself, save by way of the propinquity which occurs between bodies. Hence indwelling is inconceivable between two creatures [men, servants]—how, then, is it conceivable between the creature and the Lord?

If indwelling and transfer and identification and being qualified by the likes of the Attributes of God—Praised and Exalted He!—in a real way are [all] false, there remains for their assertion no meaning except what we have indicated in the remarks. That prohibits the categorical affirmation that the meanings of the Names of God Most High become descriptions [qualifications] of the creature, except by a kind of limitation [reservation] devoid of deception: otherwise the unrestricted use of this expression would be misleading.

If you say: What, then, is the meaning of his [Fārmadhī's] statement that the creature, despite his being qualified by all of that, is in the way and not yet arrived? What means "being in the way"? And what means arriving" [*al-wuṣūl:* attaining, reaching]? *Then know* that "being in the way" is the refining [polishing, burnishing] of moral qualities and of actions and of cognitions—and that is a preoccupation with the building of the exterior and the interior. In all that the creature is diverted by himself from his Lord—Praised and Exalted He!—being preoccupied with the purification of his

290

interior that he may prepare himself for "arriving." And "arriving" is simply that there is disclosed to him the true state of the Truth. So if he considers his knowledge, he knows only God, and if he considers his ambition [aspiration, eager desire], he has no aspiration other than God. Thus he will be totally preoccupied with His totality [all of Him], in sight and desire [seeing and desiring], without attending in that to himself, so that he may build up his exterior by [acts of] worship, or his interior by moral cultivation. All that is "purity"—and this is the beginning. And the culmination [end] is simply that he slough off himself completely and strip himself [become stripped] for Him, so that he will, as it were, be He—and that is "arriving."

If you say: The words [expressions] of the Sufis are based on mystical visions revealed to them in the stage of friendship [with God]. But reason [man's intellect] fails to [is unable to] grasp that, whereas what you have mentioned is an exercise of the intellectual wares. *Know that* there cannot appear [be manifest] in the stage of friendship anything which reason judges to be impossible. To be sure, there can be manifest what reason fails [to grasp] in the sense that one cannot grasp it by reason alone. An example would be that there can be disclosed [revealed] to a friend [of God] that so-and-so will die tomorrow: and that cannot be perceived by the wares of reason—nay but reason is incapable of perceiving it. But it cannot be disclosed that God—Praised and Exalted He!—tomorrow will create the like of Himself, for reason declares that impossible, and it is not a case of reason's being unable [to grasp] it. More farfetched than this is that a man say: God—Great and Glorious!—will make me become Himself, i.e. I shall become He," because it means that I am an incipient and God—Exalted and Blessed!—will make me preeternal, and that I am not the Creator of the heavens and the two earths [upper and lower worlds ?], but God will make me the Creator of the heavens and the two earths.

291

THE NAME AND THE NAMED

This [latter statement] is the meaning of [Bisṭāmī's] utterance "I looked, and lo! I was He," if it be not interpreted. One who believes in the like of this has indeed been stripped of his native wit and finds indistinguishable what he knows and what he does not know. So let him believe that a "friend" [of God] may have it revealed to him that the Law [al-Sharīʿa] is untrue [false], and that, if it was true, God has changed it into untrue and has made all the utterances of the Prophet a lie. One who says it is impossible for the true to be changed into a lie says that simply through the use of reason's wares. For the changing of the true into a lie is not more unlikely than the changing of an incipient into [some thing] preeternal, and of a creature into [the] Lord. One who cannot distinguish between what reason declares impossible and what reason can attain is too contemptible [base, mean, vile] to be spoken to—so he should be left alone with his ignorance!

Chapter Two

Explanation of How These Many
Names Come Back to [Are Reducible to] One
Essence and Seven Attributes, according to the
Doctrine of the Partisans of the Sunria [pp. 172–74]

Chapter Three

Explanation of How All That Is
Reducible to One and the Same Essence according
to the Doctrine of the Muʿtazilites
and the Philosophers [pp. 175–77]

[p. 179]   SECTION THREE

On the Consequents and Complements
It Contains Three Chapters

Chapter One

Explanation of the Fact That
the Names of God Most High, with
Respect to Positive Determination [al-
tawqīf], Are Not Limited to Ninety-nine [pp. 181–83]

Chapter Two

Explanation of the Benefit of
the Enumeration and Specification by [as]
Ninety-nine
In This Chapter There Are Re-
flections [Considerations] on [Several]
Matters: So Let Us Present It in the
Form of Questions [pp. 184–91]

Chapter Three

Are the Names and Attributes
Applied to [Predicated of] God—Great
and Glorious!—Based on Positive Determination,
or Are They Possible [Allowable] by Way of Reason?
[pp. 192–96]

[End of the *Maqṣad*]
[p. 179]

293